# THE
# CALIFORNIA
# REAL ESTATE PRIMER

### Ray D. Westcott

Essentials for Broker and
Salesperson License Examinations
&
For Buyers and Sellers
of California Real Estate

**Forty-First Revised Edition**

This text is revised in accordance
with latest law changes.

ISBN: 0-940745-03-8
Library of Congress Catalog Card No. 91-092487
COPYRIGHT © 1992

**Real Estate Primer Publishers**

Distributor to the Book Trade:
**Publishers Group West**
(415) 658-3453
(800) 788-3123

# Foreword

For over forty years, the *Primer* has been a valuable aid to persons preparing for the California real estate license examinations. It has also been used in basic courses on California real estate including "California Principles of Real Estate." This course is required of applicants for the salesperson's license examination. Also, the *Primer* is valuable for buyers and sellers and others who deal in California real estate.

The *Primer* is to the point. It eliminates legal language as much as possible, and is written so the average person may understand it without difficulty. When legal terms are used, they are explained in everyday language. No claim is made that the *Primer* is a complete text on real estate law.

The *Primer* has boiled-down the various subjects to a minimum. There are no lengthy discussions of minor points or exceptions to the rule to confuse the reader. Therefore, the *Primer* is not to be relied upon as an in-depth statement of the law. You should refer to the statutes, or consult with an attorney, for complete and accurate information when making important legal decisions. Purchase of the California Department of Real Estate's *Reference Book* and *Real Estate Law* are recommended for in-depth information.

You will find reference notations in the *Primer*. Where a section number is given, it pertains to the California Real Estate Law. Where a regulation number is given, it pertains to a Real Estate Commissioner's regulation. CC numbers pertain to the California Civil Code. All of these are contained in the *Real Estate Law* book.

Material for broker or salesperson license cannot be separated. The same general ground is covered in both examinations; therefore, all of the information provided by the *Primer* is important to both.

At the end of each chapter there are "check questions," which are keyed to the paragraphs containing the answers. It is important to the learning process that the student answer these questions, and then refer to the applicable paragraphs for the answers when necessary. By doing this you will not only learn the specific answer, but will gain a better understanding of the subject matter so that you will be able to answer related questions. Mark your answers to the check questions in pencil so that you can erase them after you have gone through the entire book. Then go back and answer them all again after completing the Sample Examination should you feel that you need more work. The Sample Examination will further help you in learning and retaining the material in the *Primer*, as will reading each definition in the Combination Index and Brief Definitions of Real Estate Terms and Phrases.

Some persons are able to take the State license examinations and feel perfectly relaxed. They are fortunate, as their examination papers reflect their knowledge of the subject. Others, less fortunate, are badly handicapped by becoming extremely nervous and making many errors, although they really understand the subject. There is no perfect formula for correcting this condition, but these persons may be helped by the following suggestions. Remember that you are not pressed for time. At present 5 hours are allowed for the brokers all-day license examination, and 3 1/4 hours are allowed for salespersons. This is a very adequate amount of time, so don't feel rushed. Also, don't get bogged down on questions for which you are not sure of the answers. This may cause you to become flustered. Just let these questions go until after you have answered all of the questions for which you have good knowledge. In the State examinations, which are multiple choice, incorrect answers do not count against you. Therefore, it is best to answer all of the questions. Of four choices of answers, if you can eliminate, say two of them you have a 50-50 chance of answering the question correctly. Read the questions very carefully. Be sure you understand exactly what is being asked. It is very easy to misread a question. Another tip, do not sit up late studying the night before and come to the examination tired. Do your studying well in advance and retire early the night before the examination. Arrive at the designated place early. Fear of being late is harmful.

The late author was closely identified with California real estate for many years in the capacity of broker, Real Estate Board Executive Secretary, organizer of real estate classes, and for several years as Chief Deputy Real Estate Commissioner. His son, David, who has been active in the California real estate industry for over thirty years, is now the editor of the *Primer* and updates each new edition. He is presently an independent real estate appraiser in San Diego.

# Acknowledgments

The editor expresses his appreciation to the several real estate professionals who have reviewed chapters which deal with their particular areas of expertise. Their help has been of great value. Also, he expresses his appreciation for the guidance provided over the past several years by Realtor and Professor Dan Thren who has used the *Primer* in his real estate classes since the 1950's. He is a member of the San Diego Association of Realtors and heads a San Diego real estate investment company. His help has been invaluable.

# CONTENTS

**CHAPTER**

# California Real Estate Law

## LICENSES

**A1**    The State of California requires persons who engage in the real estate business as agents to be licensed. The **California Real Estate Act** was adopted in 1919 and has been amended at various sessions of the State Legislature since that time. Adoption of a license law was sponsored by persons engaged in the business as a means of raising its standards. Since that time all fifty states have passed similar laws. All these laws seem to have the same fundamental purposes. California and its neighboring states, Oregon, Nevada and Arizona, have real estate license laws which are very similar in their provisions. The California law was codified in 1945, and is included in the Business and Professions Code along with laws governing other businesses and professions. It is known as **The Real Estate Law**. A code is a grouping of laws related to the same general subject.

**A2**    A **Real Estate Commissioner**, the chief officer of the California State **Department of Real Estate (DRE)**, appointed by the Governor, is charged with licensing real estate agents. Dealing in "business opportunities" is covered by a real estate license.

**A3**    Two kinds of licenses are issued to engage in the real estate brokerage business, namely broker and salesperson. Either may, upon qualifying, obtain a license good for four years and may renew it every four years without further examination, but must satisfy Continuing Education requirements.

**A4** Mineral, Oil and Gas broker licenses are also issued; however, this type of salesperson license has been discontinued. (Section 10500, et seq.)

**A5** Nearly everything a person ordinarily does in engaging in a real estate brokerage business **for, or in expectation of, a commission or fee**, requires a real estate license. A person requires a license if he: (Section 10131)

• Sells or offers real estate for sale.

• Buys or offers to buy.

• Solicits prospective sellers or purchasers.

• Solicits or obtains listings.

• Negotiates the purchase, sale or exchange of real property.

• Negotiates new real estate loans.

• Buys and sells and exchanges mortgage or trust deed notes (existing loans).

• Deals in loans on existing mortgage or trust deed notes.

• Leases real estate, or negotiates the sale or exchange of leases.

• Rents, places for rent, or collects rents.

• Assists with filings on State or federal lands.

• Charges "advance fee" for promoting sale, lease, or financing.

• Solicits borrowers or lenders, negotiates loans, or collects payments for lenders on real estate or real estate liens (mortgages or trust deeds).

• Deals in real property sales contracts.

• A real estate license is needed to perform as an agent in doing any of the above acts in connection with business opportunities.

**A6**     If a person uses his own funds (acts as a principal) in buying or selling trust deed notes or sales contracts, he needs a license in some cases. The law requires a person who is "in the business" as a principal to be licensed. A principal is one who buys, sells, or exchanges sales contracts, trust deed or mortgage notes with the public. This applies whether one deals in loans directly secured by real estate, or loans secured by existing trust deed or mortgage notes (secured collaterally). (Section 10131.1)

**A7**     A person is considered to be **"in the business"** if he **buys eight or more, or sells eight or more** of these investments in any calendar year, provided he bought them for resale to the public and not as a personal investment.

**A8**     However, if some of these investments were purchased by a person through the services of a licensed agent, they are excluded in determining the total number purchased for resale. (Section 10131.1)

**A9**     Usually it is only when a person performs these various acts for others for compensation, or in anticipation of compensation, that he needs a license. The compensation may be anything of value.

**A10**     Some of the persons who are **not required** to have a license are: (Section 10133)

• A person handling his own property (with exceptions).

• An officer of a corporation, or general partner of a partnership, in dealings with property owned or leased, or proposed to be purchased or leased by his company.

• Employees of banks, savings and loan associations, credit unions, insurance companies and other financial institutions which operate under State or federal law.

• Anyone acting under a "power of attorney" (to be explained later).

• A lawyer who does these things as part of his legal services (otherwise he is not exempt).

- A trustee selling under a deed of trust.

- Persons acting under order of a court.

- Resident managers of apartment buildings, hotels, motels, trailer parks, and their employees, who rent or lease these properties. (Section 10131.01)

**A11** A person holding an option is usually classed as a principal and can deal with a property without a license.

**A12** An unlicensed person cannot make even one deal requiring a license without violating the law. Anyone who acts as a real estate broker or salesperson without being licensed, if convicted, can be fined up to $10,000, or imprisoned in the county jail for a term not to exceed six months, or both. A corporation may be punished by a fine not to exceed $50,000. This also applies to the party without a license who advertises using words that indicate that he or she is a licensed real estate broker. The dollar amounts were increased as of January 1, 1988. (Section 10139)

**A13** The Commissioner's Regulation No. 2726 requires a broker to have a written contract with each salesperson and with any broker with whom he has a broker-salesperson arrangement. Such agreement must include provisions relating to supervision of license activities, duties, compensation, etc. These signed contracts **must be kept on file for 3 years** from termination.

**A14** Only licensed brokers may collect commissions from escrow or from other brokers or individuals. A salesperson must be paid his share by the broker who employs him. Anyone, including escrow officers, who pays a commission to anyone but a licensed broker may be fined $100 in court. A licensed person who is in violation of this may lose his license (have it revoked or suspended). (Section 10138)

**A15** Two salespersons working for different brokers cannot legally divide commissions directly. They may have their licenses revoked for doing this. Commissions must be divided through their brokers. Remember, **a salesperson is an employee** and must work for some broker. He cannot be licensed under two brokers at the same time. (Section 10137)

## OBTAINING A LICENSE

**A17**   For complete information on obtaining a license, obtain a copy of the Department of Real Estate's pamphlet entitled "Instructions to License Applicants." The following provides general information on this subject.

The Rules and Regulations state that both broker and salesperson applicants must be at least 18 years old. U. S. citizenship is not required. Applicants must meet the following education and experience requirements before the Department will schedule them for an examination. All applicants must pass a written examination.

**A18**   Qualification for a broker license includes the applicant's having been actively engaged as a licensed real estate salesperson in California for at least two years within a five-year period immediately prior to the date of application for the broker license. Qualification in lieu of the two years' salesperson experience may possibly be obtained by having at least one of the following: the equivalent of two years' general real estate experience, a degree from a four-year college, or membership of the bar in any state of the United States. Applicants lacking the active two-year salesperson experience and claiming equivalent experience or college education must submit substantiating evidence.

**A19**   Merely holding a salesperson license for two years is not enough. The applicant must secure certifications from employing brokers that he devoted two years of **full time** employment to the business.

**A20**   Persons claiming "equivalent experience" will be required to show the equivalent of two years' full time employment as a salesperson in the business. Employment in appraising, real estate development, title or escrow work, etc., or experience in the real estate brokerage business in other states may be acceptable, or at least earn credit toward the required two years. A combination of California salesperson experience, equivalent experience, and college work will be considered by the Commissioner in meeting the required two years' active salesperson experience requirement. This requirement must be satisfied before the applicant will be scheduled for the broker examination. The DRE Equivalent Experience Form must be submitted in applying for equivalent experience credit.

**A21** An applicant for an original broker license examination must also have successfully completed eight courses in real estate at an accredited institution (college or approved private school). An applicant for the salesperson license examination must have successfully completed a course in Real Estate Principles, and must complete two additional courses within 18 months of being licensed, or his license will be suspended. A copy of Sections 10153.2 and 10153.3 giving the details of this is provided on pages 373 and 374.

## THE QUALIFYING EXAMINATIONS FOR ORIGINAL LICENSES

**A22** The original license applicant files his application for examination on a special form provided by the Department of Real Estate and pays the examination fee. This is $50 for the broker applicant and $25 for the salesperson. These sums do not include the license fees which are payable only after the applicant has been notified that he has passed the examination. If he fails this first test, he may take another by paying another examination fee. There is no limit to the number of re-examinations to qualify; however, the applicant must pass within two years from the date of his application or file a new one and start all over again. When notified that he has passed, the original broker applicant pays his four-year license fee of $165, and the original salesperson applicant pays $120 for his four-year license if he qualified for the examination with all three courses. These are the Real Estate Principles and the additional two courses which must be completed within 18 months of being licensed. If he qualified for the license exam with only the Principles course, then his license fee is $145.

**A23** The salesperson examination is a half-day affair, with a 3 1/4 hour session in the morning or in the afternoon. Questions are multiple choice. The Department can change the rules and schedules to suit its convenience, but at present the salesperson test goes something like this:

• General weighting: Real property and laws relating to ownership 11%, tax implications of real estate ownership 8%, valuation/appraisal of real property 15%, financing real estate 17%, transfer of property 10%, real estate practice 22%, brokerage: responsibilities and functions of salespersons 17%. All salesperson examinations will include a real estate form and form related questions.

• A salesperson candidate must correctly answer 70% of 150 questions in order to pass.

**A24** The broker's examination is an all-day test with 2 1/2 hours allotted in the morning and 2 1/2 hours in the afternoon.

• General weighting: Real property and laws relating to ownership 9%, tax implications of real estate ownership 8%, valuation/appraisal of real property 15%, financing real estate 16%, transfer of property 9%, real estate practice 21% and broker's responsibility for agency management 22%.

• A broker candidate must correctly answer 75% of the 200 questions in order to pass the examination.

**A26** License examinations are given frequently. They are given in Sacramento, San Francisco, Fresno, Los Angeles, San Diego, and Santa Ana.

**A27** Examinations are given by assignment. No one will be admitted who does not have an examination schedule notice received by mail from Sacramento. If for some reason the applicant cannot appear at the stated time, he may fill out the bottom portion of the examination schedule notice requesting another examination date, and return the notice to the Department with the appropriate fee.

**A28**    Upon passing the examination, the applicant is mailed an application for license. The application must be completed and returned within one year with the license fee and, if required, an acceptable fingerprint card and fingerprint processing fee.

**A29**    Licensees receive their licenses by mail. Salespersons are to deliver their licenses upon receipt to the employing broker, who sends a "salesperson change form" to the Department stating that he is to employ the salesperson.

## RESTRICTED LICENSE

**A30**    A restricted license is sometimes issued to persons by the Commissioner when he is not entirely satisfied as to their qualifications for "honesty, truthfulness, and good reputation," provided they have met examination and other requirements. In effect, these are probationary licenses. If, after a period of time, the holder satisfies the Commissioner that he merits a regular license, one may be issued. The Law states that restricted licenses carry no property right or right of renewal. One may be issued to a new applicant after a hearing, or to a person whose license has been suspended or revoked, if the Commissioner agrees to do so. (Section 10156.5, et seq)

**A31**    A restricted license permits the Commissioner to give a borderline applicant a chance to prove his worth, whereas otherwise his request for a license would have to be summarily denied. A bond may be required, also periodical reports to the Commissioner of business done. Salespersons may be limited to the employ of a particular broker. The Commissioner specifies the restrictions. These licenses are also issued for four years, however the Commissioner may restrict the license to a limited term. The fees are the same as for regular licenses. If the conduct of the restricted licensee indicates he should not be licensed, the

Commissioner may call a formal hearing, and suspend the restricted license pending final determination after the hearing.

## MORE ABOUT LICENSES

**A32**  While brokers are encouraged to maintain their offices in business locations, the Commissioner does not undertake to enforce local zoning regulations. Some jurisdictions strictly enforce these, others do not. The Real Estate Law says every licensed real estate broker shall maintain a definite place of business as his office. Said office is the place where licenses are displayed and client consultations are held. The address of an answering service, for example, does not comply. (Section 10162)

**A33**  A broker may have as many branch offices as he desires by securing branch office licenses for them. (Section 10163)

**A34**  The broker's license, and those of all of his salespersons, must be available for inspection at his main office, even though the salespersons are working out of branch offices. The only license which must be available in the branch office is the broker's branch office license. (Section 10160 & Regulation 2753)

**A35**  The State Real Estate Department must operate on the fees it collects. All licenses require a fee, and fees are charged for all examinations. Fees are also charged in connection with the regulation of subdivisions.

**A36**  All of the license fees collected go into the **Real Estate Fund**. Eight percent of these fees are placed in the Education and Research Account of the Real Estate Fund and 12% is credited to the Recovery Account (See A98). The Legislature may appropriate money from the Education and Research account to be used by the Commissioner in the advancement of real estate education and research at the University of California, State colleges and community colleges. Private universities may also receive research contracts.

**A37**   A broker or salesperson license may be renewed every four years upon filing of a proper application, payment of the required fee, and satisfying Continuing Education requirements for the renewal of real estate licenses. A total of 45 hours of approved Continuing Education within the four year period immediately prior to renewal is required. This must include a three-hour course in Ethics, Professional Conduct and Legal Aspects of Real Estate, a three-hour course in Agency Relationships and Duties in a Real Estate Brokerage Practice, and a minimum of 18 hours of Consumer Protection courses. Successful passing of appropriate testing is required. An exception to this is that salesperson licensees, **for their first license renewal**, need only satisfy the requirement of a three-hour course in "Ethics" and a three-hour course in "Agency." However, as part of the salesperson's qualifying for his original license, he must also successfully complete two additional approved courses within 18 months of being licensed. Failure to do this will cause automatic suspension of his license.

**A38**   Licenses must be renewed before they expire, or 1 1/3 times the fee must be paid. This makes the broker four-year license fee $220 instead of $165, and the salesperson license fee $160 instead of $120.

**A39**   The licensee may renew the license within two years of the expiration date. After the two-year period he is treated as a new applicant.

**A40**   Salesperson licenses may be transferred from one broker to another as often as desired. When a salesperson leaves the employ of a broker, the broker must immediately notify the DRE headquarters in Sacramento. The broker gives the license certificate to the salesperson, who strikes out the former broker's name and address, replaces them with those of the new employing broker, and gives the certificate to him. Using a special DRE form, the new broker must inform the DRE in Sacramento within 5 days that he is employing the salesperson. (Regulation 2752)

**A41**   The law requires that all nonresident applicants for licenses in California must file an **irrevocable consent** with the Commissioner, so that a valid service may be made upon them by delivering a process to the Secretary of State if personal service cannot be made. Briefly, this means that residents of other states, holding a license here cannot escape being sued in California as a result of their real estate transactions. The same filing of consent to be served must be made by out-of-state subdividers who seek permission to sell subdivision parcels in this State. (Section 10151.5)

**A42**   A broker may be licensed under a **fictitious name** provided it is not misleading and conforms with other rules. It must be properly registered in the county where the broker plans to operate. A fictitious name is one which does not definitely identify the broker, such as "Apex Realty Co." These are also called dba's (doing business as). A broker named John Brown for instance, will not be issued a license with a dba Brown and Smith, unless he is actually in partnership with a Smith. Certain exceptions are made when a partner has died or severed his connection with the firm, and the name is retained because it has advertising value.

**A43**   A real estate broker or salesperson who enters the military service of the United States may secure reinstatement of his license upon leaving the service. The law requires him to notify the Commissioner within six months after entering the service. The military licensee is not required to renew his license until he resumes business, or within one year of his discharge, whichever is earlier. If he neglects to give the six-months' notice, he can furnish proof of service upon return and be reinstated. (Sections 10460 through 10463)

## CORPORATION LICENSES

**A44**   At the outset of this chapter, we stated that there are two basic types of real estate licenses: namely, real estate broker and real estate salesperson. Broker licenses may be divided into two types: individual and corporation. There is just one kind of salesperson license: the individual salesperson license.

**A45** Any corporation engaged in the real estate business must have a corporation real estate broker license. At least one officer must be licensed to engage in the business on behalf of the corporation. It may be the president, vice-president, secretary, etc. This officer must have the status of a broker. He can only transact business on behalf of the corporation under his license as an officer of that corporation. He may also have an individual real estate broker license.

## PREPAID RENTAL LISTING SERVICE (PRLS) LICENSE

**A46** There is a special license for those who confine themselves to a prepaid rental listing service business. They must provide the Department of Real Estate with a surety bond of $2,500 for each office. Licensed brokers who engage in this type of business are exempt from the bond and license requirements. A prepaid rental listing service is the business of supplying prospective tenants with listings of **residential** property for tenancy, while collecting a fee at the same time or in advance of when the listings are supplied. A PRLS licensee may not negotiate rentals between prospective tenants and landlords. Licensed real estate agents of course, may do this. (Section 10167 through 10167.8)

**A47** A prepaid rental listing service license is $100 for 2 years and $25 for each additional office. **The law requires written contracts with prospective tenants. These must contain certain minimum information, and the contract forms must be approved by the DRE prior to use.** A licensee, other than a real estate broker, must refund the full advance fee if **at least 3 listing**s of available rentals meeting the specifications are not given **within 5 days** after execution of the contract. The prospective tenant must demand return of the fee **within 10 days** of the expiration of the 5-day period. Also, licensees must refund any amount over $25 if the prospective tenant obtains a rental other than through the services of the licensee during the term of the rental listing contract, or does not obtain a rental. The prospective tenant must make demand for the refund **within 10 days** after expiration of the contract. (Section 10167 through 10167.17)

## REGULATION OF LAND LOCATORS

**A48** Those persons who charge an advance fee, usually so much per acre, for assisting or offering to assist persons to locate or make filings on state or federal lands to purchase, lease, or enter are required to hold a real estate broker license. (Section 10131)

**A49** A land locator must enter into a written contract with the applicant before accepting any compensation. Commissioner's Regulation 2960 describes various items of information which the contract must contain. These include a description of the services to be performed by the broker.

## REAL PROPERTY SECURITIES DEALERS LAW

**A50** In the past, some firms would buy second trust deeds, resell them to the public, and make very substantial profits. Purchasers of these trust deed notes were enticed by relatively high rates of interest on their investments. However, in many cases buyers were not informed as to the high risk character of these trust deeds. This type of business became so profitable for the dealers that they found it difficult to secure enough trust deeds to meet the demand. This resulted in the making of poorly secured second loans on properties such as over-financed tract houses and vacant subdivision lots. Eventually, the bubble burst and some of the firms were thrown into bankruptcy. The public lost heavily. Operators who did this type of business have been referred to as "discount brokers" or "ten-percenters." Measures were taken by the 1961 legislature to control this type of business, as well as other abuses. Laws were passed to closely regulate these practices without damaging the legitimate business of real estate brokers in handling trust deed and real property sales contract transactions.

## SALES OF GUARANTEED NOTES OR
## REAL PROPERTY SALES CONTRACTS

**A51**  In order to deal in these, one must first be a licensed real estate broker. Then he must secure a **Real Property Securities Dealer endorsement** to his broker's license to permit him to deal in these "guaranteed securities." The fee for this is $100, and it must be paid each time the broker's license is renewed. Also, he must maintain on file with the Commissioner a surety bond of $10,000 for the public's protection. The sale of **real property securities** under the jurisdiction of the DRE **pertains only to sales to the public** and does not include sales to corporations, institutional lenders, pension funds, real estate brokers, attorneys, etc. Do not confuse these "real property securities" with those for which the Corporations Commissioner issues permits. (Section 10237.3)

**A52**  The sale of a "guaranteed" real property security differs from the sale of the usual trust deed note or real property sales contract because of the acts, promises and guarantees of the broker which create a real estate security for which a Real Property Securities Dealer endorsement is required. This type of real property security is created if the broker agrees to do any of the following:

**(1)**  Guarantee the purchaser against loss.

**(2)**  Guarantee that payment of principal and interest will be made in conformity with the terms of the note or contract.

**(3)**  Personally assume payment to protect the security of the note or sales contract.

**(4)**  Take partial payments on the purchase price of the security.

**(5)**  Guarantee a specific yield of interest.

**(6)**  Pay with his own funds any interest or premium for a period prior to actual purchase and delivery of the note or contract.

**(7)**  Agree to repurchase the note or real property sales contract under certain conditions. (Section 10237.1)

**A53**  Before the broker sells any of these "guaranteed" real estate securities, **a permit must be obtained** from the Commissioner, who may set the amounts to be sold, the terms, conditions, etc. A permit may be denied if the proposed sale is not considered fair, just, and equitable to the public. In this case the broker may petition for a hearing on his application for a permit. A fee is charged for permits which are good for one year. (Sections 10238.3 & 10238.4 and Regs. 2975 & 2976)

**A54**  There are many other requirements imposed on real estate securities dealers in the sale of these trust deeds and sales contracts. Prior to the sale, the broker must give the investor a **detailed statement on the real estate** which secures the investment, and keep a copy on file for four years. The statement must be signed by both the investor and the dealer, and must be on a form approved by the Commissioner. An appraisal of the property must be made by the broker or independent appraiser, and a copy given to the investor unless the investor indicates on the form that he will obtain his own appraisal. A copy of the appraisal must be kept on file by the agent for four years. (Sections 10232.5, 10237.4, et seq & Reg. 2977)

**A55**  A dealer must annually file with the Commissioner an audited financial statement which includes the number of sales and the total dollar volume of sales made as a Real Property Securities Dealer. (Section 10238.1)

**A56**  Advertising material used in offering real property securities must be filed with the Commissioner for his approval 10 days prior to its use. (Sections 10235, 10237.7 & Regs. 2978 & 2847.1, et seq)

**A57**  The Securities Dealer endorsement is not required for dealing in **promotional notes**; however the other requirements stated above for guaranteed securities must be complied with, including the permit and appraisal.

**A58**  A "promotional note" is a note which is **not over 3 years old** and basically is:

**(a)** One of a series of notes secured by **trust deeds** on separate parcels **in one subdivision**.

**(b)** One of a series of **real property sales contracts** pertaining to separate parcels of real property **in one subdivision**, all of which are executed by one person or persons associated together as owners. (Section 10237.1)

**A59** Although not in a category of a security instrument, **the sale or lease, or the offering for sale or lease, of lots, timeshare estates or timeshare uses in an "out-of-state" subdivision** as in Nevada, Hawaii, or Arizona is subject to some of the same requirements as guaranteed securities. A Securities Dealer endorsement is not required for dealing in these; but the same type of permit must be secured, an appraisal of the property must be made, and a copy must be given to the client, etc. (10249.2 and Reg. 2806)

## ADVANCE FEE OPERATORS

**A60** To correct unfair practices on the part of some operators who charge an "advance fee" for listing, advertising, offering to sell or lease, or to arrange a loan on a property, the State Legislature passed a law to enable the Commissioner to control these activities more effectively. The Commissioner may require that all contract forms and certain advertising material to be used by advance fee operators be submitted to him for approval at least ten days before being placed into use. He may then order that they not be used if they are unfair or misleading or do not meet various requirements. Advance fees for advertisements in newspapers of general circulation, published primarily for the purpose of promoting the sale or lease of business opportunities or real estate are not included. (Sections 10026, 10085, 10131.2)

**A61** Every broker who collects "advance fees" must place them in a trust account and keep them intact unless spent for the benefit of the principal, or until five days after a final accounting is made to the person furnishing the funds. While the funds are in trust, the broker must give his principal a verified accounting at the end of each calendar quarter, and also when the contract has been completely performed by the licensee. (Section 10146)

**A62** Failure of the broker to comply with these provisions of the law may result in the principal collecting treble damages, plus attorney's fees, in addition to possible loss of license. The same requirements apply when either real estate or business opportunities are involved. (Section 10146)

## MINERAL, OIL, AND GAS LICENSE

**A63** Agents dealing with the public in the sale or lease of land involving petroleum or mineral values, must secure a Mineral, Oil, and Gas broker's license. The M.O.G. broker's examination requires a knowledge of the rudiments of geology regarding minerals, oil, and gas, as well as all of the information needed for the regular broker license examination. There is no salesperson license in this classification. Persons are exempt from the license requirement who deal only with persons or companies engaged in producing or marketing oil, gas, or minerals. Generally, the rules applying to real estate brokers as described in this chapter apply to these brokers. Comparatively few of these licenses have been issued. (Sections 10500 through 10566)

**A64** Licensed real estate brokers are not required to have an M.O.G. license to engage in transactions wherein the transfer of mineral, oil, or gas property is purely incidental to the sale, lease, or exchange of real property. A real estate broker who occasionally negotiates a transfer of mineral, oil, or gas property other than one which is purely incidental to a real property transaction, but which still is only incidental to his real estate brokerage business, may secure a permit for such transactions from the Commissioner, and is not required to have a Mineral, Oil, and Gas license. Only one permit may be secured in any calendar year. Not more than 10 transactions may be performed under a permit by the broker and his salespersons. The fee for each permit is $50. A licensee who has occasion to negotiate more than 10 mineral, oil, or gas transactions within any one calendar year must secure a Mineral, Oil and Gas broker's license. (Section 10507)

## MOBILEHOMES

**A65** Real estate licensees are permitted to deal in mobilehomes which have been properly registered. Mobilehomes which have been placed on permanent foundations and legally converted into real property are excluded from this requirement.

**A66** A broker is prohibited from maintaining a place of business at any location where **two or more mobilehomes are displayed and offered for sale**, unless the real estate broker is also licensed by the State Department of Housing and Community Development to sell mobilehomes.

**A67** A real estate broker is prohibited from advertising or offering a mobilehome for sale unless it is in place in an established mobilehome park, or on a lot where it may legally remain and be used for at least one year. The licensee must withdraw any advertising of a mobilehome for sale, lease, or exchange within 48 hours of being notified that it is no longer available. He may not advertise or represent a mobilehome as being a new mobilehome. He may not advertise or represent that no downpayment is required when in fact one is required, and the buyer is induced to finance the downpayment by a loan in addition to the primary loan financing the purchase price of the mobilehome. (All the above pertaining to mobilehomes is under Section 10131.6, et seq.)

**A68** There is a great deal of law pertaining to mobilehomes. Besides that in the Real Estate Law, some is also included in the Health and Safety Code, Vehicle Code, Civil Code, and others. In the above we have touched very lightly on the law pertaining to mobilehomes in the Real Estate Law.

# HEARINGS

**A69    Licenses may be revoked** (taken away completely) or **suspended** for various periods by the Commissioner if the person holding the license has been dishonest, or has otherwise violated any of the provisions of the Real Estate Law. In some cases the Commissioner, at his discretion, may accept the payment of a monetary penalty in lieu of suspension of a license.

**A70**    An important thing to remember is that the Commissioner cannot revoke or suspend any regular broker or salesperson license issued by him until he has first served notice of the charges in writing, called the accusation, and a **formal hearing** has been held. After being served, the respondent has 15 days to file a notice of defense with the Department. The notice of defense serves two functions: first as a formal denial of the charges in the accusation and secondly, as a request for a hearing. A failure to file a notice of defense allows the Department to proceed to disciplinary action (usually a license revocation) without a hearing.

**A71**    A formal hearing is one where witnesses testify under oath. It should not be confused with an informal conference which is often called as part of the investigation of the charges. Accused licensees are entitled to a fair and impartial hearing and may have their lawyers present. An **administrative law judge**, provided by the Office of Administrative Hearings, presides over the hearing.

**A72**    Both the Commissioner and the accused person have the right to call and examine witnesses, introduce documents, and cross-examine opposing witnesses. The hearing is recorded by a court reporter who will prepare a transcript if requested. A transcript is a written record of the testimony.

**A73**    The Commissioner may subpoena witnesses and documents needed at the hearing. The same right is given to the respondent, and the Commissioner must furnish subpoenas if the respondent requests.

**A74**    After the hearing is concluded, the administrative law judge prepares a proposed decision which is sent to the Real Estate Commissioner. The Commissioner has three options: adopt the proposed decision as his/her own, reduce the penalty, or reject the decision.

**A75**    When the Commissioner makes his decision, a copy must be sent to the respondent. If it is adverse to him, he may request reconsideration. If this is denied, he may present the matter in Superior Court through his attorney, and ask the court to set aside the Commissioner's order.

**A76**    A person whose license is revoked or suspended may petition the Commissioner to be reinstated or have the penalty reduced, but this cannot be done until one year has passed.

**A77**    The law governing the method of holding these hearings is called the **California Administrative Procedure Act**.

**A78**    The Commissioner may deny a license or give a restricted license to any new applicant after a hearing if the results of the hearing show that the applicant is not honest, truthful, and of good reputation.

## VIOLATIONS OF THE LAW

**A79**    The Commissioner may revoke or suspend licenses for definite reasons set out in the Real Estate Law. In some cases the Commissioner may, at his discretion and in lieu of suspension, impose a fine of $250 for each day of suspension stayed with the total not to exceed $10,000, providing the licensee requests consideration of the fine. (Section 10175.2) Some of these causes are as follows: (Mostly in Section 10176)

1. Making substantial misrepresentation.

2. Making false promises of a character likely to influence, persuade, or induce.

3. Continuing a flagrant course of misrepresentation or making of false promises through agents or salespersons.

4.   Representing more than one party to a transaction without the knowledge and consent of all parties.

5.   Commingling (confusing or mixing) the money or property of any party to a transaction with his own.

6.   Using exclusive listings that are for an indefinite period, that is, which do not have a definite termination date.

7.   Making secret profits at the expense of the principal.

8.   Failing to give a true copy of any listing agreement or any contract pertaining to the sale, purchase, exchange, or leasing of real property to the person signing same **at the time the signature is obtained**.

9.   Using "net listings" without telling the principal the amount of the broker's commission (earnings) before the principal signs the sale contract.

10.   Using a combination listing and option form, and exercising the option without notifying the principal of the amount of profit from resale and securing his written consent thereto.

11.   Any conduct which constitutes fraud or dishonest dealing.

12.   Abandoning or moving the office (in case of broker) without notifying the Commissioner.

## OTHER CAUSES FOR REVOCATION AND SUSPENSION OF LICENSE

**A80**   If the Commissioner learns that any licensee has done any of the following acts within the past three years, he may revoke, suspend, or deny a license: (Mostly in Section 10177)

13.   Willfully violated any section of the Real Estate Law.

14.   Procured a license for himself or any salesperson by dishonest means, such as cheating at an examination, not revealing a criminal record, etc.

15.   Been convicted of a felony or a crime involving moral turpitude. (See A81)

16.   Made false statements in advertising about his business or any property. Any person found guilty of making false or fraudulent statements in advertising of lots in a subdivision may also be sentenced to jail for as long as one year and fined as much as $10,000. (Sections 11022 and 11023)

17. Willfully used the term "Realtor" or any trade name or insignia of membership in any real estate organization of which he is not a member.

18. Has been found guilty of fraud in any civil case involving a transaction in which he acted as a real estate broker or salesperson.

19. Failed to report to the Commissioner **immediately** when he discharged a salesperson for dishonesty or any other reason which is a violation of the Real Estate Law.

20. Failed to give, or cause to be given by the escrow holder, both buyer and seller written closing statements within one month of close of a transaction setting forth the selling price and, if an exchange, descriptions of the properties exchanged and the amount of any added money consideration. This applies to brokers only. (Section 10141)

21. Demonstrated negligence or incompetence in the business.

22. Failed, as a broker, to reasonably supervise his salespersons.

23. Charged excessive fees, or failed to give statements of costs and expenses to borrower when making a loan.

24. As an employee of a government agency in a capacity given access to records other than public records, used this information in such manner as to violate its confidential nature. (To prohibit such brokers and salespersons from having an unfair advantage.)

25. Failure of a "land locator" to meet special requirements. (See A48)

26. Failure of "advance fee" licensee to meet special requirements. (See A60 and A61)

27. Failure to register as a "Real Property Securities Dealer" when required (A51)

28. Used "blind advertising" in acting as an agent, except as permitted by law.

29. Inducement to panic selling. This is to induce the listing or sale of a residential property by instilling fear of decrease in property values, increase in crime, or decline in quality of schools due to the present or prospective entry into the neighborhood of persons of another race, color, or national origin.

30. It is grounds for the revocation or suspension of a license for a broker or salesperson to fail to disclose his/her direct or indirect ownership interest in any property to a prospective purchaser **prior** to his/her showing of the property.

**A81**  Number 13 above is rather far reaching. It includes failure to have licenses available as required by law. It includes failure to make a filing of a subdivision with the Commissioner, paying commissions to unlicensed persons, or payment of commissions by a broker directly to salespersons of another broker. Number 18 is highly important. If a licensee is sued and a fraud judgment is rendered against him and becomes final, the Commissioner can attack his license and there is very little defense. The judgment must be in connection with a deal in which the broker or salesperson was acting as an agent by virtue of his license, not some matter unrelated to his brokerage business. A hearing may be called any time within three years from the time the judgment becomes final. In connection with number 15, a crime involving moral turpitude covers any crime which is "bad within itself," or, as the attorneys say, "malum per se." These are crimes which are morally wrong and which should be so recognized by the wrongdoer, such as forgery. Although such a crime may be a misdemeanor, the Commissioner may still proceed to revoke or suspend a license.

**A82**  Any broker or salesperson who acts or conducts himself in a manner which would have warranted the denial of his license at the time he applied for it may have his license revoked or suspended. Denial, revocation, or suspension of a license by another agency for acts, which, if done by a real estate licensee would be grounds for the suspension or revocation of a California real estate license, could result in the loss of the real estate license. (Section 10177{f})

**A83**  Blind advertising has been a controversial subject among real estate brokers, the public, and publishers for many years. Some brokers would advertise properties for sale in the classified advertising sections of newspapers which gave the impression to the reader that the owner had inserted the ad, only to find out later that a broker was involved. The Real Estate Law prohibits this practice. In any advertising in which he is offering a service requiring a license, the broker must make it clear that an agent is doing the advertising. There is an exception in the case of a rental, where in classified advertising the broker may give only the telephone number or address of the premises to be rented. (Section 10140.6)

**A84**   The title **Realtor** is controlled by the National Association of Realtors. Unless a broker is an active member of a local real estate association affiliated with this national association, he may not use the title.

**A85**   A broker or salesperson is required to give a copy of any listing he gets signed to the person who signs it. **The same applies to any contract he gets a person to sign**. This includes sales agreements, exchange agreements, lease documents, etc. Failure to give a copy may mean loss or suspension of a license. **A copy must be given to each person who signs at the time the signature is obtained**. For example, if four prospective buyers sign a deposit receipt form, each must be furnished with a copy.

**A86**   A broker must keep papers in connection with his business **for at least three years**. These include listings, deposit receipts, cancelled checks, trust records, or any other documents incidental to his dealings as a licensed broker. The three-year period runs from the date of closing of the transaction, or in case no deal results, from the date of the listing. If there appears to the Commissioner to be sufficient cause, these may be inspected and audited by his representatives, which are usually Deputy Commissioners.

**A87**   **Commingling** has been one of the common causes for loss of license. Every broker is required to keep a trust account in a bank and deposit all trust funds in it, unless he puts the money in a neutral escrow, or turns it over to a principal who is entitled to it. Trust funds may be deposited in an interest-bearing account in a bank, savings and loan, or credit union if the broker is requested to do so by the owner of the trust funds, and if certain requirements are complied with. The broker must keep records showing the amounts and who gave him trust funds, which may be inspected by the Commissioner's representatives. Trust funds are such receipts as deposits on sales or leases, and also rent collections. "Commingling" in brief, is the confusing or mixing of a client's funds with those of the agent. These must be kept separate and apart from the broker's own funds and be readily available. (Section 10145 and Reg. 2830, et seq.)

It is recommended that the student read the Commissioner's *Revised Code of Ethics for Real Estate Licensees*, Regulation 2785, which was adopted on June 10, 1990, and which clarifies and applies Sections 10176 and 10177 to some particular situations. Following this is the Commissioner's *Suggestions for Professional Conduct*. These are included at the end of this book.

## ORGANIZATION OF DEPARTMENT OF REAL ESTATE

**A88    The Real Estate Law** is administered by the **Real Estate Commissioner**. The Commissioner is appointed by the Governor to serve at his pleasure during the Governor's term of office. The Commissioner is head of the **State Department of Real Estate**. The Commissioner must be bonded for the sum of $10,000.

**A89**    The Commissioner must have his principal office in Sacramento and may have branch offices in San Francisco, Los Angeles and other cities where they are required. At present they are also maintained in San Diego, Fresno and Santa Ana. (Section 10077)

**A90**    He is charged with the enforcement of the Real Estate Law, the issuance of licenses, and also their revocation or suspension for cause. He must have been a real estate broker actively engaged in the real estate business for at least five years in order to be eligible for appointment. A non-broker may qualify with related experience.

**A91**    The Commissioner is permitted to bring a court action to stop anyone from violating the Real Estate Law. Such an order by a court is called an **injunction**.

**A92**   The Commissioner, his Deputies, and other Department of Real Estate employees may not engage in the real estate business or have any interest in such a business while holding office. They must take an oath of office and file it with the Secretary of State. They are restricted from engaging in any businesses for which the Department issues licenses. The Civil Service law requires that all employees of the Department of Real Estate except the Commissioner must be employed under the Civil Service system.

**A93**   The Real Estate Law provides that the Commissioner may adopt rules and regulations. These must be published before adoption, and the members of the Real Estate Advisory Commission must receive 30 days' notice before adoption. These regulations become a part of the Administrative Code and have the force and effect of law. They are for the purpose of clarifying and applying the law to particular situations. They cannot give the Commissioner new powers not provided by the law; that is, they cannot amount to new legislation.

**A94**   The Commissioner often needs legal assistance. The Attorney General of the State is his legal advisor according to law. Persons whose licenses are revoked are constantly suing the Commissioner to have them restored. The Attorney General must defend these suits. He also interprets the law for the Commissioner. For his work he makes a charge to the Department of Real Estate. (Section 10079)

## THE REAL ESTATE ADVISORY COMMISSION

**A95**   The Commissioner must appoint a Real Estate Advisory Commission comprising ten members, six of whom are to be licensed real estate brokers and four of whom are to be public members. The Commissioner presides at Commission meetings. The members serve at the will of the Commissioner. They receive per diem compensation and are allowed their necessary expenses in the discharge of their duties.

**A96**  The Law requires that the Commissioner shall meet, consult and advise with the Commission on the functions and policies of the Department, and how it may best serve the people of the State while recognizing the legitimate needs of the industry and the licensees of the Department which it regulates. The Commission may make such recommendations and suggestions of policy to the Commissioner as it deems beneficial and appropriate. At such meetings the views and suggestions of the public and of the licensees of the Department are solicited.

**A97**  The Commissioner must call meetings of the Commission at least four times each year, and written notice of the time and place of each meeting must be given to the members and to other persons who have requested notice at least 10 days before a meeting.

## RECOVERY ACCOUNT

**A98**  The State protects the public within certain limits and conditions against loss suffered as the result of fraud, misrepresentation, deceit or conversion of trust funds by a licensee in a real estate transaction in which a license is required. Funds to provide for this come from a special account in the Real Estate Fund which is called the Recovery Account. Twelve percent of all license fees collected are credited to the Recovery Account. A claim against this special fund must be made to the Department of Real Estate within one year after final court judgment, and after the injured party has exhausted all legal remedies to recover. The claimant must post a bond to assure payment of costs and legal fees. Then the Commissioner may pay the injured party up to $20,000. Not more than $100,000 may be paid because of the acts of any one licensee. In the event there are several claimants whose total of valid claims amount to more than $100,000, the Law provides for prorating the maximum sum among them. In the Department of Real Estate's fiscal year 1990-91, claims in the amount of $867,938 were paid. Since July 1964, 2,343 claims have been filed, and 1,236 claims have been paid at a total amount of $15,026,031. (Sections 10470-10481)

## CHECK QUESTIONS

**NOTE:** A few questions are given following each chapter as a check for the student. The Key Number refers to the paragraph in the chapter which contains the answer.

1. A business opportunity broker is required to have a:
   (A) Real estate broker license    (B) Business opportunity permit
   (C) A $5,000 bond            (D) Loan broker endorsement.
                                                        ( )    **A2**

2. A regular broker or salesperson license, either original or renewal, is issued for a period of:
   (A) One year                  (B) Two years
   (C) Three years            (D) Four years.          ( )    **A3**

3. A principal is considered to "be in the business" if he:
   (A) Sells 6 trust deed notes in a year
   (B) Buys mortgage notes through a broker
   (C) Buys 12 mortgage notes in a year as a personal investment
   (D) None of the above.                                      ( )    **A7**

4. A person need not be licensed if he:
   (A) Charges advance fees
   (B) Offers real estate for sale
   (C) Acts under the order of a court
   (D) Assists in filing for federal lands.                      ( )    **A10**

5. An option holder is usually classed as:
   (A) An agent                (B) A principal
   (C) An employee          (D) None of the above.     ( )    **A11**

6. Payment of a commission to an unlicensed person may result in:
   (A) Loss of license           (B) $1,000 fine
   (C) $5,000 fine             (D) $10,000 fine.        ( )    **A14**

7. All applicants for the original salesperson license are required by law:
   (A) To be citizens
   (B) To be twenty-one years old
   (C) To pass a written examination
   (D) To be bonded.                                           ( )    **A17**

8.  Broker license candidates must prove that they have:
    (A) 4 years experience
    (B) 2 years experience and 18 college units
    (C) 2 years experience only
    (D) 2 years salesperson experience and successful      A18
        completion of 8 approved courses.            (  )  A21

9.  The type of license which may be limited to less than four years is:
    (A) Regular salesperson license
    (B) A restricted license
    (C) A regular broker license
    (D) A renewal salesperson license.               (  )  A31

10. Licenses of salespersons working out of branch offices must be available
    for inspection in the:
    (A) Branch office              (B) Main office
    (C) Broker's home              (D) Salesperson's home.   (  )  A34

11. The number of branch offices which the Commissioner will license to
    any one broker is limited to:
    (A) Two                        (B) Ten
    (C) Twenty                     (D) Unlimited.            (  )  A33

12. A broker must have a Real Property Securities Dealer endorsement to
    his license if he sells guaranteed real property securities to:
    (A) His dentist                (B) Another real estate broker
    (C) An attorney                (D) A corporation.        (  )  A51

13. When transferring a salesperson license, notification must be sent to the
    DRE in Sacramento by:
    (A) The new broker
    (B) The salesperson
    (C) The old broker
    (D) Both former and new broker.                  (  )  A40

14. An individual and corporation broker license:
    (A) Must be held by each officer
    (B) Must be held by one officer
    (C) May not be held at the same time
    (D) May be held concurrently.                    (  )  A45

15. Persons who charge a fee for giving aid in making filings on federal or
    State lands:
    (A) Need a federal license
    (B) Need no license of any kind
    (C) Need a State real estate broker license
    (D) Need a California Department of Corporations permit.  (  )  A48

16. A permit must be obtained from the DRE before which of the following may be sold to the public?
    (A) 5 year old trust deed notes on subdivision lots
    (B) FHA insured trust deed notes                                      A53
    (C) Subdivision lots in Idaho                                         A58
    (D) All of the above.                                        (  )    A59

17. Fraudulent advertising of lots in a subdivision may result in a jail sentence of:
    (A) One year
    (B) Two years
    (C) Five years
    (D) No jail sentence, just a fine.                           (  )    A80
                                                                         (16)

18. A PRLS licensee must provide the prospective rental tenant with what number of satisfactory listings within how many days or refund the full advance fee?
    (A) 3 listings within 5 days
    (B) 5 listings within 4 days
    (C) 10 listings within 7 days
    (D) 5 listings within 5 days.                                (  )    A47

19. An endorsement on his license as a "Real Property Securities Dealer" is most likely to be required of a broker when he:
    (A) Sells a lot zoned for business
    (B) Guarantees payment of interest on a trust deed he sells
    (C) Guarantees against termites
    (D) Sells a purchase money trust deed on a home he has sold.
                                                                 (  )    A52

20. A real estate broker may secure only one permit in any calendar year to engage in mineral, oil, or gas transactions. How many transactions may he engage in under such a permit?
    (A) 100        (B) 5          (C) 25          (D) 10        (  )    A64

21. The cost of special permits for real estate brokers to sell oil properties is:
    (A) $10 each                  (B) $20 each
    (C) $30 each                  (D) $50 each.                 (  )    A64

22. Failure to give a copy of an agreement to all parties at the time of signing:
    (A) Will automatically revoke your license
    (B) May cause loss of license
    (C) Will cause certified copies to be delivered later
    (D) None of the above.                                      (  )    A85

23. A broker is guilty of commingling if he deposits clients funds:
    (A) In a special trust account
    (B) In his company's checking account
    (C) Gives them to a principal who is entitled to them
    (D) In a neutral escrow. ( ) **A87**

24. The official group appointed by the Commissioner to consult with him is the:
    (A) Real Estate Board
    (B) Real Estate Commission
    (C) Realty Advisory Board
    (D) Real Estate Advisory Commission. ( ) **A95**

25. Members of the Real Estate Advisory Commission are appointed for a period of:
    (A) Two years
    (B) Four years
    (C) Three years
    (D) At the will of the Commissioner. ( ) **A95**

26. Persons defrauded by real estate brokers may in some cases secure relief from the:
    (A) Local real estate association
    (B) State Realty Association
    (C) Recovery Account of the Real Estate Fund
    (D) Insurance companies. ( ) **A98**

27. A real estate broker is prohibited from maintaining a place of business where what number of mobilehomes are displayed and offered for sale?
    (A) 6 or more          (B) 2 or more
    (C) Three or more      (D) None of the above. ( ) **A66**

28. Mobilehomes must be properly registered for what period of time before real estate licensees may list and sell them?
    (A) No time limit       (B) 2 years
    (C) 3 years             (D) 4 years. ( ) **A65**

29. Broker and salesperson licenses must be renewed on time. If they are not, what multiple of the regular renewal fee must be paid?
    (A) 2.0      (B) 1.5      (C) 1.33      (D) 1.25      ( ) **A38**

**NOTE:** After answering the chapter check questions, refer to page 288 for the correct answers. Where you have answered a question incorrectly, refer to the paragraph which contains the answer.

This page intentionally left blank.

# PROPERTY

**B1**    All property is divided into two classes, **real property** and **personal property**.

**B2**    **Real property** is the land and anything permanently affixed to it. Therefore, houses, barns, fences, trees, etc. are real property. It includes the space above the earth and the space beneath the earth along with any minerals which may exist there.

**B3**    **Personal property** is any property which is not classed as real property, or real estate, as it is commonly called. Therefore, furniture, musical instruments, clothing, etc. are personal property.

**B4**    Laws and practices governing personal property and its transfer will be commented upon later in the *Primer* as they are different in many respects from those governing real property. They are of particular interest to those expecting to deal in "business opportunities."

**B5**    **Emblements** are the growing crops of the vegetable production of the soil produced annually by labor, and are a special type of personal property. This would pertain to a field of corn, wheat, oats, potatoes and other similar crops. This does not apply to tree crops, such as fruits, nuts, etc. These are real property until picked. Trade fixtures are generally considered to be personal property, and usually may be removed by the tenant before his term of occupancy is up. Any improvement to real estate may be designated personal property by agreement.

**B6**    Things can change from one type of property to the other. Coal is real property before it is mined; but when taken from the ground and piled, it is personal property. A door lock in the hardware store is personal property; but when installed in a home, it becomes real property. You may be asked a question regarding **the tests** to determine if certain property is real or personal in borderline cases. The tests are:

(1) What was the **intention** of the person when incorporating the personal property into the real property?

(2) How is it **attached** to the real property?

(3) What is its **adaptability** to the real property to which it is attached?

(4) What is the **relationship between the parties** involved in answering the question as to whether a property is real or personal?

(5) What is the **agreement** between the parties? Disputes often occur between sellers and buyers and between landlords and tenants as to whether a property is real or personal. In borderline cases, courts tend to favor tenants over landlords and buyers over sellers.

**B7**    Any interest a person may have in real property is called an estate. The greatest interest a person may have is an **estate in fee** (also called a "fee" or "fee simple estate"). It is of indefinite duration, and the owner can dispose of it in his lifetime by sale, gift, or by will upon death. The estate in fee is the estate normally transferred in the sale of real property. While not in common usage, estates in fee are also classified as estates of inheritance, or perpetual estates.

**B8**    An estate in fee with no limitations or conditions on the ownership of a property is referred to as an **estate in fee absolute**. The holder of an estate in fee absolute has all of the rights and interests in a parcel of real estate (except some held by the government including taxation, police power and eminent domain). These rights and interests are referred to as a "bundle of rights". They include the rights of use, possession, encumbering and disposition. Various rights in this bundle of rights are transferred by a fee owner to others when a property is leased, mortgaged, an easement granted, etc. Deed restrictions (see D30) may also limit the owner's rights in a property. When one or more of the rights in a property are in the hands of others, the term **estate in fee qualified** is correct. In actual practice in the real estate business, the terms above in B7 are commonly used for all forms of fee ownership.

**B9**     One who has the use of real property merely during his lifetime has a **life estate**. Life estates, like other interests in real property, may be sold, leased, or encumbered, unless the deed granting the life estate contains restrictions pertaining to these. The holder of the life estate is duty-bound to keep any improvements in repair, and to pay taxes and other legal charges against the property. If the person holding the life estate dies, then any lease in which he was the lessor would terminate. The right to the fee interest in the property after the person dies is called the **reversionary interest**.

**B10**     A fee simple estate or life estate is sometimes referred to as a **freehold estate**. The term **less-than-freehold-estate** applies to estates owned by tenants who rent or lease property. A person who leases real property (the lessee) is said to have a **leasehold estate**. A leasehold estate is a form of personal property, and is governed by laws applicable to personal property.

**B11**     Land owners by law are entitled to reasonable use of water from rivers or streams running through their land, in adjoining lakes, or underground waters. They cannot waste the water, divert it, or deprive other landowners of their share. These reasonable rights to such water are called **riparian rights**. The State may grant nonriparian owners permission to take water from the above named sources. This is referred to as the **right of appropriation.**

**B12**     An owner cannot obstruct or change a natural water course so as to cause the water to flow onto the land of another.

He can build a bridge over it or make other improvements as long as he does not divert or obstruct the water to the damage of other owners. He cannot build a dam or dike which would cause any water flowing over his land to gather on a neighbor's land. If it appears necessary to divert the flow of water, the local flood control district should be consulted, and under some circumstances, the district can authorize certain changes in the flow.

**B13** Water rights in the form of stock in a water company are sometimes attached to land so that they cannot be sold separately, and can only be sold with the land they are placed on. Such water rights, or stock, are said to be **appurtenant to the land**.

**B14** Any right which goes with the land, such as a riparian right, or the permanent right of a neighbor to cross it, is called an **appurtenance**. The term also includes improvements firmly attached so as to become a part of the real estate. Example: houses, barns, fences, etc.

**B15** An **easement** is the right to enter and use another's land within certain defined limits. Thus, a farmer may give an easement to a neighbor to drive his cattle across a certain field to reach a pasture. The neighbor's land could be adjoining that of the farmer's, or there could be intervening properties. A lot owner may give a gas company an easement to run a pipeline across the rear of his lot. If easements were not given generally, public utility services would be difficult to provide. An easement is an estate in real property.

**B16** An easement may be obtained by securing a grant deed from the fee owner, or by reserving an easement when a property is deeded to another. They also may be secured by operation of law. For example, if an owner sold a part of his land which could not be reached except by crossing a part of his remaining land, the court might very well award the buyer an easement. Easements secured in these three ways do not become invalid for lack of actual use. An easement may also be acquired by prescription. Continuous and uninterrupted use for five years will create an **easement by prescription** where such use is hostile and adverse (i.e., without permission from the fee owner), open and notorious (i.e., the owner may be presumed to have notice of the use), exclusive (i.e., although the use is not by one person only, yet it is such as to indicate to the owner that a private right is being asserted), and under some claim of right. Failure to use such an easement continuously for five years may result in losing it. Owners of easements are not assessed for taxes on the land on which the easement exists.

**B17** Easements are usually created for the benefit of other land. The land benefited is called the **dominent tenement**. The land subject to the easement is called the **servient tenement**. Easements which are attached to a dominent tenement are appurtenant to it, and are transferred along with the ownership transfer of the dominent tenement. It is said that they "run with the land." Purchasers of the servient tenement acquire the property subject to all valid easements.

**B18** Some easements are not attached to any dominent tenement, such as a power line easement. These are referred to as **easements in gross**, and are considered to be personal rights because they are held by a person (or company) and are not attached to any particular land.

**B19** Sometimes a person will build a house too near the property line, and the eaves of the house will overhang a neighbor's lot. This is one example of an **encroachment**.

**B20** Sometimes an encroachment is not discovered until several years after it occurred, as when a property is surveyed. By that time the encroachment may be legally justified by title having been gained to the area encroached upon by **adverse possession**, or by having acquired an easement by prescription. The encroachment may, of course, be in violation of the law. In such case, the party encroached upon may sue for damages and the removal of the encroaching improvements. Where the encroachment is very slight, is done innocently, and the cost of removal is large, the court may award a monetary damage amount instead of requiring removal of the encroaching improvements.

**B21**    Real estate brokers and salespersons are interested in the transfer of real property, or at least some interest in it. It is in this way that they may serve property owners and buyers, and thus get paid for the services they render. The laws of California govern the methods of transferring property rights, and they are quite extensive to cover all conditions. The *Primer* will discuss the more common laws and practices applying to real estate transfers.

# Property

## CHECK QUESTIONS

1. The land and anything permanently affixed to it are:
   (A) Real and personal property
   (C) All real property
   (B) All personal property
   (D) Combined property ( ) **B2**

2. Which of the following is usually considered personal property:
   (A) The house (C) Fences
   (B) The garage (D) Trade fixtures ( ) **B5**

3. Which of the following are tests to determine whether an item is real or personal property:
   (A) The method of attachment to the property.
   (B) Specific adaptability/Agreement of the parties
   (C) Relationship of parties/What was intended
   (D) All of the above ( ) **B6**

4. When the overhanging eaves of a house protrude over a neighbor's lot, the condition is called:
   (A) An easement (C) An encroachment
   (B) A trespass (D) Accession ( ) **B19**

5. The greatest interest one may have in land is called:
   (A) Leasehold estate (C) Fee simple estate
   (B) Life estate (D) Estate for years ( ) **B7**

6. Landowners having reasonable use of underlying or adjacent waters are said to be enjoying:
   (A) Water rights (C) An encroachment
   (B) Riparian rights (D) Deed rights ( ) **B11**

7. The right given to a water company to lay and maintain water mains along the rear of a lot is called:
   (A) An easement (C) An encroachment
   (B) A trespass (D) Accession ( ) **B15**

8. A widow who is willed the use of the family home for the rest of her natural life is said to hold:
   (A) Leasehold estate (C) Fee simple estate
   (B) Life estate (D) Estate for years ( ) **B9**

9. The property which benefits by an easement is known as the:
   (A) Servient tenement      (C) Appurtenant tenement
   (B) Adverse tenement      (D) Dominant tenement      ( )   **B17**

10. Any right which goes with the land and cannot be separated from it is in the classification of:
    (A) An appurtenance      (C) Estate for years
    (B) Leasehold estate      (D) Life estate      ( )   **B14**

11. Which of the following are clearly a part of the real property:
    (A) Fences      (C) Trees
    (B) Shrubs      (D) All of the above      ( )   **B2**

12. The holder of an estate in fee absolute does not have which one of the following rights.
    (A) Right of use
    (C) Right of eminent domain
    (B) Right of possession
    (D) Right of disposition      ( )   **B8**

13. Which one of the following is not an estate in real property?
    (A) An easement
    (B) Ownership of the fee
    (C) Right to use the property for the remainder of one's life
    (D) A leasehold estate      ( )   **B10**

14. Which one of the following is classed as real property?
    (A) A growing crop of corn
    (B) A growing crop of almonds
    (C) A harvested crop of wheat
    (D) Potatoes still in the ground      ( )   **B5**

# VARIOUS WAYS PROPERTY IS OWNED & ACQUIRED

**CHAPTER**

**C1**    This subject is of much importance to persons in the real estate brokerage business; for unless one understands some of the fundamentals, he or she can encounter difficulty in some real estate transactions.

**C2**    An individual may own the fee simple estate in a property without anyone else having an interest in it. The term applied to such ownership by an individual is called **ownership in severalty**. This may be misleading because the term would indicate that several persons own it, which is not the case.

**C3**    If two or more persons buy property and own it together, they are called **tenants in common** (unless the property is acquired as community property, joint tenancy property, or partnership property). They may own equal or unequal shares. No one of them can point out the particular part of the property he owns, since his individual share is in the whole of the property. He owns an undivided interest with others. If any one of the tenants in common should die, his interest is not acquired by the remaining tenants in common, but by his heirs. The interests of the tenants in common may be obtained at different times. Consent of the other owners is not necessary in order to sell one's share. All have equal rights of possession. One tenant in common may bring a partition lawsuit to cause a court supervised sale of the property with the proceeds divided among the co-owners. This can be a disadvantage should the other tenants in common not want to sell the property.

**C4**    Real estate may be owned by a partnership. A partnership is an arrangement by contract between two or more persons to pool their assets and efforts in a business venture with each to share in the profits. Each partner becomes a **tenant in partnership** which is very similar to being a tenant in common, although partnership property is subject to certain regulations imposed by law. Partnership property may be held in the names of all parties, or by one or more partners in trust for all partners.

**C5** If two persons, such as a husband and wife, own property as **joint tenants**, they always own an undivided equal interest and have the same rights to the use of the whole property. If either dies, his or her interest immediately becomes the property of the remaining joint tenant. Therefore joint tenants have the **right of survivorship**. The fact of death must be established for the records. This may now be done in two ways, either by court decree, or by merely recording an affidavit of survivorship and a certified copy of the death certificate with the county recorder. No probate is necessary, which provides for savings on probate costs and eliminating long delays.

**C6** Usually only persons very close to each other hold property in this way, such as husband and wife, brothers, sisters, etc. It would not be practical for others to be joint tenants since their families and relatives would not be benefited in case of their deaths. It may be done, however. **Joint tenancy property cannot be willed to another person.**

**C7** More than two persons may be joint tenants, but this is not common. If there are three and one dies, the others acquire his interest and still remain joint tenants.

**C8** A joint tenancy ownership is always created by a single grant deed which names the grantees as joint tenants. Tenants in common may deed to themselves as joint tenants, or husband and wife may deed community property to themselves as joint tenants. Also, a sole owner may deed property to himself and another or others as joint tenants.

**C9** A joint tenancy is destroyed if one of two joint tenants deeds his interest to another. The remaining joint tenant and the new owner would become tenants in common. There would no longer be any right of survivorship.

**C10**    There are said to be four criteria to a joint tenancy: unity of **interest**, unity of **title**, unity of **time**, and unity of **possession**. In other words, the parties have the same equal interest, acquired by the same deed, commencing at the same time, and have the same right of possession.

## OWNERSHIP BY MARRIED PERSONS

**C11**    Married persons present another classification as far as owning property is concerned. Several states, including California, have community property laws. Briefly, these laws give husband and wife equal interest in property they acquire together during their marriage. This is termed **community property**.

**C12**    If either the husband or wife had property before marriage, it is not community property. It is called **separate property**, and each person can deal with his own as he wishes. The same is true if either inherits or is given property during the marriage.

**C13**    Any increase in value or earnings from the separate property of either is also separate property. Thus, if the wife owns an apartment house as separate property, the rents from it are also her separate property.

**C14**    Community property is often owned by husband and wife as joint tenants, but not necessarily so. If it is, either acquires full ownership upon the death of the other. The same is true if the community property is not held as joint tenants, provided the deceased spouse has not provided for the disposition of his or her share by will. Either one is entitled to do this, if the property is not held in joint tenancy.

**C15**    A spouse is either one of a married couple. If either dies, the other is referred to as the remaining spouse.

**C16**    Neither spouse may sell community real estate without the consent of the other. Both must agree and sign any instrument to convey, mortgage, or lease (over one year) the community real property. The agent should have both parties sign any listing agreement which pertains to this type of property ownership.

**C17**    Community property includes both real and personal property. Both husband and wife must get a fair price for community personal property sold, and cannot give away items such as furniture, clothes, etc. without the other's consent.

**C18**    Separate property which is commingled with community property is usually classified as community property.

**C19**    There can be many ramifications due to the way title is held, both as to legal matters and income tax liability. It is the wise agent who advises his client to seek the advice of an attorney or an accountant if there is any question as to how title should be taken to a property.

## OTHER ENTITIES WHICH MAY OWN REAL ESTATE

**C21**    The **corporation** is a form of entity created by statute. When legally established, it can act as a person. The details of forming a corporation are a job for an attorney. Articles of incorporation must be drawn and filed with the Secretary of State, and the necessary permits must be secured from the Corporations Commissioner for the issuance of shares of stock. While the shareholders own the corporation, the death of any of them does not affect the corporation as far as continuing its business. This is one advantage of doing business with a corporation instead of an individual. The corporation doesn't die. For this reason they are favored to act as trustee under a deed of trust. If an individual trustee dies, there is the trouble and expense of having the court appoint another. A corporation cannot be a joint tenant as it would always outlive an individual.

**C22**    A board of directors controls the affairs of the corporation. They are elected by the stockholders. Officers of the corporation cannot enter into any contracts on behalf of the corporation without consent of the directors. This consent is shown by a resolution included in the minutes of a meeting which has been legally called and at which a quorum is present.

**C23    Limited Partnership**. This type of partnership is provided for by law. A Limited Partnership certificate must be filed—another job for an attorney. The names of limited partners cannot be used in conducting the business, and they cannot manage it. At least one of the partners in the firm must be a "general partner" with unlimited liability. The main advantage of a limited partnership over the usual partnership, is that the limited partners have less liability. In the event the business "goes broke," the limited partners are not responsible for the firm's debts beyond their investment. In a **general partnership**, each partner is personally liable for the debts of the partnership, and all of the partners share responsibility for management of the business enterprise.

**C24    Real Estate Investment Trusts** (REITS). Real estate investment trusts make it possible for the small investor to enjoy some of the advantages of an investment in desirable large properties. He may purchase only a few shares if he wishes. They may be purchased through stock exchanges. These trusts are created in accordance with special provisions of the Internal Revenue Code. If a REIT distributes 95% of its earnings, it only has to pay a tax on any additional retained earnings. Shareholders must pay a tax on trust distributions as ordinary income. There are equity trusts which invest in real estate. There are mortgage trusts, and combination trusts which invest in both real estate and mortgages. They are regulated by both state and federal governments. In California, the Corporations Commissioner has jurisdiction over them. There are many requirements of these companies to qualify as REITS. Some of these are:

1. Must be beneficially owned by at least 100 investors.

2. No fewer than six persons may hold more than 50% of the beneficial interest.

3. A minimum of seventy-five percent of the gross income must come from real estate investments.

## VARIOUS WAYS REAL ESTATE IS ACQUIRED

The acquiring of title to real estate most commonly occurs through the purchase or exchange of property. Some other ways by which property may be acquired are discussed in the following.

C25   If for any reason real property has no owner, the title reverts to the State. The property is said to **escheat** to the State. This may happen in cases where a person dies and leaves no will and has no legal heirs. The procedure for the State to acquire unclaimed property is set forth in the Unclaimed Property Act in the Code of Civil Procedure. During the process, claimants have a certain period of time in which to make their claims, and infants and persons of unsound mind have special consideration. A person who dies without leaving a will is said to die **intestate**. However, he may have legal heirs. If so, then one or more of the heirs acquires the property through **intestate succession** in proportions as prescribed by law.

C26   Real property given by will is known as a **devise**, and the recipient is a **devisee**. Personal property given by will is a **bequest**. A man who makes a will is a **testator**, and a woman is a **testatrix**. A man named in a will to handle the disposition of a deceased person's estate is termed an **executor**; if a woman is named, she is called an **executrix**. If the will names no one and the court makes the appointment, that person is termed an **administrator** or **administratrix**.

C27   When a river gradually deposits silt and forms additional land, it belongs to the person whose land borders on the river. Such a gradual formation of land is called **accretion**. The silt or material which forms the added land is called **alluvion**. If a flood should cause a stream to suddenly wash away land from along its banks, the process is called **avulsion**.

**C28   Condemnation**. Condemnation is the lawful taking of private real estate for public use. The owner must be given **"just compensation"** for the property, which is its **fair market value**, and the property must be acquired only for some actual public need such as a school or highway. The right of the federal government, a state or its political subdivision to condemn property is called the **right of eminent domain**.

**C29   Dedication of real property** to the city, county, or State means in effect, the giving of an easement or fee simple estate for its use for some public purpose. If for some reason, the political subdivision no longer uses a dedicated property for that purpose, theoretically it reverts to the person who made the dedication. Dedications may be voluntary, as when a landowner dedicates a park site for public use. Perhaps he wants to leave it as a memorial to himself. If the park is abandoned, title would probably revert to his estate. This would be a case of **voluntary dedication**.

**C30**   On the other hand the law requires a property owner to dedicate land in some cases, as when he creates a subdivision and streets must be provided. When the law requires it, it is a **statutory dedication**. A statute is a law enacted by a legislative body, such as the State Legislature.

**C31**   Anything permanently attached to the land legally becomes a part of the land and cannot be removed without the owner's consent. If one unintentionally builds a house, fence, or other improvement on another's land, it becomes the property of the landowner, and the latter is said to acquire **title by accession**. Fixtures installed by a tenant and not removed by him upon vacating the property provides another example of the landowner acquiring title by accession.

**C32**   The law provides that if a person openly occupies another's land continuously for a period of five years, claiming it as his own in defiance of the legal owner's rights and paying all taxes on the land during that time, he may **acquire title by adverse possession**. This is accomplished by suing the owner of record in a quiet title lawsuit. An absentee owner should visit his property at least once a year to make sure that it isn't being used without his permission.

## Property Ownership and Acquisition

### CHECK QUESTIONS

1. Ownership of a parcel of real estate by two or more persons is called ownership in:
   (A) Severalty
   (B) Tenancy in common
   (C) Escheat
   (D) Accession
   ( )  C3

2. The one equal right always enjoyed by a tenant in common is the right of:
   (A) Equal shares
   (B) Equal possession
   (C) Equal title
   (D) Same time
   ( )  C3

3. The principal feature of joint tenancy ownership is the:
   (A) Right of survivorship
   (B) Equal rights to use
   (C) Equal interest
   (D) All of the above
   ( )  C5

4. The death of a third party joint tenant will result in the two survivors becoming:
   (A) Tenants in common
   (B) Life tenants
   (C) Separate property
   (D) Joint tenants
   ( )  C7

5. Which one of the following is a unity of joint tenancy?
   (A) Same time
   (B) Same interest
   (C) Equal possession
   (D) All of the above
   ( )  C10

6. Property accumulated by husband and wife during marriage by their combined efforts:
   (A) Is community property
   (B) Is separate property
   (C) Is joint tenancy property
   (D) Is personal property
   ( )  C11

7. Property received prior to marriage and any proceeds therefrom will remain:
   (A) Separate property
   (B) Community property
   (C) Common property
   (D) Joint property
   C12
   C13
   ( )

8. Without his wife's consent, the husband has the right on his separate real property to:
   (A) Sell it
   (B) Lease it for two years
   (C) Manage it
   (D) All of the above
   ( )  C12

9. Separate property which is commingled with community property is usually classified as:
   (A) Husband's or wife's separate property
   (B) Community property
   (C) Common property
   (D) Joint property
   ( )  C18

10. Real property given by a will is referred to as a:
    (A) Bequest          (C) Intestate
    (B) Devise           (D) Escheat          (  )  C26

11. A man who makes a will is known as:
    (A) A testator       (C) Executor
    (B) A probator       (D) Administrator    (  )  C26

12. When title to real property reverts to the State for lack of heirs, the property is said to:
    (A) Revert           (C) Escheat
    (B) Intestate        (D) None of the above (  )  C25

13. Acquiring title through adverse possession requires:
    (A) Paying the taxes on the property
    (B) Openly occupying the land in defiance of the legal owner's rights
    (C) Occupying the land continuously for five years
    (D) All of the above                      (  )  C32

14. The main advantage to the limited partners in a limited partnership is:
    (A) Less investment is required
    (B) They have a voice in the management
    (C) Limited responsibility for the firm's debts
    (D) Greater income tax benefits           (  )  C23

15. The disposition of real property by will is prohibited if the manner of ownership is:
    (A) Tenancy in common  (C) Community property
    (B) Joint tenancy      (D) Separate property (  )  C6

16. The formation of land by the gradual depositing of silt on land bordering a river is called:
    (A) Accretion        (C) Avulsion
    (B) Alluvion         (D) Alleviate        (  )  C27

17. The local school district offered Mr. and Mrs. Chang $150,000 for the rear 5 acres of a 10-acre parcel of vacant residential zoned land which they owned. The land was needed for the expansion of an adjacent school. The Chang's refused the offer and the school district filed a lawsuit under its power of:
    (A) Escheat          (C) Eminent domain
    (B) Dedication       (D) Legal acquisition (  )  C28

This page intentionally left blank.

# DEEDS

**D1** By **title** to land is meant the condition of ownership, or evidence of ownership. It is the existing proof of a person's interest or ownership. A document which shows the condition of ownership is also referred to as the title.

**D2** When title to a real estate interest is transferred from one party to another, it is done by a document called a **deed**.

**D3** There are various kinds of deeds, but all are for the purpose of passing or conveying title to real property. A transfer of property is often referred to as a **conveyance**.

**D4** Some of the more common deeds are: grant deed, quitclaim deed, gift deed, tax deed, and sheriff's deed.

**D5** A **grant deed** is ordinarily used to transfer title of real property. The **grantor** conveys the property and the **grantee** receives it.

**D6** All deeds must be in writing and must contain certain essentials, as follows:

- Name of the grantee (person receiving title)
- Name of grantor (person conveying title)
- Description of property (enough to identify it)
- A granting clause
- Signatures of grantors

**D7** The actual consideration or purchase price, if there is one, need not be mentioned in the deed. You will find that most deed forms in use today state, "for a valuable consideration, receipt of which is hereby acknowledged."

**D8**   The description in the deed should be the legal description of the property, although any description which definitely identifies it will do. It is not necessary to mention any buildings on the land conveyed because they are considered part of the land.

**D9**   The **granting clause** means the wording "I hereby grant." The words "convey" or "transfer" also may be used.

**D10**   Signatures of the grantors are essential. If there is more than one owner, all must sign. For instance, both husband and wife must sign deeds to community property. The deed is said to be **executed** when it is signed by the owners.

**D11**   A deed does not transfer ownership until it is **delivered to the grantee and is accepted by him**. By delivery is meant formally handing him the deed or making arrangements for delivery, as through escrow.

**D12**   A person who gives a grant deed warrants that he has not previously conveyed the property, and that he has not mortgaged or otherwise encumbered the property except as disclosed to the grantee. These are not written into the deed, and are therefore known as **implied warranties**.

**D13**   Provisions in the deed cannot restrict the new owner from selling the property to someone else. Such a provision is said to "restrict the right to alienate", and is void. Alienate merely means to dispose of.

**D14**   Deeds should be dated, but the absence of a date does not void them. If a date is missing, it is presumed to be dated on the day it was signed.

**D15**   The signature of at least one of the grantors should be **acknowledged** before a notary public, otherwise the grantee cannot record the deed. The deed would be valid, but the buyer is handicapped if he cannot record it as will be explained later.

**D16**   An acknowledgment is the grantor's formal declaration that the deed was signed by him, and that it was his own act and deed.

**D17**   A notary public usually takes an acknowledgement, but the law permits others to do so, such as judges and court clerks.

## OTHER DEEDS

**D18**   A **quitclaim deed** is unlike a grant deed in that the grantor makes no real or implied guarantees or warranties. He does not warrant that he owns the property and has not encumbered it. He merely transfers any interest he may own, or any rights he may have in the property. Quitclaim deeds are used to clear the title of "clouds" and defects.

**D19**   A **gift deed** is similar to a grant deed, except for the consideration. Instead of money, property, or something valuable, the consideration is love and affection. A father who wishes to distribute his property among his children would use this type of deed.

**D20**   A **valuable consideration** consists of money, property or an obligation. A **good consideration** is love and affection. It meets legal requirements.

**D21**   A **joint tenancy deed** is merely any deed conveying property to two or more persons as **joint tenants**. Such a deed makes the grantees joint tenants as far as that particular property is concerned. It is not necessary to use the phrase "with right of survivorship" in such a deed, as the joint tenants acquire this right anyway.

**D22**   A **tax deed** is one given as a result of a tax sale of property.

**D23**   A **sheriff's deed** is one given by the sheriff upon court order when property is sold to satisfy a debt. It contains no warranties or representations whatsoever.

**D24**   A **trust deed** is for the purpose of pledging a property as security for a note.

**D25**   A deed cannot be assigned (transferred by endorsement). If property is sold, a new deed must be given. Merely handing a deed back to a grantor does not transfer the property back to him.

**D26**   A forged deed is always void, even in the hands of an innocent purchaser.

**D27**   If the grantor is unable to sign his name to a deed, he may have a witness write his name and he may then make his mark. One witness is enough to make a valid deed, but the deed cannot be acknowledged and recorded unless two witnesses sign when the grantor signs by mark (usually a cross).

**D28**   A minor is a person under 18 years of age. A minor is either emancipated or unemancipated. Under the **Emancipation of Minors Act**, minors such as those who have entered into a valid marriage, or are on active duty in the U. S. armed forces, are considered as being over the age of majority for certain purposes, including entering into contracts to sell, lease, etc., real estate. Also, minors who are at least 14 years of age and who willingly live apart from their parents or guardian with their consent, and who are managing their own financial affairs, may petition the superior court for a declaration of emancipation. An unemancipated minor cannot legally make a contract relating to real property. Should the unemancipated minor enter into real property contracts, they possibly may be voided up until a reasonable time after his/her reaching majority. This is a tricky area of law and an attorney should be consulted. All minors, however, may acquire title to real property by gift or inheritance.

**D29**   In California, a person who has been judicially determined to be of unsound mind, or who is entirely without understanding, has no power to enter into real estate contracts. It may be possible to deal with an incompetent's guardian with court approval of a contract. The incompetent person may acquire title by gift or inheritance.

**D30** Certain property use restrictions may be inserted in deeds by which the buyer is bound, but they may not be unreasonable or limit his ability to sell (alienate). These restrictions in deeds are usually referred to as **conditions and covenants.** They may cover such things as building setback, type of dwelling, keeping animals, etc. Such restrictions are usually accompanied by a forfeiture provision in event of violation of them. Subdividers usually record a **declaration of covenants, conditions and restrictions (CC & R's)** instead of stating them in each deed, as they are usually rather lengthy. The purpose of a declaration of CC & R's is primarily to help provide for future conditions in a subdivision which will be beneficial to all owners as to the use, enjoyment and values of their properties.

**D31** Restrictions, either by deed or declaration, against sale of property to anyone because of race, color or religion have long been held unconstitutional by the courts. These restrictions may still be set forth, but they are unenforceable in any court action.

**D32** No one may deed his property away to keep it from being legally seized and sold to satisfy his debts. There have been cases where persons have conveyed property to friends or relatives when they expected to go through bankruptcy. Such conveyance may be set aside by the courts.

# Deeds

## CHECK QUESTIONS

1. In general use in California are quitclaim deeds, gift deeds, tax deeds, sheriff's deed, and:
   (A) Warranty deeds      (C) Surveyors deed
   (B) Grant deeds      (D) Partnership deed      ( )    **D4**

2. A transfer of the title of real property is said to be:
   (A) A lease      (C) A conveyance
   (B) An option      (D) A homestead      ( )    **D3**

3. In order for a deed to be valid it is required to be:
   (A) Dated      (C) Verified
   (B) Acknowledged      (D) Signed by grantors      ( )    **D10**

4. The transfer of ownership requires that the deed be:      **D11**
   (A) Delivered      (C) Verified      **D14**
   (B) Acknowledged      (D) Dated      ( )    **D15**

5. One who conveys real property by grant deed is called:
   (A) A conveyancer      (C) A payor
   (B) A grantee      (D) A grantor      ( )    **D5**

6. A deed cannot be recorded unless:
   (A) It is dated      (C) It is acknowledged
   (B) It states consideration      (D) All of the above      ( )    **D15**

7. A good consideration consists of:
   (A) Money      (C) An obligation
   (B) Property      (D) Love and affection      ( )    **D20**

8. A gift deed conveying title to real property to keep it from being legally seized may possibly be set aside or voided by:
   (A) Grantor's creditors      (C) A subsequent buyer
   (B) Grantor's debtors      (D) The courts      ( )    **D32**

9. The document which transfers title with no warranties, expressed or implied, is a:
   (A) Grant deed      (C) Quitclaim deed
   (B) Warranty deed      (D) None of the above      ( )    **D18**

10. A deed made by an unmarried person between the ages of 18 and 21 is:
    (A) Voidable                    (C) Valid
    (B) Void                        (D) Unenforceable          (  )  **D28**

11. The deed given upon court order when property is sold to satisfy
    a debt is:
    (A) A sheriff's deed            (C) A court deed
    (B) A quitclaim deed            (D) A trust deed           (  )  **D23**

12. A deed can be legally:
    (A) Assigned
    (B) Signed by a mark
    (C) Executed by an unemancipated minor
    (D) Signed by the grantee                                 (  )  **D27**

This page intentionally left blank.

# COUNTY RECORDS

**E1**    State law provides that the county recorder of each county shall record various documents, including those which affect any real estate in that particular county. The law also provides that he shall set up certain index records so that the public may determine if certain documents are recorded.

**E2**    Recording of documents and instruments has many advantages since the law considers that recording gives notice to the public of their existence. This is called **constructive notice**. If an owner actually resides in a property, he is said to give **actual notice** of ownership.

**E3**    Failure to record some instruments is actually dangerous to one's interests. For instance, if you fail to record a mortgage and another should be given by the owner at a later date and recorded, the second one usually would have priority over the first.

**E4**    Similarly, a person holding an unrecorded deed to property **he does not occupy** takes the chance of another deed being given and recorded, which would put him in a very unfavorable position. In conflicting claims to the same parcel of land, priority of recordation will ordinarily determine the rights of the parties, unless actual notice is given by a grantee who occupies the property prior to the recording of the deed of another.

**E5**    Buyers, mortgage lenders, title companies and others rely upon the public records for information as to condition of titles. The law recognizes this and favors those who record their documents.

**E6**     In order to be eligible for recordation, signatures to most real estate instruments must be acknowledged, and in some cases, must be verified (sworn to), otherwise the recorder will not accept them. The recorder is permitted to charge a fee for his services.

**E7**     In some cases, it is necessary to send deeds and other instruments affecting real estate to some other state for signature, and they are acknowledged by a notary public in that state. These are acceptable for recordation in California.

**E8**     Must all signatures to a real estate instrument be acknowledged in order that it may be recorded? When an instrument is executed by two or more persons, the acknowledgment of just one of their signatures is sufficient for it to be eligible for recordation.

**E9**     At one time the recorder's staff copied information from all instruments submitted for recordation by hand or typing. Now in use is a photographic method which has advantages in saving time and accuracy, and in showing actual signatures and insignia.

**E10**     Every county in this country has provisions for recording real estate documents and other instruments. As a general rule, unless real estate deeds, liens, etc., are recorded **in the county where the property is located,** they do not affect the title. An innocent buyer or lender who has no knowledge of them is protected against their effect by law if they are not recorded.

## ACKNOWLEDGMENTS AND VERIFICATIONS

**E11**     An **acknowledgment** is a formal declaration that a person has executed an instrument and that he has done so of his own free will. An acknowledgment must be declared before someone authorized by law to take acknowledgments, usually a notary public.

**E12**   Others are authorized to take acknowledgments, such as a justice of the peace, certain judges, court clerks, and county recorders.

**E13**   A notary public must have an official seal containing the words "Notary Public" and use it on acknowledged instruments which he or she notarizes.

**E14**   No notary public or other official may take an acknowledgment if he/she is an interested party in the document being acknowledged.

**E15**   When a notary public takes an acknowledgment, the person whose acknowledgment is taken must appear before him/her in person and be known to be the person whose name is signed.

**E16**   A **verification** is an oath or affirmation made before a notary public or other qualified person that the contents of an instrument are true. No oath or affirmation is taken when instruments are acknowledged.

**E17**   Certain instruments must be verified instead of simply being acknowledged. Among them are notices of non-responsibility, mechanic's liens, notices of completion, and others.

**E18**   An **affidavit** is a statement or recital of circumstances in writing to which a person takes an oath that they are true. For instance, a person may swear to an affidavit (verify it) that he saw a certain person at a certain place at a specified time.

# County Records

## CHECK QUESTIONS

1. County Recorders are required by law to:
   (A) Assess all real property      (B) Collect property taxes
   (C) Keep index records            (D) None of the above.      ( )      E1

2. An owner is said to give constructive notice if he:
   (A) Resides in the property      (B) Posts a sign
   (C) Advertises a sale            (D) Records a deed.            ( )      E2

3. The failure to record some instruments can result in:
   (A) Danger to interest           (B) Loss of priority                   E3
   (C) Loss of property             (D) All of the above.         ( )      E4

4. Which one of the following instruments must be verified rather than simply being acknowledged?
   (A) Grant deed                   (B) Notice of non-responsibility
   (C) Trust deed                   (D) Lease.                    ( )      E17

5. If an instrument is recorded in a county other than the one in which the property is located, it:
   (A) Does not affect title        (B) Gives constructive notice
   (C) Gives actual notice          (D) None of the above.        ( )      E10

6. A notary public is required to have a device to use in connection with the acknowledging of instruments known as:
   (A) A stamp                      (B) A level
   (C) A seal                       (D) A sextant.                ( )      E13

7. A sworn statement made before a qualified officer as to the truth of an instrument is called:
   (A) An affidavit                 (B) An alluvion
   (C) A verification               (D) An acknowledgement.       ( )      E16

8. A statement or recital of circumstances in writing to which a person takes an oath as to the truth of a matter:
   (A) A verification               (B) An affidavit
   (C) An acknowledgment            (D) None of the above.        ( )      E18

9. A declaration that a person has executed a document and has done so of his own free will is:
   (A) A verification               (B) An affidavit
   (C) An acknowledgment            (D) An avulsion.              ( )      E11

# TITLES
# &
# TITLE INSURANCE

CHAPTER

**F1** Originally, all real estate was owned by some government or sovereign power which subsequently transferred title to private owners by grant or patent. The conveyance was made subject to reservation of sovereign right. In California, title originated to a great extent with the Spanish Crown by way of land grants which were recognized when the United States government acquired the territory. Over the years these titles have been conveyed and encumbered in various ways by subsequent private owners. As described in the previous chapter, county records have been set up under supervision of county recorders, so that records of all instruments affecting California land are kept for public reference.

**F2** Practically everyone who buys real estate insists that he or she be furnished evidence that the title is good. For that reason it is necessary to search public records to ascertain the condition of title to properties. These searches include the county recorder's records, tax records and others. County records are the greatest source of title information. Because the average person is not expert in determining the effect of recorded instruments, he rarely attempts to search the records himself, but utilizes the services of a title company.

**F3** Modern title companies have the capability of making a computer search to find items of public record against a particular property. When certain documents are identified, copies are secured from the county recorder's office unless they are available in the company's microfiche files. Years ago title companies kept records of public recordings in large books which were known as **lot books**. These are still sometimes referred to when it is necessary to search the records prior to the time records were begun to be stored in a computerized system. A title company's facilities and records which enable it to make searches are called a **title plant**.

**F4**     Private title companies do this work in California. Their systems and services are considered to be among the best in the nation. These companies are regulated by the Insurance Commissioner under the provisions of the California Insurance Code. They must have at least $500,000 paid-in capital and must maintain a substantial guarantee fund. Loss of property due to defective title is relatively scarce in this State. These title companies back up their work to various degrees, depending upon the kind of service ordered.

**F5**     You may order various kinds of information from a title insurance company. A lot book report will give you the ownership vesting of a property, any trust deeds still in effect, and anything that has happened to them such as assignments, notices of default, etc. A chain of title report would provide you with a list of all documents which have transferred title to a property, such as grant deeds, quitclaim deeds, etc. A judgment and tax lien report would provide you with this kind of information on a particular individual or corporation. There are several other types of specialized information which may be ordered. Some title companies refer to these as reports, and others call them guarantees. Even though they are called guarantees, the title company's liability is minimal on these, like $100 in some cases. The purpose of these is primarily to provide information. Where real protection from title defects is wanted, a policy of title insurance must be ordered.

**F6**     A preliminary title report shows the condition of title of a property at a certain time on a certain date. It is ordered by the escrow officer for review and approval of a buyer or other party in a transaction. It is issued for the purpose of facilitating the issuance of a policy of title insurance, and the title insurance company assumes no liability because of it.

**F7**     A **policy of title insurance** is what its name implies. It provides insurance against many title defects. **The California Land Title Association (CLTA) Standard Coverage Policy** of title insurance insures against matters disclosed by public records, lack of capacity or authority of parties, forgery in the chain of title, defective delivery of a deed, and some other types of nonrecorded risks. The standard policy **does not** protect the policyholder against defects in the title known to the holder to exist at the date of the policy and not previously disclosed to the insurance company; nor against easements and liens which are not shown by the public records; nor against rights or claims of persons in physical possession of the land which are not shown by the public records (since the insurer normally does not inspect the property); nor against rights or claims not shown by public records, yet which could be ascertained by physical inspection of the land, or by inquiry of persons on the land, or by a correct survey.

These limitations do not involve as much risk as they might appear to. They can be mostly eliminated by careful inspection of the property involved, inquiry as to the status of persons in possession, and by employing a licensed surveyor to make a survey of the property.

**F8**    Policies of title insurance are often written for others than buyers and owners of property. For example, they are written for the benefit of persons lending money on property under a mortgage or trust deed.

**F9**    The **ALTA** (American Land Title Association) policy is one written to protect non-resident lenders, such as out-of-state mortgage companies. The title insurance company issues such a policy only after itself obtaining a competent survey and making a physical inspection of the property. The ALTA policy covers additional risks which the local lender might investigate for himself through a physical inspection of the property. It insures against things covered by the standard policy of title insurance, and in addition it covers such things as possible errors in surveys, liens not of record, unrecorded easements, claims to water and mineral rights, rights of parties in physical possession, etc.

**F10**    An **extended coverage policy of title insurance** refers to a special policy which covers certain specified risks not covered by the standard policy of title insurance. It provides buyers with basically the same protection that the ALTA policy provides to lenders, and is called the ALTA Owner's Policy.

**F11**    In special cases, companies will insure against unusual risks, but arrangements must be made in each case and a premium must be paid commensurate with the risk. However, no policies will provide protection as to the legal occupancy and use of a property. These include a property's zoning and general plan designations. These are subject to change from time to time and can be easily checked with the city or county having jurisdiction over the property. Whether or not occupancy has been approved for a building can be checked with the department having jurisdiction over this.

**F12**    Policies of title insurance state the **exceptions** to the clear title which they are insuring. These may include encumbrances which do not adversely affect a property such as a tax lien, where the taxes are not yet due and payable, and boundary line utility easements. There may be, however, encumbrances which have serious adverse effect on a property's utility and value. A title report may briefly refer to the exceptions, usually giving a document recording date and number and perhaps legal descriptions of easements. A property purchaser or lender should insist on completion of a transaction being subject to his approval of all such exceptions as shown in the preliminary title report. Where a particular document is mentioned under an exception, and the party is not sure as to what it contains, he should ask the title company to provide him a copy of it. Also, if easements are mentioned but he isn't sure of their locations, he should ask the title company to plot them on a plat map of the property for him. A title insurance company may be liable for damages if it fails to include in a policy of title insurance encumbrances as exceptions, which adversely affect a property's value.

**F13**    An **abstract of title** is merely a summary of a file of documents which affect the title to a certain property. When examined by an attorney skilled in these matters, it is the basis for an opinion as to the status of the title. This method of studying the records and preparing summaries or "abstracts of title" of all pertinent documents discovered in the search is cumbersome and not used to any extent in California.

**F14**    A **chain of title** is a detailed account of all actions and events affecting the title to a property as far back as the original government patent, if possible.

# Titles/Title Insurance

## CHECK QUESTIONS

1. A search of the title will include checks on:
   (A) Recorder records          (B) Tax records
   (C) Lien records              (D) All of the above.          ( )    F2

2. A lot book report will provide you with information as to:
   (A) Any liens against a corporation
   (B) Any trust deeds in effect on a property
   (C) The size of a lot
   (D) The property's zoning classification.          ( )    F5

3. A preliminary title report provides:
   (A) Minimal insurance
   (B) Coverage varies with amount of the premium
   (C) No insurance coverage
   (D) None of the above.          ( )    F6

4. A summary of a file of the documents which affect the title to a certain property is known as a:
   (A) Guaranty of title          (B) Title policy
   (C) Abstract of title          (D) Patent.          ( )    F13

5. Out of state lenders requiring a policy of title insurance ask for:
   (A) A guaranty of title
   (B) An ALTA policy
   (C) A certificate of title
   (D) A torrens title.          ( )    F9

6. The standard coverage policy insures against:
   (A) Forgery in the chain of title
   (B) Lack of capacity
   (C) Defective delivery of a deed
   (D) All of the above.          ( )    F7

7. Title policies in California are issued by:
   (A) County recorder          (B) Banks
   (C) County assessor          (D) Private companies.          ( )    F4

8. An ALTA policy does not insure against:
   (A) Liens not of record
   (B) Unrecorded easements
   (C) Errors in survey
   (D) Default by a mortgagor.                    (  )    F9

9. An abstract of title insures against:
   (A) Unrecorded liens          (B) Mechanics' liens
   (C) Nothing                   (D) Forged documents.    (  )    F13

10. A buyer of a parcel of land should require:
    (A) His approval of a preliminary title report
    (B) A certificate of title
    (C) An abstract of title                               F6
    (D) None of the above.                    (  )    F12

11. An out of state buyer of raw subdivision land would have the greatest
    protection by requiring which type of title insurance?
    (A) A standard policy
    (B) An ALTA owner's policy
    (C) An A.M.A. policy                                   F9
    (D) An ALTA policy.                       (  )    F10

This page intentionally left blank.

G

CHAPTER

# ESCROWS

**G1**   The handling of all papers and funds in connection with real estate transactions is complicated and requires someone skilled in this work to handle the matters promptly and accurately. For this reason the custom has grown in California of entrusting some able person with these details. **He/she carries out instructions agreed upon by both parties to a transaction, and is called an escrow holder.**

**G2**   While all these documents, funds, and instructions are in the hands of the neutral "third party," they are said to be "**in escrow.**"

**G3**   The two essential requirements for a valid sale escrow:

1.   A **binding contract between buyer and seller.** This can be in the form of a sale agreement, deposit receipt, exchange agreement, or mutually agreed-upon escrow instructions of buyer and seller.

2.   **The conditional delivery of transfer instruments and funds to the escrow holder.** A simple example of this is where a seller deposits a signed deed, and the buyer deposits funds, signed trust deed and note documents in an escrow, all of these to be used by the escrow holder according to the conditions of the mutually agreed-upon escrow instructions.

**G4**   Escrows may be opened for any purpose to carry out the wishes of two or more parties to a contract. They may involve the completion of a lease, the transfer of personal property, placing of a mortgage, etc. The selection of an escrow company to handle a transaction is a matter of mutual agreement of the parties. The escrow holder is the mutual agent of both parties, and therefore must be impartial. All information concerning the escrow must be kept confidential by the escrow holder.

**G5** The typical escrow takes care of the preparation of all papers involved in a real estate transfer, getting them properly signed, delivered, recorded, and accounting for all funds involved. A more detailed listing of the functions of an escrow is as follows:

- Serves the buyer and seller as an impartial stakeholder, or depository of documents and funds.

- Serves as a communications link to the various parties involved in a transaction.

- Prepares escrow instructions for signatures of buyer and seller.

- Secures a preliminary title report which will show the current condition of title to the property.

- Requests a beneficiary's (lender's) statement if loan is to be assumed by buyer, or is to be paid off.

- Responds to the lender's requirements.

- Receives purchase funds from the buyer.

- Prepares the deed and other documents, and coordinates the flow of documents and funds.

- Prorates insurance, taxes, interest and rents, etc.

- Obtains releases of contingencies (contingencies could include, for instance, buyer approval of an inspection report on the condition of a building).

- Records the deed and loan documents as per instructions.

- Closes escrow when all of the instructions of buyer and seller have been complied with.

- Disburses funds, including charges for broker's commission, loan payoffs, recording fees, title insurance, amount due the sellers, etc.

- Prepares final statement accounting for the disposition of all funds deposited in escrow, and provides copies to buyer and seller.

**G6** When all instructions, money and documents are placed in escrow so that it can be completed, it is a **complete or perfect escrow**.

**G7** When the escrow officer has performed in accordance with his instructions, the escrow is completed and he/she is released from further liability.

**G8** When the escrow instructions are properly drawn and signed, they become an enforceable contract binding on all of the parties. These instructions may supplement or modify the original contract of sale. If the terms of the escrow instructions are in conflict with those of the original contract, the instructions will usually control since they constitute the latest contract agreement between the parties.

**G9** Escrow companies, with certain exceptions, must be licensed by the State. Only corporations organized for this purpose may secure a license. The Commissioner of Corporations issues the licenses in accordance with the provisions of the Escrow Law. He must make an investigation in connection with each new application for an escrow license. Applicants must be financially solvent and of good character. This applies to officers, directors, and employees. The company must furnish a surety bond in the range of $25,000 to $50,000, and employees entrusted with money and valuables must also meet bonding requirements.

**G10** Each main escrow business location must have a manager or officer with at least five years of responsible escrow experience, and each branch office must have a manager with at least four years experience.

**G11** Certain firms and individuals are granted limited exemptions from the license requirement, including banks, savings and loan associations, title insurance companies, attorneys and real estate brokers. The latter may only hold escrows which are incidental to transactions in which they are acting as agent. They must keep escrow funds in a trust account, and keep records available for inspection by the Real Estate Commissioner.

**G12**
- Escrow companies are prohibited by law from paying fees or giving gifts for the referral of escrow business to them, except for the normal compensation of their own employees.

- Accepting signed blank instructions to be filled in later is prohibited.

- Also prohibited is the permitting of any alteration of signed instructions without the initialing of all parties who signed.

- A copy of the instructions must be given to everyone who signs or initials them.

- Escrow companies may not pay out advances on brokerage commissions.

- The escrow licensee must keep receipts in a trust fund, and must submit annual audits prepared by a qualified accountant to the Commissioner of Corporations.

**G13** Remember, an escrow officer is not a "closer." The details of your transaction should be worked out completely, with the seller and buyer signed to a binding sales contract before going to escrow.

**G14** Developers of single family dwellings are prohibited by law from requiring that purchasers use an escrow company in which the developer has an ownership interest of 5% or more. (CC 2995)

# ESCROW CLOSING STATEMENT

**G15**    Although the escrow closing statement is prepared by the escrow officer, it is very important that the broker or salesperson has an understanding of the various items included in it, and knows which charges are normally the responsibility of the seller and of the buyer. In the following some of the common charges are discussed.

In the sale of real estate, the seller usually pays the broker's commission. Whether or not he pays for the title insurance policy to insure that the buyer receives good title, depends somewhat upon the locality and the arrangement between the parties to the transaction. In southern California, and in some places in northern California, the seller usually pays for the policy of title insurance. In other northern California areas the buyer usually pays for this. The charge for the service of the escrow holder is usually divided on a 50-50 basis, but not always.

The fees for drawing trust deeds, notary fees for them, title policies to insure lenders and other loan costs are paid by the buyer. The seller pays for drawing and notarizing the deed, and also the deed transfer tax with a charge of 55 cents for each $500 of equity (or fraction thereof) conveyed. The buyer pays for recording his deed.

Real estate taxes and insurance are prorated to the date of close of escrow. If impounds have been paid to the lender to take care of future expenses such as taxes and insurance, any balance at close of the sale should be credited to the seller. Since interest on loans is not paid in advance but at the end of a certain period, the seller usually owes some interest on the trust deed note and should be charged.

In examinations, a closing statement question will usually state which charges the seller is to pay and which charges the buyer is to pay.

In constructing an escrow closing statement for the seller, you list in one column the charges to the seller (called debits) and, in another column, those items with which he is to be credited. First, of course, you credit the seller with the total selling price, and then charge (debit) him with the balances of the trust deeds and other liens the buyer agrees to assume as well as any trust deeds he is taking back as part of the purchase price.

Let's take a typical problem of this kind which is sometimes found in license examinations.

Broker Green negotiates the sale of Jones' home to Robinson. The price is $150,000 and Robinson agrees to assume a first loan with a balance of $60,000, and gives a purchase money second trust deed for $50,000 to the seller. He pays the balance of the purchase price and incidentals to the escrow in cash. (The types and amounts of the charges, of course, will vary from case to case.) **How much cash does Jones get from the escrow upon close of the transaction, considering the following charges?**

| | |
|---|---|
| Broker's commission | $9,000.00 |
| Unpaid taxes at close of escrow | $345.00 |
| Unpaid trust deed interest at close of escrow | $280.00 |
| Advance insurance premium paid | $160.00 |
| Drawing deed | $ 30.00 |
| Notary fee (deed) | $ 10.00 |
| Recording deed | $ 25.00 |
| Title policy (paid by seller) | $650.00 |
| Various fees in connection with the loans | $200.00 |
| Total escrow fee (to be split 50-50) | $240.00 |
| Transfer tax on deed | $ 99.00 |

The best way to solve this problem is to set up two columns, seller's credit and debit as shown on the following page. Of course you could add or subtract each item from the selling price, but this would be lengthy and confusing.

# SELLER'S CLOSING STATEMENT

| ITEM | DEBIT (CHARGE) SELLER | CREDIT SELLER |
|---|---|---|
| Selling price | | $150,000.00 |
| First trust deed assumed | $60,000.00 | |
| Second trust deed given | 50,000.00 | |
| Broker's commission | 9,000.00 | |
| Unpaid taxes to close of escrow | 345.00 | |
| Trust deed interest accrued to close of escrow | 280.00 | |
| Insurance paid in advance | | 160.00 |
| Drawing deed | 30.00 | |
| Notary fee-deed | 10.00 | |
| Title insurance policy for buyer | 650.00 | |
| Escrow fee (one-half) | 120.00 | |
| Transfer tax | 99.00 | |
| | $120,534.00 | $150,160.00 |
| Cash to seller (answer) | 29,626.00 | |
| | $150,160.00 | |

In examinations, this type of problem is sometimes made more difficult by requiring the calculation of proration of taxes, interest, insurance, and possibly rents. In the Real Estate Arithmetic chapter on page 298 you will find instruction and practice problems on calculating prorations. We have given you the various figures to simplify this problem.

# BUYER'S CLOSING STATEMENT

| ITEM | DEBIT (CHARGE) BUYER | CREDIT BUYER |
|---|---|---|
| Purchase price | $150,000.00 | |
| First trust deed assumed | | $60,000.00 |
| Second trust deed to seller | | 50,000.00 |
| Rebate to seller for insurance paid in advance | 160.00 | |
| Unpaid taxes to close of escrow | | 345.00 |
| Trust deed interest accrued to close of escrow | | 280.00 |
| Recording deed | 25.00 | |
| Various fees in connection with loans | 200.00 | |
| Escrow fee (one-half) | 120.00 | |
| Cash deposited into escrow | | 39,880.00 |
| TOTAL | $150,505.00 | $150,505.00 |

## Escrows

# CHECK QUESTIONS

1.  Someone skilled, prompt, and accurate, who carries out instructions from both parties to a transaction is known as a:
    (A) Management counselor    (B) Title holder
    (C) Power of attorney       (D) Escrow holder.          (  )  G1

2.  A transaction is said to be "in escrow" when all documents, funds, and signed instructions are in the hands of a qualified:
    (A) Title holder            (B) Title officer
    (C) Third party             (D) Buyer.                  (  )  G2

3.  For which of the following purposes may an escrow be opened:
    (A) The completion of a lease
    (B) The transfer of personal property
    (C) The placing of a mortgage
    (D) All of the above.                                   (  )  G4

4.  When an escrow officer has performed in accordance with his instructions, he is released from further liability and it is said:
    (A) The transaction is endured
    (B) The trustee is now liable
    (C) The escrow is completed
    (D) All of the above.                                   (  )  G7

5.  When all instructions, money and documents are placed in escrow so that it can be closed, it is a:
    (A) Complete escrow         (B) Perfect escrow
    (C) Good escrow             (D) Both (A) and (B).       (  )  G6

6.  The Commissioner of Corporations issues escrow licenses to financially solvent:
    (A) Partnerships only       (B) Individuals and corporations
    (C) Corporations only       (D) Individuals only.       (  )  G9

7.  Which of the following is not a prohibited practice under the Escrow Law:
    (A) Paying fees to non-employees for referral of business
    (B) Accepting signed blank instructions to be filled in later
    (C) Altering signed instructions without initialing
    (D) Placing funds in a trust account.                   (  )  G12

8. Which of the following firms and individuals are exempt from the escrow license requirement:
(A) Title companies
(B) Banks
(C) Attorneys
(D) All those in (A), (B), and (C)                                    (  )  G11

9. When escrow instructions are properly drawn and signed by all parties, they form:
(A) A binding contract          (B) A surety contract
(C) A revocable contract        (D) A prima facie contract.  (  )   G8

10. It is the custom in the southern part of the State that the cost of the buyer's title insurance policy is paid by:
(A) The seller                  (B) The buyer
(C) The broker                  (D) The trustee.             (  )  G15

11. A valid sale escrow requires:
(A) Approval of the escrow instructions by the broker
(B) A binding contract between buyer and seller and the conditional delivery of transfer instruments and funds to the escrow holder
(C) Approval by the Department of Real Estate
(D) Signing of escrow instructions by the buyer only.        (  )   G3

# SUBDIVISIONS

**H1**  New land subdivisions are regulated by the State, and also by the city or county. Promotional (recreational) lot subdivisions are regulated by the State and federal governments.

**H2**  The State, through the Real Estate Commissioner, regulates them so that there will be no fraud in their sale. The city or county, whichever has jurisdiction, is primarily interested in the physical aspects of a subdivision. This includes size of lots, street plan, utility improvements, open space, satisfaction of environmental concerns, etc. The federal regulation is the Interstate Land Sales Full Disclosure Act.

**H3**  The authority of the State to regulate subdivisions is set forth as part of the Real Estate Law, and is referred to as the **Subdivided Lands Law** (Sections 11000 - 11200). The authority of the cities and counties is set forth in the **California Subdivision Map Act**, which gives cities and counties the right to pass local laws (ordinances) to control the development of subdivisions. The city council or the board of supervisors (county) administers the subdivision ordinances with the aid of a planning commission. The Map Act is part of the California Civil Code.

## CALIFORNIA SUBDIVISION MAP ACT

**H4**  The California Subdivision Map Act, which provides the framework of law under which cities and counties govern the physical aspects of subdivisions, defines a subdivision as any division of land into **two or more parcels or units** for the purpose of sale, lease, or financing. The Map Act requires, with some exceptions, that division of property into **five or more parcels or**

**units requires tentative and final subdivision maps**. There is no exemption under the Map Act for parcels which are 160 acres and larger, although there is in the Subdivided Lands Law. The subdivider must first get approval of a tentative map. When this is approved, there are usually many conditions attached to the tentative map, such as grading, street and utility requirements that must be met before approval of a final map can be obtained. After the final map is approved, it is recorded by the county recorder.

**H5** Under the Map Act, **divisions of four or fewer parcels or units**, and other divisions exempted from the tentative and final map process, can be accomplished by getting approval of a **parcel map**, which is usually a less difficult and costly process.

## SUBDIVIDED LANDS LAW

**H6** The regulations enforced by the Real Estate Commissioner under the Subdivided Lands Law are the thing with which we are primarily concerned in this chapter, as it is the law upon which applicants for license will be mostly quizzed in their examinations. The Subdivided Lands Law is designed to protect the purchasing public from misrepresentation, deceit and fraud in the sale of subdivisions. It requires subdividers to provide potential buyers full disclosure of important facts about the subdivision in which they are considering buying property. This full disclosure is provided in a **Final Subdivision Public Report**.

**H7** A subdivision, according to the Subdivided Lands Law, is either improved or unimproved land divided into **five or more parcels** for sale, lease or financing. Improved land means land upon which buildings have been erected. This law pertains to both standard and common interest subdivisions. In a **standard subdivision** there are no common or mutual rights of either ownership or use among the owners. Each owner has rights in his individual lot and nothing more. In **common interest subdivisions** individuals own or lease a separate lot or unit, and have an undivided interest in the common areas of the subdivision, such as a recreational area. Parcels of 160 acres or more in size are not considered as subdivided parcels. This law applies not only to subdivided land within California, but to out-of-state subdivisions which are offered for sale or lease in California.

**H8**     Before subdivided land can be offered for sale or for lease, the subdivider must secure a Final Subdivision Public Report from the Commissioner. In order that he may receive a Final Public Report, a **Notice of Intention** to sell or lease, along with a completed questionnaire, supporting documents, and a fee, must be delivered to the closest Department of Real Estate office which deals with subdivisions. This would be Sacramento or Los Angeles. The DRE then makes an investigation of the proposed subdivision. (Section 11010)

**H9**     The questionnaire provided by the DRE contains numerous questions regarding the new subdivision. These include questions about the title, encumbrances, number and sizes of the lots, nature of the improvements, plans for furnishing public utility services, topography, soils and ecological information, etc. A title report, copy of a survey map, copies of any mortgages or trust deeds against the land and other documents must be filed with the completed questionnaire. The latter must be signed and acknowledged by the person who makes the filing. This may be the owner of the land, the subdivider, or an agent.  The filing fee is $500 plus $10 for each lot in a "standard subdivision." It is $1,600 plus $10 per lot or unit for a "common interest subdivision."

**H10**     Expressly zoned commercial and industrial subdivisions which are limited to commercial and industrial uses are exempt from the requirement of filing a Notice of Intention. Also exempt are standard subdivisions within city limits with completed residential structures and other improvements necessary for occupancy, provided certain requirements of the Real Estate Law have been complied with. (Sections 11010.3 and 11010.4)

**H11** Providing all requirements are met, the Commissioner issues the Final Subdivision Public Report upon completion of his investigation. These reports are good for **five years only**, unless renewed. Copies of the Final Public Report must be given to buyers prior to the execution of a binding contract, and receipts must be obtained from buyers on a form approved by the Commissioner. The receipts must be retained for **three years** for the Commissioner's inspection. (Section 11018.1)

**H12** A copy of the Public Report must be given to any member of the public who requests one. A copy of the Public Report and a statement advising that copies are available must be conspicuously posted in the subdivision sales office. (Section 11018.1)

**H13** As stated previously, the offering of subdivided property for sale or for lease is prohibited until the subdivider has made a complete filing and a Final Subdivision Public Report is issued. However, the Commissioner will in some instances issue a **Preliminary Public Report** providing a qualifying minimum application filing package is submitted. The Preliminary Report only allows the subdivider to take deposits in connection with advance parcel reservations before he has completed his filing due to various reasons. Either the subdivider or potential buyer may cancel the reservation at any time. Such deposits must be impounded in an escrow subject to withdrawal by proposed purchasers without any deductions until such time as the Final Public Report is issued, furnished to prospective purchasers, and binding contracts entered into. It typically takes many months for the subdivider to obtain a Final Public Report. A Preliminary Report can help him start his sales effort sooner, and buyers still have the protection of receiving the full information about the subdivision in the Final Report when it becomes available. The Preliminary Report does not contain the same full disclosures as a Final Report. The Preliminary Report is good for one year, or until the Final Public Report is issued.

**H14** The Commissioner may, on the basis of the particular circumstances of a proposed offering, waive the requirement of the submission of a completed questionnaire if the Commissioner determines that prospective purchasers or lessees of the subdivision interests to be offered will be adequately protected through the issuance of a Public Report based solely upon information contained in the Notice of Intention.

**H15 Common interest subdivisions** are condominium developments, community apartment projects, stock cooperatives, planned developments and others. Common interest subdivisions must meet the same basic requirements as standard subdivisions, and must meet additional requirements necessitated because of the undivided common interests of the owners. Common interest subdivisions also come under the Commissioner's jurisdiction when there are five or more lots, or units. (CC1351, 1364 et seq)

**H16** Civil Code Section 1351 recognizes the term **condominium**. This is a term applied to an individual unit in a building development wherein various owners own particular spaces in fee and share an undivided interest in common areas such as walks, corridors, parking spaces, etc. The condominium may be in a residential, commercial, or industrial development. When it is residential, the recreation areas, clubhouse, swimming pool, etc, may be owned as tenants in common, with each apartment owner having an undivided interest in these portions of the development. The living unit however, is individually owned, and may be financed, sold and taxed as a separate unit. It gives the owner many of the safeguards and privileges enjoyed by the owner of a dwelling on a standard lot. The condominium form of ownership has especially gained popularity in areas where land values are high. Legislation regarding condominiums goes into much detail concerning the management, assessments, and other matters connected with this form of ownership. This differs from ownership of the average **"own your own,"** where an undivided interest in the whole property is owned with the right of occupying a certain unit. Condominium units are unique in that the purchaser owns the "air space" which he occupies, bounded by the interior surfaces of the outer walls, ceiling and floor. Even the ground below is a part of the property in which he owns an undivided interest. You can see that in the case of a two or three-story building where others also own apartments above the ground floor, this would have to be so. Condominium developments are governed by a board of directors elected by the owners.

**H17** Another popular type of common interest subdivision is the **planned development**, which is also called a **planned unit development (PUD)**. These differ from condominiums in that each building is on a separate lot. The buildings may have common side walls along the lot lines. There are certain areas which are owned in common by the owners of the individual lots. Cities and counties use several variations of these terms, such as planned residential development (PRD), and planned industrial development (PID). These developments are governed by a board of directors elected by the owners.

**H18** The law gives jurisdiction over common interest subdivisions to the Real Estate Commissioner. A subdivision public report is required if **five or more lots** are involved in a "planned development", or if **five or more units** are involved in the other types of common interest subdivisions. The law requires persons offering common interest subdivision interests for sale or lease under the authority of a Public Report to provide the prospective buyer with copies of the governing instruments of the subdivision, including the declaration of covenants, conditions, and restrictions (CC&R's), articles of incorporation, bylaws and operating rules of the owners' association, the latest financial report for the development, and a statement of any delinquent owners' association assessments against the interest being offered. (CC1368)

**H19** Because members of the public often do not have satisfactory knowledge of all that is involved in common interest developments, the law requires that a certain statement describing these be given to prospective purchasers at the same time they are given the Public Report. This statement is entitled **Common Interest Development General Information**. This statement gives information about homeowners' associations, common areas and facilities, common area assessments, the possibility that your unit could be liened and sold for non-payment of an assessment, etc. (Section 11018.1{c})

**H20** Time-share projects in resort areas have become very popular in recent years and have been highly promoted. An example of a time-share project is an oceanfront apartment house where the time-share purchaser acquires the right to occupy a certain apartment unit for the first two weeks in August for the next ten years. Rights to occupy this apartment would be sold to others for the remaining 50 weeks.

According to Section 11003.5 of the Real Estate Law:

- A **"time-share estate"** is a right of occupancy in a time-share project which is coupled with an estate in the real property.

- A **"time-share use"** is a contractual or membership right of occupancy in a time-share project which is not coupled with an estate in the real property.

**H21** Time-share projects are considered to be subdivisions, and Subdivision Public Reports for them must be obtained from the Department of Real Estate providing the project consists of **12 or more** time-share estates or time-share uses having terms of **5 years or more.** The most common types of time share projects are apartment units, and hotel and motel rooms.

**H21.1** A person who has made an offer to purchase a time-share estate or time-share use in a time-share project as defined in Section 11003.5, has the **right to rescind** any contract resulting from the acceptance of the offer until midnight of the third calendar day following the day on which the prospective purchaser executed the offer to purchase. (Section 11024(a))

**H22** If any material changes are made in the set-up of a subdivision after the Final Public Report is issued, the Commissioner must be notified. (Section 11019)

**H23** After a subdivider is issued a Public Report and starts selling, if the Commissioner finds that he is violating the law, he may issue a **"desist and refrain"** order, stopping further activities. The subdivider may then request a hearing. He has 30 days in which to do this. Then he must be given a hearing within 15 days, unless he himself requests a delay. After the hearing, if the Commissioner does not make a decision within 30 days, the desist and refrain order is rescinded. (Section 11019)

**H24** False or misleading advertising of subdivision lots is banned by law. A person found guilty of this may be sentenced to jail for up to 1 year, and be fined as much as $10,000. (Sections 11022 and 11023)

**H25** Under the Subdivided Lands Law, if any land being subdivided is subject to any mortgage, there must be provision to release any lot or parcel sold from the mortgage or trust deed upon payment of a certain release price. Such a provision is called a **"release clause."** Without such a provision, the seller could not give clear title when the purchaser has paid for his lot in full, so the law requires these clauses. As a general rule, all deposit money paid by purchasers of subdivided parcels must be impounded and not drawn upon until the subdivider conveys the property interest purchased free from any **"blanket lien"**, which is a trust deed or mortgage covering more than one lot. Under the law however, the subdivider may post bond, put title in trust, or meet other requirements for the protection of the purchaser's deposit, and thus secure release of the deposit for his use.

**H26** Anyone who fails to make a required subdivision filing and pay the filing fee may be sued by the Commissioner for an amount equal to **three times the usual fee**.

**H27** The Commissioner requires that subdividers comply with the city and county regulations affecting subdivisions. The final subdivision map must be approved by the planning commission and the governing body of the city or county, and recorded by the county recorder.

**H28**  Some cities and counties do not permit lots in new standard subdivisions to be less than 5,000 square feet in area. Others have even larger minimum area requirements, particularly if cesspools or septic tanks are to be used. On the other hand, lots in planned developments may be quite small, but there are common areas in addition to the individual lots.

**H29**  Residential subdivision lots usually may not be sold unless there is an assured domestic water supply, or unless potable well water can be developed at reasonable cost. Potable means suitable for drinking.

## LAND PROJECTS

**H30**  In order to protect the public from abuses in the sale of **unimproved recreational lots,** or lots located in sparsely populated areas of the State, laws were passed giving the Commissioner additional authority to control their sale. This type of subdivision is called a **Land Project.**

**H31**  A Land Project is a subdivision which contains 50 or more unimproved parcels with fewer than 1500 registered voters within two miles. (Section 11000.5)

**H32**  A subdivision will not be subject to Land Project special regulations if all the lots are to be offered for sale only to builders or developers, or if they are not to be sold by substantial direct mail advertising with no more than 10% of the price allowed for overhead and advertising, and no more than conventional brokerage commissions. (Section 11000.5)

**H33**  The Commissioner will deny the issuance of a Public Report for a Land Project unless he is satisfied as to a number of things. These include sewage disposal, water system, utilities, other community facilities to adequately provide for the projected population of the entire subdivision, and provision for protection against flooding. Also, the Commissioner wants to be sure that the continued financing of these improvements bears a reasonable relationship to the value of the lots, and that the method of financing the lots, including balloon payments, is reasonable.

**H34**   Any contract to buy or to lease in a Land Project may be rescinded by the buyer without cause of any kind by written notice before midnight of the 14th calendar day following execution. The subdivider must conspicuously disclose this right to rescind the contract. (Section 11028)

**H35**   Every Land Project subdivider must submit reports to the Commissioner each calendar quarter giving the names and addresses of all buyers who subsequently withdrew or attempted to withdraw by notice, by failure to make payments for 90 days, by claim of rescission, or otherwise. (Section 11029)

**H36**   The federal regulation of Land Projects is substantially the same as the State regulation. It applies only to projects with 50 or more recreational lots and is called the **Interstate Land Sales Full Disclosure Act**. A Statement of Record must be filed with the Secretary of Housing and Urban Development (HUD) together with a fee. A copy of the filing with the State is acceptable as well as a copy of the State Public Report.


## WATER SUPPLY

**H37**   Water service for subdivisions is furnished by various types of organizations, including public utility water companies, mutual water companies, irrigation districts, county water districts, municipal water services, and municipal utility districts. In some cases, the land purchaser must develop his own supply of potable water from a well or spring.

**H38**   A **mutual water company** is a non-profit company organized by water users in a certain district to develop and furnish water to its stockholders at reasonable rates. Articles of incorporation are filed with the California Secretary of State. Stock is distributed to water users. A permit must be obtained from the State Department of Corporations to do this. The company is run by a board of directors elected by the stockholders. Water costs depend upon the expense of providing the service. Assessments may be levied if more money is needed for development of facilities. This type of water company is common in suburban areas. In most cases the stock is made appurtenant to the land. That is, each share of stock is attached to a particular parcel of land, and cannot be sold separately.

H39    A **public utility** or **public service corporation** is a private enterprise conducted for profit to its owners. They are under supervision of the State Public Utilities Commission. They may provide service only in the district allotted to them. The Commission issues them a "certificate of public convenience and necessity."

H40    An **irrigation district** is a district created under a special law for the purpose of developing and furnishing water, primarily for agricultural purposes. It has many of the characteristics of a local government, such as a municipal government. Bonds for development of facilities may be voted by residents of the district, subject to validation by a court.

H41    The term **water table** denotes the distance from the surface of the ground to the depth to which ground waters have risen. A high water table is often unfavorable as it brings salts to the surface, makes drainage difficult, rots tree roots, etc. A very low water table means deeper and more expensive well drilling, with higher power costs for pumping.

## Subdivisions

# CHECK QUESTIONS

1. New land subdivisions are regulated by:
   (A) The State                 (B) Cities and counties
   (C) Federal law               (D) All of the above      ( )    H1

2. Subdivision layout, street plan, size of lots and improvements are the responsibility of:
   (A) The State                 (B) The federal government
   (C) Real Estate Commission    (D) Cities and Counties     ( )    H2

3. The authority of the Commissioner to regulate subdivisions is set forth in the:
   (A) Subdivision Map Act      (B) Real Estate Law
   (C) Federal Law              (D) Planning Ordinance.    ( )    H3

4. A subdivision is defined in the Subdivided Lands Law as land divided into:
   (A) Three or more parcels    (B) More than four parcels
   (C) Five or more parcels      (D) Two or more parcels.    ( )    H7

5. The Map Act usually considers a subdivision to be a minimum of:
   (A) 3 lots                 (B) 4 lots
   (C) 2 lots                 (D) 5 lots.                 ( )    H4

6. Which of the following is not required in a subdivision filing with the Commissioner?
   (A) Information on encumbrances
   (B) Filing fee
   (C) Title information
   (D) Appraisals of properties.                 ( )    H9

7. The California Subdivision Map Act requires:
   (A) Delivery of the Final Subdivision Public Report to
        prospective buyers
   (B) The filing of a Notice of Intention to sell or lease      H4
   (C) The filing of a Final Map                    H8
   (D) Blanket mortgages shall have release clauses for      H11
        individual lots                          ( )    H25

8. A subdivision lot may be offered for sale when the Commissioner has issued a:
   (A) Final Subdivision Public Report
   (B) Letter of Approval
   (C) Final Subdivision Permit
   (D) Tentative Map. ( ) **H8**

9. A Final Subdivision Public Report is valid for a period of:
   (A) One year            (B) Two years
   (C) Five years          (D) Ten years. ( ) **H11**

10. The signed receipt of a copy of the Public Report must be kept on file for a period of:
    (A) One year            (B) Two years
    (C) Three years        (D) Four years. ( ) **H11**

11. The purpose of a condominium project may be:
    (A) Residential use       (B) Commercial use
    (C) Industrial use        (D) Any of the above. ( ) **H16**

12. Condominium developments are classified as subdivisions by the Commissioner if they have:
    (A) Two or more units
    (B) Four or more units
    (C) Five or more units
    (D) Fewer than four units. ( ) **H18**

13. Subdivision Public Reports are required for time-share projects where there are 12 or more time-share estates or uses which have terms of:
    (A) 1 year or more       (B) 3 years or more
    (C) 5 years or more      (D) No time requirement. ( ) **H21**

14. For which one of the following events must the Commissioner be notified regarding a subdivision for which he has issued a Public Report?
    (A) Each sale made
    (B) Change of subdivision documents
    (C) Change of sales agent
    (D) Single sale of 4 lots. ( ) **H22**

15. If subdivided lands are covered with a blanket mortgage, which of the following is required by the Commissioner?
    (A) Waiver Form        (B) Release clause
    (C) Record of Survey    (D) Subordination Clause. ( ) **H25**

16. Failure to make a subdivision filing and pay the fee can result in a suit by the Commissioner for:
    (A) $500
    (B) $1000
    (C) Three times the usual fee
    (D) Six months in jail.                                    (   )  H26

17. A non-profit company organized by water users is called:
    (A) A public utility
    (B) A water district
    (C) Mutual water company
    (D) Irrigation District.                                   (   )  H38

18. The formation of a mutual water company requires a filing with the:
    (A) Real Estate Commissioner
    (B) City Council
    (C) Board of Supervisors
    (D) Secretary of State.                                    (   )  H38

19. The ownership of the "air space" in a multiple story office building along with an undivided interest in the building's common areas is termed the ownership of a:
    (A) Planned development office
    (B) Own-your-own office
    (C) Condominium office
    (D) PUD office.                                            (   )  H16

20. The Interstate Land Sales Full Disclosure Act is administered by:
    (A) DRE       (B) FHA       (C) FNMA       (D) HUD.   (   )  H36

21. To be considered a Land Project, a subdivision must contain a minimum of what number of lots?
    (A) 50        (B) 25        (C) 5          (D) 10.    (   )  H31

# Agency & Power of Attorney

**I 1**     Since 1872 Civil Code Section 2295 has provided that, "An **agent** is one who represents another, called the **principal**, in dealings with third persons. Such representation is called **agency**." The agency status of a real estate broker is most often created by a written contract, such as a listing contract. However, an agency relationship also can be caused to exist because of oral statements and actions of the parties.

**I 2**     The relationship between an agent and his principle is termed a **fiduciary** relationship. This means that the agent has an obligation to be loyal, and to provide diligent and faithful service to his principal. He must not profit by virtue of the agency, except for agreed compensation for service rendered. Specific fiduciary obligations of the agent to the principal include obedience, loyalty, confidentiality, disclosure, reasonable care, diligence, and accounting of all monies belonging to the principle. The broker/agent must disclose all material facts to his principal, **including all offers** received prior to the sale of a property, unless he is instructed otherwise.

**I 3**     The principal is liable to third persons who have sustained injury through a reasonable and prudent reliance upon his agent, where the agent has acted within the scope of authority granted to him.

**I 4**     A broker is most often the agent of the seller, but in some cases is the agent of the buyer. Or, he may be a dual agent, where he is the agent of both the seller and the buyer. Where this is the case, the broker must disclose this fact to both parties and must obtain their consent. The Real Estate Law specifically forbids licensees from acting as **undisclosed dual agents**. Further, principals of an undisclosed dual agent may rescind a sale or lease agreement even without showing actual fraud and injury. The broker could lose his license and commission and be liable for damages. There are many cases of record in which a broker was penalized for violation of this law of agency. (Section 10176d)

I 5    A real estate salesperson, to the same extent as the salesperson's broker, is subject to the obligations arising out of the fiduciary relationship between the broker and the broker's principal. The salesperson is the supervised employee of the broker and is employed to carry on licensed activities on behalf of the broker.

I 6    A real estate licensee who is the agent of a seller or buyer also has a duty of fair and honest dealing to the other party. For example, an agent of the seller must not withhold from a prospective buyer material facts regarding the property which are unknown to the buyer, and which are not ascertainable by the buyer through diligent observation.

I 7    The licensee should be familiar with the Commissioner's *Code of Ethics and Professional Conduct for Real Estate Licensees*, which has the force of law, and his *Suggestions for Professional Conduct*. These are reprinted at the end of this book. (Regulation 2785)

## AGENCY DISCLOSURE LAW
### Civil Code Section 2373-2382. Applies to 1-4 dwelling units.

I 8    The above information pertains to all classes of real estate. A new agency disclosure law was effective as of January 1, 1988 and applies to sales, and leases for more than one year, of real property improved with one to four dwelling units whether to be owner-occupied or not. This legislation applies to real estate licensees in transactions where a listing is executed or an offer to purchase is obtained.

I 9    Often in the past people dealing with real estate licensees in residential properties have not had a clear understanding of the agency relationship, and whether or not the person they were dealing with was actually their agent. This new law provides for the informing of sellers and buyers of residential property that there are three types of agent, namely seller's agent, buyer's agent, and dual agent, and what the duties and obligations are of licensees in these agency positions. This information must be disclosed to buyers and sellers by means of a form, and signed acknowledgements that the form has been received must be obtained. The California Association of Realtors has a form which is designed for this use.

I 10    The second step is for the broker to make an election as to whose agent he is going to be. If he takes a signed listing, he has to be the agent of the seller. He can be the agent of the seller exclusively, or he can elect to be the agent of both the seller and the buyer. If he is working with a buyer and is not the listing agent, he can elect to be the agent of the buyer exclusively, or of the seller exclusively, or of both the buyer and seller.

I 11    As soon as practicable, the listing agent must disclose to the seller and buyer whether the listing agent is acting in a real property transaction exclusively as the seller's agent, or as a dual agent representing both the buyer and the seller. After the selling broker, who is not the listing agent, makes his election as to whose agent he is going to be, he must provide that information in writing to the buyer and seller "as soon as practicable," but always before buyer or seller enters into a transaction. This may be done in the contract to purchase and sell real property (deposit receipt form), or it may be done in a separate form designed for this purpose, such as the California Association of Realtors form which is entitled *Confirmation-Real Estate Agency Relationships*. The law requires a check-box format like the following:

_____ is the agent of (check one):
(Name of Listing Agent)

[ ]  the seller exclusively; or
[ ]  both the buyer and seller.

_____ is the agent of (check one):
(Name of Selling Agent; not the same as the Listing Agent)

[ ]  the buyer exclusively; or
[ ]  the seller exclusively; or
[ ]  both the buyer and seller

This *Confirmation-Real Estate Agency Relationships* form must be signed by the broker, and the buyer and seller.

**I 12**    This law was sponsored by the California Association of Realtors (CAR) "after more than seven years of studying the complex legal and practical issues concerning agency in a real estate transaction." The above information concerning this important law is very brief. The practicing broker and salesperson should become fully knowledgeable regarding all of its features in order to properly comply with it. CAR publishes a *Compliance Manual* which provides important information regarding compliance with this law.

## DUTY OF DISCLOSURE TO PROSPECTIVE PURCHASER OF RESIDENTIAL PROPERTY BY BROKER

**I 13**    The State legislature enacted additional "full disclosure" law which became effective on January 1, 1986. It came about because of the court's findings in the well-publicized Easton case. This law requires that a real estate licensee disclose to a prospective purchaser all facts materially affecting the value or desirability of a property an investigation would reveal, subject to the following limits of responsibility of the agent. (CC 2079 through 2079.5)

**I 14**    Following is a very brief summary of this law as it pertains to the duties of a real estate licensee:

1. It mandates only a reasonably competent and diligent **visual inspection** of the accessible areas of the property.

2. The duty to make the visual inspection is limited to **residential real property of one to four units**.

3. It defines the standard of care owed by an agent to a prospective purchaser as the degree of care a reasonably prudent real estate licensee would exercise, and is measured by the degree of knowledge through education, experience and examination required to obtain a real estate license under California law.

4. It applies the duty only to a broker who has entered into a written contract with the seller to find or obtain a buyer, and to a broker who acts in cooperation with such a (listing) broker to find and obtain a buyer.

5. It provides that the duty of inspection does not include or involve areas that are reasonably and normally inaccessible, nor to inspection of common areas in common interest subdivisions if the seller or broker supplies the prospective buyer with the documents and information required by law.

6. It established a two-year statute of limitations which runs from the date of recordation, close of escrow, or occupancy, whichever occurs first. Legal action for breach of duty imposed by this law must be commenced within this two year period.

7. It provides that the buyer or prospective buyer has a duty to exercise reasonable care to protect himself or herself, including knowledge of adverse facts which are known to, or within the diligent attention and observation of the buyer or prospective buyer.

## DISCLOSURE UPON TRANSFER OF RESIDENTIAL PROPERTY - BY SELLER

I 15    More law to protect buyers of one to four dwelling units, whether to be owner occupied or not, became effective January 1, 1987. This is contained in the Civil Code Section 1102, et. seq. This applies to transfers of real property by sale, sales contract, ground lease coupled with improvements, or exchange. Exempted are certain transfers, including those ordered by courts, foreclosure sales, where a Subdivision Public Report is provided, etc.

I 16    This law requires that the **seller** fill out, sign, and provide the buyer with a form entitled **Real Estate Transfer Disclosure Statement**. This form must be delivered to the buyer as soon as practicable before transfer of title, or execution of the contract. The form lists the many items found in a dwelling, such as a dishwasher, trash compactor, air conditioner, etc. The seller checks which of these that the property has, and is required to provide information on any that are not in operating condition. The seller must also indicate any defects in the various building components such as the roof, foundation, electrical system and plumbing. He must also indicate whether there are any of a number of other things such as building additions made without permits, settling or other soil problems, flooding or drainage problems, noise problems, presence of environmentally hazardous substances or materials, and neighborhood nuisances, etc. The form provides a check-off list for the many items to be covered.

**I 17**  The form states that it contains a disclosure of the condition of the property within the personal knowledge of the seller, and is not a warranty of any kind by the seller or agent, and is not a substitute for any inspections or warranties the buyer may wish to obtain.

**I 18**  Additionally, Section III of the form must be completed by the agent representing the seller, and Section IV by the agent who obtains the offer, if he or she isn't the seller's agent. These portions of the disclosure statement must set forth the licensee's findings as a result of having made a reasonably competent visual inspection of the property. Sections III and IV of the form are designed to assist licensees in carrying out their duties as described in Civil Code Section 2079, et seq. See I 13 and I 14.

**I 19**  Under this law the seller or his agent shall not be liable for any error, inaccuracy or omission of any information if it was not within his or her personal knowledge. This also holds true if the information was provided by a public agency, or in a report or opinion delivered to the buyer which was provided by an expert, such as a licensed engineer, geologist, structural pest control operator, etc.

**I 20**  The disclosure statement provides the prospective transferee with important information about the property upon which to base his buying decision. If the disclosure statement is provided to him after he executes the offer to purchase, or if there are any significant changes made in it, then the transferee has a period in which he may terminate his offer by written notice to the transferor or his agent. He has three days in which to do this if the disclosure was delivered in person, or five days after delivery by deposit in mail.

I 21    No transfer shall be invalidated solely because of the failure of any person to comply with any provision of the law. However, any person who willfully or negligently violates it shall be **liable in the amount of actual damages suffered by a transferee**. The right of termination as stated in paragraph I 20 is not a contradiction of this, since transfer has not yet taken place.

I 22    In the past, a seller of this type of property has been in a more favorable position than the buyer, since he has lived with the property for some time, and is usually well aware of its shortcomings. Now he must share his knowledge with a prospective buyer, putting both on a more equal basis.

I 23    Any agent dealing in one to four unit residential properties should read the entire text of this very important law.

## "AS IS" CLAUSE

I 24    Real property may be sold with an "as is" clause in the contract. The "as is" clause is used to tell the buyer that the property is being sold in its existing condition, and that the buyer must accept it with whatever physical shortcomings it may have. This is legal and ethical because the basic rule in the sale of real property under California law is "caveat emptor" - let the buyer beware. Still, in California the buyer is given some protection. A seller may not intentionally or negligently misrepresent the condition of a property. A seller has the duty to disclose known facts materially affecting the value or desirability of the property which are not within the knowledge or reach of the buyer after diligent attention and observation. In order to avoid future liability, sellers and their brokers would do well to err on the side of overdisclosure. Buyers should be asked to confirm in writing that the disclosures were made. The two full disclosure laws discussed in this chapter pertaining to 1 to 4 dwelling units give additional protection to buyers of this class of property.

# POWER OF ATTORNEY

I 25    A **power of attorney** is a written instrument (document) which authorizes one person to act for another in his stead.

I 26    The person who confers this right upon another is called the **principal**, and the person authorized to act for the principal is called his **attorney-in-fact**.

I 27    The power of attorney may be either **general** or **specific**. The general power of attorney permits the attorney-in-fact to do all acts for his principal. The specific power of attorney permits him to do only those things which are specifically set forth in the instrument.

I 28    Any person capable of contracting may act as an attorney-in-fact. When he signs any instrument on behalf of his principal, he should sign in this manner: John Smith, by William Jones, his attorney-in-fact.

I 29    The power of attorney should always be recorded with the county recorder of the county in which the conferred power is to be used.

I 30    The principal may revoke the power of attorney at any time by recording a declaration revoking it. Death of either party also revokes it.

I 31    There are certain things an attorney-in-fact cannot do. He cannot give away his principal's property, convey or mortgage it without receiving adequate consideration; deed or mortgage property to himself; or otherwise use the principal's property for his own benefit. Such acts are voidable. He must have no interest adverse to his principal in order to act as an attorney-in-fact.

I 32    The power of attorney is a convenient instrument in many cases, particularly where business must be transacted when the principal is absent from the country, ill, etc.

# Agency
## Power of Attorney

## CHECK QUESTIONS

1. The broker enters into a position of trust and owes his loyalty to his principal. Such a relationship is called:
(A) Power of attorney      (B) Fiduciary
(C) Bonded agent      (D) Joint venture.      ( )   I 2

2. A seller's agent takes an offer to purchase to the seller of a ten acre parcel of land. While the seller is trying to decide whether or not to accept the offer, two more offers with different terms come in. The agent should:
(A) Take the two new offers to his principal immediately.
(B) Not take the two offers to the seller since he felt they were not as desirable as the first one
(C) Take only the best of the two new offers to the seller.
(D) Take the later offers to his principal only after he had decided to reject the original one, since the first offeror should have the first chance to buy the property.      ( )   I 2

3. Where a broker is the agent of both buyer and seller, but does not inform both of them of this:
(A) The broker is an undisclosed dual agent
(B) The buyer may rescind the purchase
(C) The broker could be liable for damages
(D) All of the above.      ( )   I 4

4. A broker may be:
(A) Agent of the seller solely
(B) Agent of the buyer solely
(C) A dual agent
(D) Any of the above.      ( )   I 4

5. The agency law which requires a broker to make an election as to whose agent he is going to be, buyer's, seller's or dual, and to inform the buyer and seller in writing of his election would apply to:
(A) A residential triplex      (B) Vacant land
(C) A restaurant building      (D) An office building.      ( )   I 8

6. A listing broker of 1 to 4 residential units must disclose to a prospective purchaser all facts materially affecting the value or desirability of a property within certain limits of responsibility. He is required to:
(A) Inspect the piping and wiring
(B) Make a reasonably competent and diligent visual inspection of the property
(C) Inspect any common areas
(D) Rely on the seller for information on the property.　　( )　I 14
(1)

7. The Real Estate Transfer Disclosure Statement which sellers are required to provide to buyers does not have to contain information on:
(A) Market value
(B) Defects in electrical system
(C) Flooding problems
(D) Neighborhood nuisances.　　( )　I 16

8. A document authorizing one person to act for another in his stead is known as a:
(A) Contract of Sale　　　　(B) Joint Note
(C) Power of Attorney　　　(D) None of these.　　( )　I 25

9. The person authorized to act for another is called his:
(A) Principal　　　　　　　(B) Declarant
(C) Attorney-in-fact　　　　(D) Specific agent.　　( )　I 26

10. If an attorney-in-fact deeds his principal's property to himself, such an act is:
(A) Permissible　　　　　　(B) Valid
(C) Voidable　　　　　　　(D) Legal.　　( )　I 31

11. A power of attorney can be revoked by:
(A) Recording an appropriate declaration
(B) Destroying the document
(C) Death of either party
(D) Both (A) and (C).　　( )　I 30

12. A power of attorney permitting the attorney-in-fact to do all acts for his principal is known as a:
(A) Specific power of attorney
(B) Exclusive Authorization
(C) General power of attorney
(D) Exclusive Agency.　　( )　I 27

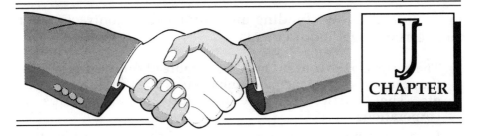

# CONTRACTS

**J1**     The real estate agent is greatly concerned with contracts, because it is through them that he is authorized to represent persons dealing in real estate. He earns his commissions by getting people to enter into contracts.

**J2**     According to California's Civil Code, a **contract** is an agreement between two or more persons to do certain things or, in some cases, not to do certain things. If the contract meets legal requirements, it may be enforced by law.

**J3**     Contracts may be oral or in writing. Both of these are termed **express** contracts. The written contract is usually more desirable, because if disagreement arises as to terms, it may be interpreted. In an **implied** contract, an agreement is shown by acts and conduct rather than words.

**J4**     Certain contracts must be in writing according to law in order to be enforced. **All agreements to buy, sell, or lease real estate for more than one year must be in writing to be enforced.** This includes listings, sale and purchase agreements, exchange agreements, etc.

**J5**     A broker's authorization to sell property must be in writing, otherwise he cannot sue for a commission. The law which requires these real estate contracts to be in writing is called the **Statute of Frauds**. It was passed because of the many controversies and suits which arose as a result of oral agreements in real estate. This law requires any real property contract to be written if it is not to be carried out within one year.

**J6**     In order to be binding and enforceable, contracts must meet certain legal requirements:

1.  The **parties to the contract must be capable of contracting**, that is, they cannot be unemancipated minors (see **D28**), insane, convicts, etc. The "parties" may be individuals, partnerships or corporations.
2.  Each party must give his **free and mutual consent**, meaning that he cannot be forced, threatened or tricked into agreeing to the terms of a contract.
3.  A **lawful object** is required, which means that any agreement to do some unlawful act cannot be enforced.
4.  A contract must have a **legally sufficient consideration**. A consideration is money, property, or an obligation of value. In other words, it should bestow mutual benefits upon the makers and not be entirely unfair to one of the parties.
5.  Most real estate contracts must be in writing to be enforceable as discussed above.

**J7**     A contract secured by duress, menace, fraud, or undue influence is voidable at law. **Duress** means use of force, such as depriving a person of his liberty or withholding his property. **Menace** means the use of threats. **Fraud** consists of making false promises, misrepresenting facts, etc. **Undue influence** means taking undue advantage of one's position or authority, or another's weakness or distress, etc. Mistakes may also make a contract unenforceable.

**J8**     To **execute** a contract means to sign and consent to carry out an agreement to completion. An **executed contract** is one where both parties have completely performed the terms of a contract. An **executory contract** is one where something needs to be done in order to bring it to completion.

**J10**     **Liquidated damages** are predetermined damages set forth in a contract to be paid by the party who defaults. This is used where it would be impractical or extremely difficult to determine actual damages if a default should occur.

**J11**     A seller or buyer may sue for **specific performance** if the other party defaults. Specific performance means compliance with the specific provisions of a contract or agreement. If a court orders specific performance, the buyer or seller is obligated to complete the terms of the contract.

**J12**    Specific performance suits often are brought by a buyer after a seller has agreed to sell and changes his mind for some reason, such as a rise in the market value of the property prior to the completion of the transaction.

**J13**    Sometimes a lawsuit is brought for the **rescission** of a contract. If the court orders rescission, the parties to the contract must put themselves in the same position they were in before they started to carry out the agreement; that is, any money paid must be returned, any property transferred must be returned, etc.

**J14**    **Cancellation** of a contract does not go that far. The parties merely cease to take any further steps in carrying out the contract, but past acts are not affected.

**J15**    A contract may be either rescinded or cancelled by mutual agreement of the parties. A contract may be terminated by fulfillment of its terms. **Novation** means a substitution of a new contract for an old one by mutual agreement of the parties.

**J16**    It sometimes happens that either the seller or buyer in a real estate transaction dies before completion of the transaction. A real estate contract properly drawn usually contains a provision which states that all the terms of the contract are to be binding upon the heirs, executors, administrators and the assigns of the respective parties.

**J17**    When the courts are called upon to interpret contracts, certain general rules are applied. To determine the intent of the parties, the whole of the contract is taken together; that is, certain statements are not considered without taking into consideration the apparent intent of the entire contract. If a printed form is used, the written parts supersede inconsistent printed parts. The intepretation is made with the idea of giving the terms of the contract a reasonable and lawful meaning.

**J18**    A person who induces another to sign a contract by making false oral promises or misrepresentations, cannot avoid the effects of this fraud by inserting a statement in the contract that there have been no promises or misrepresentations made that are not expressly set forth in the contract, or that the signer waives all rights to claim fraud because of any promises made before he signed. The fraud makes the whole contract voidable.

**J19**  A **void** contract is not a contract at all, because it lacks legal effect (e.g., an owner leased his property for gambling, but it cannot be so used, as gambling is illegal .) A **voidable** contract is one which appears valid and enforceable on its face, but one which one or more of the parties may reject (e.g., a contract induced by menace may be voided by the victim). A **valid** contract is one that is binding and enforceable. It is one that meets all legal requirements. An **unenforceable** contract is one which for some reason cannot be sued upon (e.g., a contract that cannot be enforced because of the passage of time under the Statute of Limitations).

**J20**  There are **unilateral** (one-sided) and **bilateral** (two-sided) contracts. The former is where one party is obligated only if the other performs. Advertising a reward for a lost watch is an example. A bilateral contract exists when both parties agree to carry out the terms of the contract.

**J21**  Uniform Vendor and Purchaser Risk Act. It sometimes happens, although infrequently, that after a contract is made for the purchase and sale of real property, a fire or other disaster destroys or seriously damages the property. Who shall take the loss? Under California's Uniform Vendor and Purchaser Risk Act, any contract made in this State for the purchase and sale of real property shall be interpreted as including an agreement that the parties shall have the following rights and duties unless the contract expressly provides otherwise:

(a) If, when neither the legal title nor the possession of the subject matter of the contract has been transferred, all or a material part thereof is destroyed without fault of the purchaser, the seller cannot enforce the contract and the purchaser is entitled to recover any of the portion of the price paid.

(b) If, when either the legal title or the possession of the subject matter of the contract has been transferred, all or any part thereof is destroyed without fault of the vendor, the purchaser is not thereby relieved from a duty to pay the price, nor entitled to recover any portion thereof that has been paid.

## Contracts

# CHECK QUESTIONS

1. An agreement between two persons to do or not to do certain things is called a:
   (A) Codicil          (B) Agenda
   (C) Contract         (D) Collusion.          (  )   J2

2. When a person signs a document in which he consents to carry out an agreement to completion, this is termed:
   (A) Execution of the agreement
   (B) Novation of the agreement
   (C) Rescission of the agreement
   (D) Substantiation of the agreement.          (  )   J8

3. In order to be enforceable at law, which of the following contracts usually must be in writing:
   (A) Listing agreement
   (B) Offer to purchase
   (C) Escrow instructions
   (D) All of the above.          (  )   J4

4. The law which requires real estate contracts to be in writing to be admissable in court, is called:
   (A) The Statute of Limitations
   (B) The Business and Professions Code
   (C) Statute of Frauds
   (D) Real Estate Law.          (  )   J5

5. Mr. Smith, a single man, had entered into a firm contract to purchase a store building on one acre of land. Before escrow closed and before he had signed loan documents and deposited the required amount of cash in escrow, he died. His son, who was his executor, should:
   (A) Demand that the escrow be cancelled
   (B) Try to negotiate a lower price
   (C) Perform in accordance with the terms of the contract
   (D) Require rescission of the contract.          (  )   J16

6. A contract signed under duress is:
   (A) Valid          (B) Voidable
   (C) Lawful         (D) Enforceable.          (  )   J7

7. A legally sufficient consideration is:
   (A) Money                        (B) Property
   (C) An obligation of value       (D) All of these.        (  )    J6
   
   **(4)**

8. The transfer of title by a married minor under 18 years of age is:
   (A) Void
   (B) Voidable by the grantor                                       J6
   (C) Voidable by either party                                     (1)
   (D) Legal.                                                 (  )   D28

9. Which of the following is not required for a valid contract:
   (A) Mutual consent               (B) Consideration
   (C) Lawful object                (D) Duress.              (  )    J6

10. A real estate contract may be terminated by:
    (A) Mutual consent of the contracting parties
    (B) Either (A) or (C)
    (C) Fulfillment of its terms
    (D) None of these.                                       (  )    J15

11. The parties to a contract agree to substitute a new contract for the old
    one. This is properly called:
    (A) Rescission                  (B) Novation
    (C) Bilateral                   (D) Executory.           (  )    J15

12. In the event of a breach in a sales contract, a suit for specific performance
    may be brought by:
    (A) The buyer only
    (B) The seller only
    (C) The broker
    (D) Either the buyer or seller.                          (  )    J11

13. When the parties to a contract put themselves, by court order or
    voluntarily, in the same position they were in before they entered into
    a contract, the contract has been:
    (A) Restored                    (B) Rescinded
    (C) Executed                    (D) Ratified.            (  )    J13

14. When the parties to a contract cease to take any further steps to carry out
    the contract, but past acts are not affected, the contract has been:
    (A) Novated                     (B) Rescinded
    (C) Executed                    (D) Cancelled.           (  )    J14

15. If there is any conflict in the provisions of a printed form contract:
    (A) The printed parts supersede the written parts
    (B) The contract is void
    (C) The written parts supersede the printed parts
    (D) It must be cancelled. ( ) J17

16. If a real property contract has a provision which is not to be carried out within one year, it is not enforceable if:
    (A) It is not recorded    (B) It is not in writing
    (C) It is not verified    (D) None of the above. ( ) J5

17. The use of force, such as depriving a person of his liberty in order to secure consent to a contract is termed:
    (A) Duress    (B) Depression
    (C) Unlawful detainer    (D) Forced action. ( ) J7

18. Securing consent to a contract by means of threats is:
    (A) Delusion    (B) Trickery
    (C) Overbearance    (D) Menace. ( ) J7

19. Taking advantage of one's authority or another's weakness to secure consent to a contract is termed:
    (A) Fraud    (B) Forceful detainer
    (C) Undue influence    (D) Illegal persuasion. ( ) J7

20. A contract where something still needs to be done to bring it to completion is called:
    (A) An executed contract    (B) Implied contract
    (C) Bilateral contract    (D) Executory contract. ( ) J8

21. When a contract recites the extent of damages to be paid by a party in the event he defaults under the terms of a binding contract, and the other party is stopped from claiming damages other than those specified, such damages are called:
    (A) Liquidated damages    (B) Full settlement damages
    (C) Consent damages    (D) Perverse damages. ( ) J10

22. A contract which obligates one party, only if the other elects to perform, is called:
    (A) Restricted    (B) Liquidated
    (C) Bilateral    (D) Unilateral. ( ) J20

This page intentionally left blank.

# Listings, Deposit Receipts, Options & Probate Sales

**CHAPTER**

## LISTINGS

**K1** **Listings are contracts** whereby licensed agents are authorized to find a purchaser for a specified property at a specified price and terms, usually within a certain time limit.

**K2** The consideration given by the agent is that he will use his efforts to locate such a purchaser.

**K3** A listing may merely authorize a broker to find a purchaser and not authorize him to do anything else. If he is to secure a deposit or do anything else, the listing should specifically give such authorization. The usual listing form does give authorization to the agent to both find a purchaser and accept a deposit.

**K4** When a purchaser is found during the term of the typical listing who is ready, willing and able to buy in accordance with its provisions, the broker has completed his work and is entitled to his remuneration. However, the listing may state that no commission is payable except on a completed transaction. As a general practice, the agent also usually arranges to place the transaction in escrow, smooth out petty differences between buyer and seller, arranges for a termite inspection, and many other things.

**K5** Listings fall under four general classes: open listings, exclusive agency listings, exclusive right to sell listings, and multiple listings. These should all be in writing and signed by the owners of the property to be sold.

**K6** Oral listings are not illegal, as is often said; but they give the broker no protection, and he cannot force collection of his commission if the seller refuses to pay it. Most brokers refuse to work on them. If an owner is serious about selling his property, he should be willing to give a written listing.

**K7**     An **open listing** does not prohibit a seller from giving a similar listing to as many agents as he pleases. He may give this type of listing to several brokers. The first one to find a buyer and get the seller's acceptance makes the sale. Brokers hesitate to spend much money or time in finding a buyer, since they have no assurance that another broker may not sell it first. If an owner sells a property himself, he is not obligated to pay a commission to any of the brokers to whom he gave open listings. Open listings are not required to contain a definite termination date, but sometimes they have one.

**K8**     An **exclusive agency listing** gives the exclusive right to sell the property to one broker only, but does not prevent the owner from selling it. If he does, he need not pay a commission. This type of listing must have a definite termination date.

**K9**     An **exclusive right to sell listing** makes a broker the sole person having the right to sell a property. Not even the owner may sell it while the listing is in effect without paying a commission to the broker. Brokers should not take this type of listing unless they are willing to spend time and money to find a buyer. This kind of listing must also have a definite termination date. The exclusive right to sell listing is the one preferred by agents, and is the type most often used in real estate brokerage.

**K10**     The **multiple listing** is usually an exclusive right to sell listing given to a broker who belongs to an organization of brokers, with the understanding that it will be circulated to all members of the organization giving them the right to work on it. Many real estate associations maintain this service for members. It is very effective in securing action and the highest price for sellers, and promotes business for the broker members.

**K11**     The Real Estate Law requires that a copy of any listing taken be given to the person signing it **at the time it is signed**.

**K12**   Any exclusive listing must have a **definite termination date**. It cannot for instance, be taken for a period starting with the date of the listing and state "until sold." Or, it cannot be "effective until cancelled in writing," etc. A violation occurs when the broker claims, demands or receives a fee on a listing without a definite termination date. The law applies the requirement to any exclusive listings relating to transactions for which a license is required; not only sales and exchanges, but to loan authorizations, leases, etc. (Section 10176f)

**K13**   A listing may provide that the broker be protected against sale by the owner to one of the broker's prospects for a definite period after the listing expires. The terms of a listing contract which includes such a protective clause usually requires that the broker furnish the owner of the property with a list of prospective purchasers with whom the broker has shown the property. This must be done within a certain number of days after expiration of the listing.

**K14**   In order to prevent misunderstanding where personal property is to be included in the sale of real property, it is a good idea to make a list describing the various items, and include a statement on the listing form that "the sale price shall include all personal property listed in the inventory attached hereto."

**K15**   A **net listing** is one which specifies that the owner (seller) is to receive a certain sum for a property, with all sale expenses including the broker's commission to be covered by any price the broker obtains in excess of the net figure. Sometimes the seller agrees to pay title and escrow costs from his share, but requires the broker to get his commission over and above the net figure. If a net listing is used, the meaning of the term should be thoroughly explained to the principal who should be fully informed that all monies received over and above the net price will be kept by the broker as commission on the transaction.

**K16**   Some brokers consider net listings to be unfair and will not use them. It may be seen that the broker might have the inclination to beat the seller down to the lowest possible price and then sell the property for the highest possible price in order to secure the greatest commission. This is contrary to his duty as an agent, which is to serve his principal to the best advantage.

**K17**  While net listings may lead to abuses very easily, they are legal contracts, and if the broker uses them fairly, there is no breach of the ethics of the business.

**K18**  The Real Estate Law requires that the broker, when using a net listing, tell the seller what commission he is making before signing him to a sale agreement. The broker is also required to reveal to both buyer and seller the selling price in writing within one month of the closing of the transaction. The escrow closing statement will suffice for this. Penalty for failure to do this is revocation or suspension of license.

**K19**  Sometimes a broker may not complete a sale, but carry negotiations along far enough to cause the deal to be made. In such a case, he is said to be the **procuring cause** and may be entitled to his commission.

**K20**  It is not necessary to use the legal description of a property in the listing agreement. Any description which definitely describes the property will do, such as an address or an assessor's parcel number.

**K21**  We gave the usual meaning of a listing to the average person in the business in paragraph K1. The Real Estate Law gives it a broader interpretation and applies it to various agreements entered into by brokers in the real estate and business opportunity businesses over which the Law gives the Commissioner certain controls. These include a number of things such as a list of prospective rentals for which a charge is made; an agreement by which the agent, for a fee, undertakes to promote the sale or lease of property or a business through some advertising service; the finding of a suitable property for purchase or lease, or various other assignments. A broad definition of the term "listing" might include any oral or written agreement between a real estate broker and a principal, whereby the agent is to render a service for which he is licensed to give in expectation of a fee or compensation.

## DEPOSIT RECEIPTS

**K22**   When the broker or salesperson has helped his or her client locate a property which the client would like to own, the client is encouraged to make an offer to purchase the property backed-up by an "earnest money" deposit.

**K23**   In general use in California are forms which are used to write-up the offer and provide a receipt for the earnest money. These forms are provided by the California Association of Realtors (CAR) and by some local Associations of Realtors. The proper name for these forms is **"real estate purchase contract and receipt for deposit."** However, they are commonly referred to in the business as a **"deposit receipt"**. A deposit receipt problem using a two-page form is included in the final examination. You will find this form on pages338 and 339. A four-page deposit receipt form provided by CAR would be more suitable for some transactions. Also, occasionally in unique and complicated transactions an attorney who specializes in real estate is employed to draw-up a contract for the purchase of property.

**K24**   Whichever form the agent selects for a particular offer to purchase, he should be thoroughly familiar with it since it is the basic contract for the purchase and sale of the real estate involved. The deposit receipt should set forth all of the things to be agreed-upon by buyer and seller, including price, financing, length of the escrow, time of possession of the property by the buyer, who pays which expenses of the sale, and possibly many other things. The deposit receipt also provides for agreement of the seller to pay the broker a commission of a certain amount. The terms of this document should be explained carefully to both buyer and seller.

**K25**   After the buyer executes the deposit receipt, the broker should take it to the seller as soon as possible, **because a person who submits a real estate offer may withdraw it at any time before it is accepted and the fact of the acceptance is communicated to him.** Therefore, the broker should notify a buyer at once when his offer is accepted.

**K26** If the seller changes the terms of the original offer to purchase in any way, he has made a counteroffer, and the buyer is not bound by his original offer as it is deemed rejected.

**K26.1** There are special rules which apply to liquidation clauses in deposit receipts where the contract in question is for the purchase and sale of residential real property of not more than four residential units where the buyer intends to occupy one of the units as a residence. (CC1675, et. seq.)

1. These special rules apply only to amounts actually prepaid, in the form of deposit or downpayment.

2. If the amount paid pursuant to the liquidated damages clause does not exceed 3% of the purchase price, the clause is valid unless the buyer proves that the amount paid is unreasonable.

3. If the amount actually paid pursuant to the liquidated damages clause exceeds 3% of the purchase price, the clause is invalid unless the party seeking to enforce it proves that the amount paid is reasonable.

4. The provision must be separately signed or initialed by each party to the contract, and if it is a printed contract, the provision must be set off in ten point bold type or contrasting red print in eight point type.

5. These rules do not apply to real property sales contracts as defined in Chapter M.

**K26.2** Purchase contracts commonly include contingencies which must be met before a sale can be concluded. For instance, a prospective buyer may require that the sale of his present dwelling close escrow before the purchase of a new home may close escrow. Or, a prospective buyer may require a report which shows a property to be free of harmful asbestos. There any number of conditions which may be included in a purchase contract which must be satisfactorily fulfilled before an escrow may be closed. If the escrow fails because of a contingency that is not satisfied, or for some other reason which is the fault of the seller, the buyer is entitled to the return of his deposit. New law effective January 1, 1991 (CC 1057.3) applies to this. It pertains only to one to four unit residential properties, one of which is to be owner occupied. Where the seller has wrongfully withheld consent to a return of the deposit, the buyer under this law has the right of return of his deposit, and damages of treble the amount of funds he deposited in escrow, but not less than $100 or more than $1,000. Further, the seller would also be liable for attorney's fees to enforce this statute.

**K27**   Remember that the Real Estate Law requires that brokers and salespersons must give copies of documents and agreements to all persons signing them at the time they are signed. Also, copies of these documents must be kept in the broker's file for three years.

## MISCELLANEOUS ITEMS CONCERNING BROKERAGE

**K28**   **The amount of commission an agent receives for his work is purely a matter of agreement with the principal.** There is no schedule of commission rates established by law. The rate agreed-upon is usually established by custom. Real estate associations in different communities used to suggest a schedule of rates, but no longer do so in accordance with federal government agreements to drop anti-trust charges. It is unlawful for any group to specify that members must adhere to certain rates. **The law provides that a notice of the negotiability of commissions be inserted in real estate contracts where the property is one to four residential units.**

**K29**   The property owner/seller who gives a listing and agrees to pay for the broker's services is called the broker's **client or principal**. The prospective buyer is sometimes referred to as the **customer**. A seller is also a **vendor**, and the buyer a **vendee**.

## OPTIONS

**K30**   An agreement whereby one person, **for a consideration,** gives another person the right to buy his real property within a certain time limit for a specified price and upon specified terms is called a **real estate option**. Options also may be used in connection with personal property. Options, like other real estate contracts, must be in writing and should be recorded to give constructive public notice.

**K31**   An option is not a listing, because it does not make anyone an agent. The person taking an option is a prospective buyer and, therefore, a principal.

**K32**   The person giving the right and receiving the consideration is the **optionor**. The one taking or receiving the option is the **optionee**.

**K33**   The optionee has the right to buy the property (exercise the option), but is not obliged to do so. If he does not, he merely loses his option money or other thing of value he has given the optionor for giving him the right to buy during the option period.

**K34**   If the optionee decides to buy the property, the option becomes a sales contract, and both optionor and optionee are legally bound by its terms. It is important that the option set out the details of the sale if the option is exercised. For example, if it merely sets forth the total sales price, the optionee cannot insist on financing terms when he exercises the option.

**K35**   The proposed buyer (optionee) must notify the optionor of his election to buy the property **within the time limit** set out in the option.

**K36**   Since the optionee is a principal and not an agent, he does not need a real estate license.

**K37**   The optionee must give the optionor a valuable consideration, such as a sum of money, a note, etc. The consideration need not be large. Even 25 cents on a $100,000 option price would suffice. However, the consideration must in fact, pass from optionee to the optionor for the option to be valid.

**K38**   Options may be assigned to others unless the purchase price is to consist wholly or partially of a note to be executed by the optionee. This protects the optionor, since while the optionee might be a good credit risk, an assignee may be a poor risk.

**K39**   The broker who takes an option to buy property should go out of his way to make it clear that he is not acting as an agent, but as a principal.

## PROBATE SALES

**K40**   This could get into a rather long and involved subject, but there are certain fundamentals with which the broker or salesperson should be acquainted. First of all, the executor or administrator of an estate from which property is to be sold, cannot until court approval is received, give an exclusive listing or option, fix the commission rate, or bind the estate to a sale. No commission may be paid except from the proceeds of a sale approved by the court. The amount of the commission must be approved by the court.

**K41**   After an initial purchase bid has been received and approved by the court, a public hearing is held by the court at which time further bids on the property are solicited. The original bidder is protected to the extent that a second bidder must increase the original offer by at least 10% of the first $10,000 bid, and 5% in excess of that amount. If a broker produces a client who makes the original offer and he is over-bid by someone who is not represented by an agent, the court may award him a commission on the amount of the original offer only. Effective January 1, 1991, on confirmation of sales of improved real property, the court will not approve any real estate commission in excess of 5%, without good cause shown for any larger commission.

## Listings, Deposit Receipts, Options and Probate Sales

## CHECK QUESTIONS

1. Listings are contracts whereby licensed agents are authorized to find a purchaser for a specified property at a specified price and terms and usually:
   (A) They are not in writing
   (B) Within a certain time limit
   (C) In the form of an option
   (D) They cannot be enforced.                    (   )   K1

2. Under the typical exclusive listing, the broker is entitled to his commission when:
   (A) The deed is delivered
   (B) The escrow closes
   (C) A bona-fide offer at the full price and terms is produced
   (D) The listing expires.                         (   )   K4

3. A broker has no protection and cannot force collection of his commission, if the listing he holds is:
   (A) An Exclusive Agency      (B) Oral
   (C) An Exclusive Right        (D) Multiple listing.     (   )   K6

4. A broker received an exclusive agency listing, and when the owner sold the property himself, he demanded a full commission. The broker was entitled to:
   (A) A full commission         (B) A half commission
   (C) No commission             (D) Advertising costs.     (   )   K8

5. A broker who holds an exclusive right to sell listing is entitled to his commission if the property is sold by:
   (A) Himself                   (B) Any broker
   (C) Owner                     (D) Any of the above.      (   )   K9

6. The Real Estate Law requires that a copy of any listing taken be given to the person signing it:
   (A) By the next business day
   (B) At the time it is signed
   (C) At the time the broker approves it
   (D) Within two weeks.                             (   )   K11

7. Mr. Lin agreed to give Mr. Smith his personal note for $10 as consideration for a 10-day option to purchase Smith's property. The option was invalid:
   (A) If Lin was not a resident of California
   (B) Because options must be for at least 30 days
   (C) If Lin's note was not actually delivered to Smith
   (D) Because the $10 was insufficient consideration.　　( )　K37

8. When a broker carries negotiations far enough along to cause the deal to be made even though he did not complete the sale, he may be:
   (A) Entitled to no commission
   (B) The procuring cause
   (C) Entitled to commission
   (D) Both (B) and (C).　　( )　K19

9. When using a net listing, the Real Estate Law requires a broker to:
   (A) Split his commission with the owner
   (B) Supply owner with names of all of his prospects
   (C) Divulge the extent of his commission before the seller signs a sale agreement
   (D) None of the above.　　( )　K18

10. When an optionee decides to buy the property and exercises the option, the option becomes:
    (A) Extinct　　　　　　(B) Cancelled
    (C) A sales contract　　(D) An exclusive listing.　　( )　K34

11. A broker who takes an option should make it clear to the seller and any buyer that he is acting as:
    (A) An agent　　　　(B) An optionor
    (C) A principal　　　(D) A debtor.　　( )　K39

12. A court has approved an original offer to purchase a mobilehome park from an estate at a price of $3,400,000. At the court's public hearing, what minimum additional amount must be bid in order to get the property:
    (A) $170,500　(B) $340,000　(C) $150,400　(D) $15,000. ( )　K41

13. A person who submits a real estate offer may withdraw it at any time
    (A) Within 24 hours
    (B) Before it is accepted and such acceptance is communicated to him
    (C) Within three days of acceptance
    (D) Before the close of escrow.　　( )　K25

14. If, upon receipt of an offer to purchase under certain terms, the seller makes a counter offer, the prospective purchaser is:
    (A) Bound by the counter offer
    (B) Bound by his original offer
    (C) Bound by the agent's decision
    (D) Relieved from his original offer.　　( )　K26

This page intentionally left blank.

# ENCUMBRANCES

**CHAPTER**

**L1**    Generally speaking, an **encumbrance** on real property is anything which affects or limits the title. It is a broad term and includes both important and relatively unimportant things affecting title.

**L2**    Encumbrances include such important things as mortgages and easements which have a substantial effect on a property. They also include less important things such as boundary utility easements, and other minor things which may appear when the condition of title of a property is searched.

**L3**    **Liens** are a certain class of encumbrances. They affect the property by making it security for the payment of some debt, or performance of some act. For example, real estate taxes and mortgages are liens because the property is security for the payment of a certain sum of money.

**L4**    Some examples of encumbrances which affect the physical use of a property are recorded restrictions, easements, and zoning requirements.

**L5**    Remember, all liens are encumbrances. All encumbrances are not liens.

**L6**    Liens are classified in two groups, **voluntary** and **involuntary liens**. A mortgage is a voluntary lien as the owner voluntarily puts it on his property by borrowing money. Real estate taxes are an example of an involuntary lien as they are required by law. County and State agencies are required to notify owners when an involuntary lien is recorded.

**L7**    Liens are also classified as **general liens** and **specific liens**. A general lien affects all property an owner may have. A delinquent income tax payment is an example of a cause for a general lien. A specific lien affects only some specific property held by an owner. Property taxes and a mortgage are examples of specific liens.

**L8**     A **judgment** is a lien on property which results from an order of a court as a result of a lawsuit. If you are sued for injuring someone, the court may award the person a judgment of say, $1,000. If recorded in the county where you own property, it is a lien on all properties in your name. Hence, it is a general lien. More details on judgments will be given later.

**L9**     A **mechanic's lien** is a special lien which the law permits to be recorded on real property in cases where the general contractor, subcontractor, workmen, or persons furnishing materials are not paid for their services, labor or materials. A recorded mechanic's lien can make the value of real property security for payment if all legal requirements are complied with. The following pertains to private (not government) construction projects.

**L10**     There are time limits for recording mechanic's liens; the time being different under different circumstances, but in no case less than thirty days or more than ninety days after completion of a construction project or a repair job.

**L11**     The time limit for recording these liens depends upon whether or not a notice of completion is recorded. A **notice of completion** is a notice recorded by an owner in the county recorder's office giving constructive notice that the job has been finished. To be valid concerning mechanic's liens, these must be recorded within ten days after all work is completed. Also, if work has stopped for a continuous period of 30 days the owner may record a **notice of cessation**.

**L12**     When either of these notices are recorded, the general contractor has 60 days in which to record a lien; and all subcontractors, workmen and material houses have 30 days.

**L13** Completion of work on improvements for mechanics' lien purposes is also considered to occur when:

- The improvements are occupied, or are used by the owner or his agent, and all work on the project has stopped.

- The improvements resulting from the work have been accepted by the owner or his agent.

- All labor on the project stops for a continuous period of 60 days.

**L14** If completion qualifies under one of the ways in L13, then the general contractor and everyone furnishing labor or material to the job has 90 days to record a lien.

**L15** A construction trust deed normally has priority over mechanics' liens on a construction project. However, a mechanic's lien can have priority over a trust deed lien which attaches to a property. For instance, if the foundation of a building is started, or building materials are delivered to a property before a trust deed to finance the building is recorded, then even a mechanic's lien filed by a plasterer for unpaid wages (the plasterer coming on the job several weeks later) will come ahead of the trust deed as a claim against the property. For this reason finance companies, or anyone else making a construction loan, check a property to see that no work has been done nor materials delivered just before recording their trust deed.

**L16** If a contractor does not pay his workers, or for his material, liens may be filed on the property even though the owner has properly paid the contractor. For this reason, owners often require contractors to furnish a bond to guarantee payment of debts incurred in connection with the building job, and withhold final payment to the contractor until the period for filing mechanics' liens is over.

**L17** A law designed to protect the property owner, general contractor, and construction lender from "double jeopardy" in the matter of mechanics' liens, provides that prior to recording a mechanics' lien, anyone who supplies material, equipment, services, or labor on a construction job must provide a **preliminary notice** to the general contractor, the owner, and the lender, in writing within 20 days of their first contact with the construction project, that they have a right to record a lien if they are not paid. However, a 1987 law permits the 20-day preliminary notice to be filed with the county recorder. When the notice of completion or notice of cessation is recorded, the county recorder notifies the owner, contractor, and lender, of those who have filed the 20-day notice. This preliminary notice may be given after the 20 days, however the priority of a mechanic's lien may then suffer in priority to other liens. When the owner and the others know who is involved on the job, they can verify whether or not they have been paid for their services or material.

L18    Those who record mechanics' liens must start a suit to foreclose the property within 90 days. The court may order the property sold to satisfy the claims. If enough is not secured from the sale to pay the claims, then the court may give a deficiency judgment against the owner for the balance.

L19    Mortgages and trust deeds are liens with which the broker and salesperson deal frequently. Because of their importance, a special chapter is devoted to them. Taxes and assessments are also very common and important liens. Special attention will also be given to them.

L20    A **writ of execution** is a court order directing the sheriff (or some officer) to sell property and pay off a judgment with the proceeds.

L21    A **notice of nonresponsibility** is a notice used by a person having an interest in a parcel of real estate to protect himself against mechanics' liens or other claims. For instance, an owner who has sold a property on a purchase contract, or who has leased it, may protect his interest against claims of workmen or materialmen who have furnished labor or material for improvements at the request of the contract purchaser or lessee.

If within 10 days after he discovers work is being done, his interest in the property is protected if he posts a notice of nonresponsibility on the property and records a copy with the county recorder.

**L22** He must post the notice in some conspicuous place on the property. For recording this notice, his signature must not be merely acknowledged, but must be verified. To verify a document means to take an oath or affirmation as to its correctness. If he does all of this properly, any mechanic's lien will not have priority over his interest.

**L23** The term **cloud on a title** is a general term used to denote any encumbrance on property, but usually one which does not greatly affect it. However, sometimes these clouds are serious enough to affect the conveying of a property's title.

## Encumbrances

## CHECK QUESTIONS

1. Which of the following statements is false:
   (A) An encumbrance affects the title
   (B) All encumbrances are liens
   (C) Leases and easements are encumbrances                    **L3**
   (D) All liens are encumbrances.                      (   )    **L5**

2. Which of the following is an encumbrance, but not a lien:
   (A) Mortgage                 (B) Restriction
   (C) Trust deed               (D) Taxes.               (   )    **L4**

3. Which of the following is an involuntary lien:
   (A) Real estate taxes        (B) Mortgage
   (C) Trust deed               (D) None of the above.   (   )    **L6**

4. A lien which affects all property an owner may have is known as a:
   (A) Mechanic's lien          (B) General lien
   (C) Specific lien            (D) Property lien.        (   )    **L7**

5. When an abstract of judgment is recorded it becomes:
   (A) A specific lien against one property
   (B) An easement covering one property
   (C) A general lien on all real property owned in the county
   (D) An attachment lien.                              (   )    **L8**

6. To be effective, a general contractor must file a mechanic's lien within:
   (A) 30 days after notice of completion is recorded
   (B) 60 days after notice of completion is recorded
   (C) 10 days from date money was due and unpaid
   (D) 90 days after notice of completion.              (   )    **L12**

7. Which of the following have only 30 days to file a mechanic's lien after a notice of completion:
   (A) Material Suppliers
   (B) Mechanics or other workmen
   (C) Subcontractors
   (D) All of the above.                                (   )    **L12**

8. Everyone furnishing labor or material to a job has 90 days to file the lien if:
   (A) A notice of completion is filed
   (B) A notice of abandonment is filed
   (C) There is a suspension of work for 60 continuous days
   (D) None of the above.                                      ( )   L14

9. Owner had a free and clear lot and had a load of lumber delivered to it. Later he got a construction loan for $15,000 from a pension fund which was recorded after the lumber delivery. Everyone connected with the job was paid, except that the lumber company and the painter were unable to collect $1,000 each. They both filed mechanics' liens. If the property was sold at a foreclosure sale for $15,000, the amount that the pension fund could recover is:
   (A) $15,000                    (B) $14,000
   (C) $13,000                    (D) $12,500.                 ( )   L15

10. The notice filed by an owner of real property to protect himself against liens for work and material which he has not ordered (maybe vendee or lessee did) is called:
   (A) Notice of abandonment
   (B) Notice of completion
   (C) Notice of nonresponsibility
   (D) Writ of execution.                                      ( )   L21

11. Which of the following is an encumbrance which affects the physical use of the land?
   (A) Land contract              (B) IRS lien
   (C) Trust deed                 (D) Easement.                ( )   L4

12. Mr. and Mrs. Stephens were injured in an automobile accident. The court found Mr. Mason at fault and awarded the Stephens a judgment in the amount of $175,000. The Stephens recorded an abstract of judgment. What kind of encumbrance did this create?
   (A) A specific lien            (B) A general lien
   (C) A voluntary lien           (D) A trust lien.            ( )   L8

This page intentionally left blank.

# Mortgages, Deeds of Trust & Sales Contracts

CHAPTER

## MORTGAGES

**M1**   Both mortgages and deeds of trust (trust deeds) have the same purpose, that is, to make real estate security for money owed by the owner of a property. The methods by which they do this are different, and we shall point out these differences in this chapter. First, let us consider the mortgage.

**M2**   A **mortgage** is the time honored method of securing real estate loans. It is a contract whereby property is hypothecated to secure a debt or obligation. In other words, a mortgage is a contract which makes a property legally the security, or guarantee, that a loan (note) will be paid, or that some obligation will be fulfilled in a specified time.

**M3**   **Hypothecate** simply means to give a thing as security without giving up the right to use it. The person who mortgages a home for instance, retains the use and benefits of it as long as he keeps up his part of the bargain by making the mortgage payments.

**M4**   Just two parties are involved in a mortgage, the property owner who borrows, and the lender. The borrower is called the **mortgagor**, and the lender is the **mortgagee**.

**M5**   The mortgagor does not transfer the title of his property to anyone.

**M6**   The debt is evidenced by a note signed by the mortgagor, and the mortgage contract merely makes the property the security for the payment of the note.

**M7**   Mortgages are recorded as a matter of course, so that they will come ahead of (have priority over) any liens recorded afterwards.

**M8** When it is paid off, that is, when the note is paid, the lender must make out a **certificate of discharge**, and have it recorded and sent to the borrower. (Wipes mortgage from records).

**M9** If all mortgages were paid off according to terms, we could drop the subject right here, but unfortunately people are sometimes unable to pay the principal and interest and the lender must foreclose.

**M10** To foreclose means to bring a suit in court to sell the mortgaged property to pay off the loan, accrued interest and cost of the suit. This is done under a special section of the law which sets forth the exact procedure required. This is referred to as a **judicial foreclosure**.

**M11** If the mortgage has been assigned to someone else, that person can start the foreclosure. The person holding the mortgage usually makes everyone having any interest or claim on the property a defendant in the suit. A foreclosure guarantee report may be secured from a title company which will provide the names of all such parties.

**M12** The case comes to trial and if the default is established, the court orders a sale of the property to be held by the sheriff or court commissioner. If the sale brings more than enough to pay the debt and costs of the suit, the balance goes to the junior lien holders, and then any remainder to the mortgagor (former owner).

**M13** If the property does not sell for enough to pay off the debt and costs, the lender may ask the court for a **deficiency judgment**. He must do this within three months after the foreclosure sale of the property. A deficiency judgment is a personal judgment against the debtor for either (1) the deficiency amount between the unpaid debt plus costs and the sale price or (2) the deficiency amount between the unpaid debt plus costs and the fair market value of the security as determined by the court, whichever deficiency amount is smaller. The court may determine that the property sold too low at the foreclosure sale. (CC 726) **Deficiency judgements cannot be obtained if the mortgage was a purchase money mortgage as defined by law**.

**M14** A **purchase money mortgage** is one given to the seller as part of the purchase price when buying property. It is also a mortgage given to a **third party** (usually a financial institution) that makes a loan to the buyer of real property to be used as part of the purchase price of a **dwelling of not more than four units occupied in part or entirely by the buyer**. The purchase money mortgage may be a first, or a junior lien such as a 2nd or 3rd mortgage.

**M15** Therefore, no deficiency judgment may be obtained where the mortgage was given to the seller as part of the purchase price regardless of the type of property. Nor may it be obtained where a third party made the loan to be used as part of the purchase price on one to four dwelling units to be all or partly owner-occupied. However, one may possibly be obtained on any other type of property in connection with a third-party mortgage, for example, a triplex not owner-occupied, vacant land, commercial property, etc.

**M16** The sheriff or court commissioner does not issue a deed until one year after the sale if the sale proceeds do not satisfy the amount of debt plus accrued interest and costs. If the sale proceeds do fully cover these, then this period is three months. In the meantime, the mortgagor may redeem his property any time during the year or three month period by paying the full amount of the mortgage indebtedness and all costs of foreclosure.

**M17** During the 3 month or year period, the owner is said to have an **equity of redemption**. He can retain possession of the property and reside in it. He can sell his equity of redemption.

**M18** If the owner does not redeem before the redemption period is up, the buyer in the foreclosure sale may sue him for the fair rent of the property during that period.

# TRUST DEEDS

**M20** The mechanics whereby a trust deed secures a loan are different from a mortgage. Instead of merely making the property security for the loan, the owner actually deeds it to a third party to hold until the loan is paid.

**M21** The third party, who is the stakeholder, is called the **trustee**. Under a trust deed the trustee has only the **naked legal title**, and has no other interest in the property until such time as a default is made on the terms of the trust deed note.

**M22** The borrower is called the **trustor** and the lender, the **beneficiary**. Therefore, there are three parties involved in a trust deed, or deed of trust.

**M23** The law does not specifically provide for the creation of trust deeds as it does mortgages. They came about through use.

**M24** Why did trust deeds originate? Because lenders sought a method whereby they could foreclose more quickly without court action and consequent delays. They also did not like the one-year equity of redemption.

**M25** In defense of the trust deed, lenders argue that they can risk more liberal loans on better terms if they can recover their loans more quickly in case of default. **The great preponderance of real estate financing in California is secured by trust deeds**.

**M26** The trustee is able to foreclose in case the borrower defaults, because the borrower has given him the **power of sale**. The trust deed he signed provides for it.

**M27** The loan in connection with a trust deed is also evidenced by a note. The trust deed makes the property security for payment of the note.

**M28** If the borrower under a trust deed pays off the loan, the lender (beneficiary) requests the trustee to deed back the property to the borrower. The trustee draws up and signs a **deed of reconveyance** which clears the trust deed from the records when it is recorded.

**M29**  Should the borrower (trustor) default, that is, not pay the principal and interest as required by the note, the beneficiary gives the trustee a written notice stating that the borrower has defaulted.

**M30**  The trustee then notifies the borrower that he is in default in certain respects, and that the beneficiary chooses to have the trustee sell the property to recover the debt. A copy of the **Notice of Default** is then recorded.

**M31**  The trustee must then wait three months, after which he publishes a **Notice of Sale** in a newspaper of general circulation, giving the time and place of the sale and a description of the property. The sale must be set for not less than 21 days from the day the advertisement first appears. At least 20 days before the day of the sale, a copy of the Notice of Sale must be posted prominently on the property to be sold and recorded with the county recorder.

**M32**  The property is then sold at public auction, and the lender paid from the proceeds. Bids must be in cash or equivalent, except that the amount due the lender may be used instead of cash. If there is any excess over the loan balance, unpaid interest, and costs, it goes to any junior lien holders, and then any remainder to the trustor. If the sale does not bring enough to satisfy the loan, the lender must be content. The first trust deed is satisfied first. If there are no additional proceeds available, any junior trust deeds are wiped out.

**M33**  After the sale under foreclosure of a trust deed, the trustee issues a **Trustee's Deed**.

**M34**  New law (1986) permits the default to be cured up to **five business days** prior to the sale. The borrower may reinstate his loan by making up any delinquent payments, interest, costs, etc. This is called the **right of reinstatement**.

**M35**  In the above discussion of the foreclosure of a 1st trust deed, any junior trust deeds could be wiped out. This will occur if the holders of junior trust deeds take no action. The law requires that the Notice of Default must be sent within one month of recording, by registered or certified mail, to the beneficiary or mortgagee of any recorded junior trust deed or mortgage, or to any assignee of these. This is required whether or not a **Request for Notice of Default** had been recorded by the junior lien holder. It seems however, that it would be prudent to record such a request. Also, the holder of a first lien on real property must disclose loan delinquencies of four months or more to any holder of a junior lien.

**M36**  For example, say that you are the holder of a 2nd trust deed and a Notice of Default has been recorded by the trustee of the 1st trust deed. The law provides that you can make up the back payments on the first trust deed note within 90 days after the Notice of Default is recorded, and add the amount to what is due on your second trust deed. This stops the foreclosure proceedings on the 1st trust deed. After making demand for reimbursement from the owner, if he does not do so, you may start foreclosure on your 2nd trust deed. Then if the property goes to a trustee's sale, the person who makes the successful bid is the new owner of the property - subject to the first trust deed and the note it secures. The holder of the 2nd trust deed may credit-bid the total amount owed him plus cash if he wishes. If he is outbid by another, then he is paid in cash for his interest.

**M37**  No deficiency judgment may be obtained after such a trustee's sale. Only when trust deeds are foreclosed by court action as described under mortgages, may a deficiency judgment be secured. They also may not be secured on a purchase money deed of trust. The information pertaining to purchase money mortgages (see M13, 14 & 15) also applies to purchase money trust deeds.

**M38**  Trust deeds may be foreclosed by court procedure if desired. On the other hand, mortgages are sometimes used which carry a power of sale provision. No deficiency judgment may be secured if these are foreclosed by the use of the power of sale.

# SPECIAL MORTGAGE AND TRUST DEED PROVISIONS

**M39** Sometimes a special provision is included in a mortgage or trust deed, whereby it is agreed that the owner may borrow a certain sum on another trust deed or mortgage which shall have priority over the mortgage in existence. Such a provision is called a **subordination clause**.

**M40** As an example, a home may be subject to two trust deeds, a first trust deed for $50,000 and a second trust deed for $30,000. If the first trust deed becomes due before the second trust deed was paid off, it could not be refinanced without the second trust deed becoming the first lien, unless a subordination clause kept the second lien in its place. This might be disastrous to the owner because of inability to refinance and loss through foreclosure.

**M41** A **partial release clause** in a mortgage or trust deed is a provision whereby the owner may secure the release of a portion of his property from the lien by payment of a specified amount of money. Subdividers of tracts of land need this provision to give clear title to lot buyers. As a matter of fact, the law requires release clauses in liens on property being subdivided. A mortgage or trust deed affecting an entire subdivision, or several properties under the same ownership, is commonly called a **blanket mortgage** or trust deed.

**M42** Mortgages and trust deeds may be sold and **assigned** by endorsing the note and making out an assignment form, which may be recorded.

**M43** When a person buys a mortgaged property, he can do one of two things: (1) take the property **subject** to the mortgage, or (2) **assume** the mortgage. In the first instance, the buyer assumes no personal liability for payment of the mortgage note. The property is the entire security as far as he is concerned. If he assumes it, he is personally liable in some cases, and may be subject to a deficiency judgment if the property is foreclosed by court action and does not raise enough money to pay off the debt. The same applies to trust deeds. Even though the buyer assumes, the seller remains secondarily liable and is not relieved of responsibility for the note.

**M44**   When a person pays off a mortgage or trust deed note, he is entitled to have the lien released from the records. Failure to furnish and record a certificate of discharge or deed of reconveyance within 30 days makes the responsible party subject to a penalty up to $300 payable to the mortgagor or trustor, and further, he may be liable for damages suffered as a result of failure to perform. (CC Sec. 2941)

**M45**   It is important to know the true status of a note secured by property you plan to buy. Therefore, you may want an **offset statement** from the owner of the property giving the balance due, condition of interest payments, etc. You may also want a **mortgagee's statement** so you can compare them. Or if you buy a mortgage or trust deed note you may want these statements. In the case of a trust deed, it is called a **beneficiary's statement**.

**M46**   Sometimes a mortgage or trust deed provides for the lender to advance additional money from time to time, secured by the same instrument. These are called "**open end**" mortgages or trust deeds.

**M47**   By the way, mortgages, trust deeds and contracts of sale are often referred to as **security devices** in examinations.

**M48**   An **acceleration clause** in a note and trust deed or mortgage is a clause which declares the whole loan due in case of default or some other specified occurrence. Most have this provision in case the borrower fails to keep up the payments, fails to pay taxes or assessments, neglects the property, etc. An **alienation clause** is a special kind of acceleration clause, which provides that a loan becomes due and payable if the borrower sells the property. Sometimes the lender will rely on the borrower because of friendship or reputation, but does not wish to take a chance on some stranger who may buy the property. These clauses are used widely in second trust deeds taken by the seller as a part of the purchase price. An alienation clause is also called a **due-on-sale clause**.

**M49** The law provides that any due-on-sale clause in a trust deed on four or less residential units, executed after July 1, 1972, is invalid if not printed in its entirety in both the trust deed and the note.

## REAL PROPERTY SALES CONTRACT

**M50** Numerous sales of real estate in California have been made by what is called a **real property sales contract** or **land contract**, and which is sometimes called an **installment sales contract**. This provides another means of financing the purchase of real estate. This consists of a contract whereby seller (vendor) and buyer (vendee) agree to certain terms as to the payment of the purchase in installments, and the buyer is usually given possession of the property. No deed is given or title passes until the buyer has met certain conditions of the contract, such as payment of a certain part of the purchase price in regular installments. The contract purchaser is said to be the **equitable owner** of the property.

**M51** Sometimes the contract provides for complete payment of the purchase price before the seller is required to give a deed. Other times the seller gives a deed when the buyer has paid a third or half of the purchase price, and takes a note and trust deed to secure the balance.

**M52** Sales contracts for the sale of real estate have been used extensively in the past by subdividers with lots for sale and builders of low cost homes. The seller would typically make a sale with a low down payment plus monthly installment payments. They are more likely to be used in times when the market is slow than on an active market. Liberal bank and savings and loan financing at low interest rates, and government home financing aids have substantially decreased the number of contract sales of homes.

**M53** Sales contracts sometimes contain a provision prohibiting the buyer from recording them. Such provisions are probably not enforceable. The buyer should be entitled to record his contract for his own protection in the event the seller should again contract to sell the same property, or take steps to mortgage it.

**M54** Usually, sales contracts provide that the buyer forfeits all payments made in event he defaults, as liquidated damages. The courts usually take a "dim view" on forfeitures, and may limit them to actual loss rather than to the contract terms if they feel they are unreasonable.

**M55** In the past there were some real hazards in buying a property on a sales contract. For example, since the seller held title to the property, in some cases he would encumber the property as he pleased with more liens if the contract was not recorded.

**M55.1** Provisions have been added to the Civil Code which give protection to buyers on real property sales contracts. The law defines a real property sales contract as an agreement wherein one party agrees to convey title to real property to another party upon the satisfaction of specified conditions set forth in the contract, and which does not require conveyance within **one year** from the date of the contract.

**M56** The law provides that the sales contract must contain the legal description, a list of outstanding encumbrances, and terms of the contract. If the buyer can record the contract, it gives him protection against further encumbrances. However, if the sales contract is unrecorded, the seller cannot add encumbrances which will make the total amount more than is due on the contract. Furthermore, monthly payments on the total encumbrances cannot exceed the monthly payments of the buyer, less tax and insurance impounds, if any. However, the buyer may consent in writing to the seller doing these things. (CC 2985.2)

**M57** All payments on any sales contract must first be used to pay sums as they become due on the encumbrances before the seller can use them for any other purpose. Any tax and insurance payments made to the seller must be held in a trust fund and used for no other purpose. There are heavy penalties for using the payments received on sales contracts for any purpose other than allowed by the law. Upon request, the seller must give the buyer an accounting as to how the contract payments have been used. (CC 2985.3 & 2985.4)

**M58** A fee owner who has entered into a sales contract for the sale of property cannot transfer the property title to a third party unless it is accompanied by an assignment of the sales contract. Also, if he assigns the sales contract, it must be accompanied by the transfer of title to the property. In other words, the contract and property must remain under one ownership, otherwise the purchaser under the sales contract is in a hazardous position. (CC 2985.1)

**M59** For further protection of the buyer, the law provides that every real property sales contract shall set forth (1) the number of years required to complete payment in accordance with the terms of the contract, and (2) the basis upon which the estimate of taxes was made. (CC 2985.5)

**M60** In spite of the protection given to buyers under sales contracts, these still have disadvantages for them. The vendee may have difficulty in selling and transferring his interest should he desire to do so. After fully complying with the terms of the contract he could have trouble in receiving good title to a property.

**M61** A disadvantage to the vendor under a sales contract is that he may have problems in "clearing title" and in regaining possession of the property if the buyer defaults.

**M62** Because of the various disadvantages of the sales contract, the trust deed has largely replaced it as a "security instrument."

## Mortgages, Deeds of Trust and Sales Contracts

## CHECK QUESTIONS

1. A trust deed differs from a mortgage in which one of the following :
   (A) Possession      (B) Recording      **M20**
   (C) Amortization      (D) Title.      ( ) **M21**

2. A trust deed may be released from the records by:
   (A) Recording the trust deed
   (B) Title insurance
   (C) Recording the note
   (D) Recording a reconveyance deed.      ( ) **M28**

3. A subordination clause is most often used in a:
   (A) A trust deed      (B) A grant deed
   (C) A quitclaim deed      (D) A reconveyance deed.      ( ) **M39**

4. A borrower whose note is secured by a trust deed is called a:
   (A) Trustee      (B) Beneficiary
   (C) Trustor      (D) Mortgagee.      ( ) **M22**

5. Which statement is correct:
   (A) The note is secured by the trust deed
   (B) The trust deed is secured by the note
   (C) The trust deed outlaws with the note
   (D) None of the above.      ( ) **M27**

6. Foreclosure proceedings under a trust deed by trustee's sale permits the trustor to reinstate his loan by making up the delinquent payments plus costs within:
   (A) 4 months after notice of default is recorded
   (B) Five business days prior to the trustee's sale.
   (C) 60 days
   (D) One year      ( ) **M34**

7. A blanket trust deed covers:
   (A) Two or more structures on one lot
   (B) Personal property in two or more houses
   (C) More than one real property
   (D) Equipment only.      ( ) **M41**

8. Which of the following is not a party to a trust deed:
   (A) Beneficiary      (B) Mortgagee      **M21**
   (C) Trustor      (D) Trustee.      ( ) **M22**

9. A mortgagee who finds it necessary to foreclose a mortgage would:
   (A) Notify the trustee of the default
   (B) File an attachment
   (C) Notify the mortgagor of the default, wait 90 days and publish a Notice of Default
   (D) File an action in court. ( ) M10

10. A creditor holding a note and trust deed institutes foreclosure proceeding to satisfy the debt. It will take about how long for him to receive his money?:
    (A) One month　　　　　　(B) Three months
    (C) Twelve months　　　　(D) Four months. ( ) M31

11. After a trustee's sale of real property, any money remaining after satisfying the lien holders and paying the costs and expenses of foreclosure is remitted to the:
    (A) Trustor　　　　　　　(B) Trustee
    (C) Beneficiary　　　　　(D) Mortgagor. ( ) M32

12. A trust deed which provides for the advance of additional money by the beneficiary is referred to as:
    (A) A flexible note　　　　(B) Open end trust deed
    (C) Elastic note　　　　　(D) Extendable note. ( ) M46

13. A "security device" as used in the real estate business is:
    (A) An instrument securing a loan
    (B) An office vault
    (C) A law requiring impounds
    (D) A trust account. ( ) M47

14. A clause in a trust deed which specifically makes the entire note due and payable should the property be sold by the trustor, is termed:
    (A) A sale clause
    (B) A non-merchantable clause
    (C) Personal responsibility clause
    (D) An alienation clause. ( ) M48

15. During the period following a mortgage foreclosure the debtor has what is known as:
    (A) Equity of redemption　(B) Power of Sale　　　M16
    (C) Satisfaction of mortgage　(D) Subordination. ( ) M17

16. To be able to secure a deficiency judgment in the foreclosure of a trust deed, the procedure for foreclosure must be:
    (A) By court action, the same as a mortgage
    (B) Started within 30 days after default
    (C) By trustee's sale
    (D) Approved by the trustor. ( ) M37

17. A land contract (real property sales contract) is:
    (A) The same as a mortgage    (B) Void unless recorded
    (C) A security device    (D) Similar to an option.    (   ) M47

18. The law now provides that every sales contract must contain:
    (A) The legal description    (B) Outstanding encumbrances
    (C) Terms of the contract    (D) All of the above.    (   ) M56

19. Mrs. Riddell sold a parcel of land under a real property sales contract.
    She had to raise some cash, so she sold the sales contract. The law
    required her to:
    (A) Record the sales contract
    (B) Subordinate her fee simple interest to the sales contract
    (C) Put her fee simple interest in trust until the sales contract is fulfilled
    (D) Both transfer the fee title and assign the sales contract to the buyer.
       (   ) M58

20. Advance insurance and tax payments made by the buyer under a sales
    contract to the fee owner may:
    (A) Be deposited in the fee owner's savings account
    (B) Only be kept in a trust account and be used for no other purpose
    (C) Be applied to payment of the contract
    (D) Be used for any purpose with the fee owner having the obligation of
         making the tax and insurance payments when they become due.
       (   ) M57

21. The Namaths sold their home which had a very large trust deed on it that
    was not a purchase money trust deed. They were concerned about the
    possibility of a deficiency judgment in the event of foreclosure, so they
    had the buyer assume the loan. The assumption
    (A) Relieved the Namaths of any liability
    (B) Made the property the sole security for the loan
    (C) Put the Namaths in the position of being secondarily liable for any
         deficiency judgment
    (D) Made the buyer be solely responsible for any deficiency judgment.
       (   ) M43

22. An owner gives a blanket trust deed on six of his properties with the
    right to have the various properties released from the trust deed upon
    payment of certain sums of money for each. The clause which provides
    for this right is called:
    (A) A redemption clause    (B) A partial release clause
    (C) A conveyance clause    (D) An acceleration clause. (   ) M41

23. The term hypothecate means:
    (A) To discharge a mortgage
    (B) To remedy a default
    (C) To give a thing as security without giving up the right to use it
    (D) To alienate the title of a property.    (   ) M3

# NOTES

**N1**  We spoke of notes in discussing mortgages and trust deeds, as a loan is evidenced by a note, and the mortgage or trust deed merely make certain property security for the payment of the note.

**N2**  Where there is a conflict in the note and mortgage or trust deed provisions, the provisions of the note will control.

**N3**  A **promissory note** is a written promise to pay a certain amount of money in accordance with certain agreed-upon terms.

**N4**  It must be signed by the maker and made payable to another person, or to his order. The party who makes the payments is the **payor**, and the holder of the note who receives the payments is the **payee**.

**N4.1**  The term **subrogation** refers to the substitution of one person in the place of another in regards to an obligation.

**N5**  A **straight note** is one which does not call for payment of any of the principal during the period of the loan. The entire loan is repayable on a certain due date. Interest is usually payable periodically during the term of the loan.

**N6**  An **installment note** is one which calls for periodic payments of a certain part of the principal and interest at stated intervals.

**N7**    A **fully amortized note** is one which requires equal payments including principal and interest during the life of the loan, usually monthly, to pay the amount borrowed in full. Upon each succeeding payment the amount of principal paid-off increases and the amount of interest paid decreases as the balance of the loan is gradually reduced.

**N8**    Sometimes the note calls for payment of a certain amount of the principal each month, **plus interest**. Other times the payment is a certain sum per month, say forty dollars, **including interest**.

**N9**    You can readily see that it would be a simple matter to compute the number of months it would take to pay off a loan of $10,000 at $200 per month **plus interest**, but would be difficult to figure the number of months if the $200 per month **included interest**. Watch for this type of problem in any examination for real estate license. In order to determine the payment for a level payment fully amortized loan, it is necessary to use a financial calculator or table of payments. An example of such a table is given at the end of this chapter.

**N10**    A **negotiable note** is one which meets certain legal requirements, and may be transferred from one person to another in the course of business. The holder may collect sums which are due from the maker.

**N11**    An **endorsement** is the signature of the person assigning the note.

**N12**    All notes are not negotiable, although transferable by endorsement. It must fulfill certain requirements in order to be negotiable. For instance, the promise to pay must be unconditional, that is, not based upon any future act of the payee. It must provide for the payment of a certain sum of money (called a sum certain) at a definite time or on demand, and must be payable to the bearer or his order.

**N13**   A **holder in due course** is a person who is an innocent purchaser of a negotiable note for value, and one who had no knowledge of any defect in it when he paid for it. He is the holder of a negotiable note in good faith, and the law gives him certain protection.

**N14**   Any note may be transferred, but if it is not "negotiable," the person accepting it takes it subject to any defects which may have become attached to it in previous assignments.

**N15**   If a note is signed by more than one person, it is either a **joint note** or a **joint and several note**.

**N16**   If a joint note is not paid, the makers must usually be sued together. If the joint and several note is not paid, the makers may be sued either jointly or individually.

**N17**   A note must be endorsed to be transferred to a holder in due course. How the note is endorsed (signed) is important and affects the endorser's liability. If the endorser merely signs his name without any qualifications, it has the effect of making him guarantee the note to all future holders. Such an endorsement is called an **endorsement in blank**.

**N18**   If he endorses the note using the words "**without recourse**" above his signature, he does not guarantee the payment to future holders. However, he may still have some contingent liability based on certain warranties implied by law.

**N19**   Mortgage notes outlaw (Statute of Limitations has run out) four years after they are due and payable. If a lender delays in taking action to recover his money until after that time, he cannot collect by legal action. While mortgages also outlaw four years after their notes are due, trust deeds do not even though their notes do. A trust deed is not subject to the Statute of Limitations.

**N20**   An owner's **equity**, as used in the real estate business, is his interest in property over and above liens. If the property is worth $50,000 and is subject to a $20,000 deed of trust, the owner has an equity of $30,000. An **equitable owner** is an owner who has conveyed title to his property (such as under a trust deed), but reserves all rights to its use. A buyer under a land contract is also an equitable owner.

**N21**   **Adjustable rate mortgages** (ARMs) have become very popular in recent times of high interest rates. These are amortized loans (notes) wherein the interest rate can change up or down periodically, depending on the terms of the loan. There is a maximum change that can occur at each adjustment period. There is a maximum interest rate that can be charged during the life of the loan. The rates on adjustable loans are usually tied to an index. Among the indexes used are a Federal Reserve District's cost of funds, and the 1-year and 6-month Treasury Bill rates. Section 1921 of the Civil Code requires that any lender offering adjustable-rate residential mortgage loans shall provide to prospective borrowers a copy of the most recent available publication of the Federal Reserve Board that is designed to provide the public with descriptive information concerning adjustable-rate mortgages, (entitled *Consumer Handbook on Adjustable Rate Mortgages*).

**N22**   A **prepayment penalty clause** in a note states the privileges and penalties for making principal payments in excess of the amounts called for on due dates in a note. Prepayment penalties and privileges are a matter of contract negotiation between lender and borrower, except that the law provides some controls on these in connection with owner-occupied single family dwellings.

**N23**   Civil Code 2954.9 provides that the principal balance of any loan secured by a mortgage or trust deed on a **residential property of four units or less** may be prepaid in whole or in part at any time. Also, that a prepayment penalty may be charged only during the first five years of the loan. During the first five years an amount not exceeding 20% of the original principal amount may be prepaid without penalty during any 12 month period. A prepayment charge may be imposed on any amount prepaid in excess of the 20%. The charge shall not exceed an amount equal to the payment of six months' advance interest on the amount prepaid in excess of 20% of the original principal amount. Section 10242.6 of the State Real Property Loan Law (discussed in the next chapter) provides that certain real estate loans negotiated by real estate brokers only on owner-occupied single family dwellings, may have a prepayment charge during the first seven years. Prepayment penalties are not permitted on VA and FHA loans.

**N24   Points.** You'll hear the expression, "The builder had to pay 5 points to get the loan." A point, as used in the business, is "one percent." In other words the builder had to pay a fee of 5% of the principal amount of the loan in addition to agreeing to pay the rate of interest. This, of course, increases the effective interest rate.

**N25**

TABLE OF MONTHLY PAYMENTS TO AMORTIZE $1,000 LOAN

| Term of years | 10-1/4% | 10-1/2% | 10-3/4% | 11% | 11-1/4% | 11-1/2% | 11-3/4% | 12% | 12-1/4% | 12-1/2% | 12-3/4% | 13% | 13-1/4% | 13-1/2% | 14% | 15% |
|---|---|---|---|---|---|---|---|---|---|---|---|---|---|---|---|---|
| 5..... | 21.37 | 21.49 | 21.62 | 21.74 | 21.87 | 21.99 | 22.12 | 22.25 | 22.37 | 22.50 | 22.63 | 22.75 | 22.88 | 23.01 | 23.27 | 23.79 |
| 6..... | 18.65 | 18.78 | 18.91 | 19.04 | 19.16 | 19.29 | 19.42 | 19.55 | 19.68 | 19.81 | 19.94 | 20.07 | 20.21 | 20.34 | 20.61 | 21.15 |
| 7..... | 16.73 | 16.86 | 16.99 | 17.12 | 17.25 | 17.39 | 17.52 | 17.65 | 17.79 | 17.92 | 18.06 | 18.19 | 18.33 | 18.47 | 18.74 | 19.30 |
| 8..... | 15.31 | 15.44 | 15.57 | 15.71 | 15.84 | 15.98 | 16.12 | 16.25 | 16.39 | 16.53 | 16.67 | 16.81 | 16.95 | 17.09 | 17.37 | 17.95 |
| 9..... | 14.21 | 14.35 | 14.49 | 14.63 | 14.76 | 14.90 | 15.04 | 15.18 | 15.33 | 15.47 | 15.61 | 15.75 | 15.90 | 16.04 | 16.33 | 16.92 |
| 10..... | 13.35 | 13.49 | 13.63 | 13.78 | 13.92 | 14.06 | 14.20 | 14.35 | 14.49 | 14.64 | 14.78 | 14.93 | 15.08 | 15.23 | 15.53 | 16.13 |
| 11..... | 12.66 | 12.80 | 12.95 | 13.09 | 13.24 | 13.38 | 13.53 | 13.68 | 13.83 | 13.98 | 14.13 | 14.28 | 14.43 | 14.58 | 14.89 | 15.51 |
| 12..... | 12.10 | 12.24 | 12.39 | 12.54 | 12.68 | 12.83 | 12.98 | 13.13 | 13.29 | 13.44 | 13.59 | 13.75 | 13.90 | 14.06 | 14.37 | 15.01 |
| 13..... | 11.63 | 11.78 | 11.92 | 12.08 | 12.23 | 12.38 | 12.53 | 12.69 | 12.84 | 13.00 | 13.15 | 13.31 | 13.47 | 13.63 | 13.95 | 14.60 |
| 14..... | 11.23 | 11.38 | 11.54 | 11.69 | 11.85 | 12.00 | 12.16 | 12.31 | 12.47 | 12.63 | 12.79 | 12.95 | 13.11 | 13.28 | 13.61 | 14.27 |
| 15..... | 10.90 | 11.05 | 11.21 | 11.37 | 11.52 | 11.68 | 11.84 | 12.00 | 12.16 | 12.33 | 12.49 | 12.65 | 12.82 | 12.98 | 13.32 | 14.00 |
| 16..... | 10.62 | 10.77 | 10.93 | 11.09 | 11.25 | 11.41 | 11.57 | 11.74 | 11.90 | 12.07 | 12.23 | 12.40 | 12.57 | 12.74 | 13.08 | 13.77 |
| 17..... | 10.37 | 10.53 | 10.69 | 10.85 | 11.02 | 11.18 | 11.35 | 11.51 | 11.68 | 11.85 | 12.02 | 12.19 | 12.36 | 12.53 | 12.87 | 13.58 |
| 18..... | 10.16 | 10.32 | 10.49 | 10.65 | 10.82 | 10.98 | 11.15 | 11.32 | 11.49 | 11.66 | 11.83 | 12.00 | 12.18 | 12.35 | 12.70 | 13.42 |
| 19..... | 9.98 | 10.14 | 10.31 | 10.47 | 10.64 | 10.81 | 10.98 | 11.15 | 11.33 | 11.50 | 11.67 | 11.85 | 12.03 | 12.20 | 12.56 | 13.28 |
| 20..... | 9.82 | 9.98 | 10.15 | 10.32 | 10.49 | 10.66 | 10.84 | 11.01 | 11.19 | 11.36 | 11.54 | 11.72 | 11.89 | 12.07 | 12.44 | 13.17 |
| 21..... | 9.68 | 9.85 | 10.02 | 10.19 | 10.36 | 10.54 | 10.71 | 10.89 | 11.06 | 11.24 | 11.42 | 11.60 | 11.78 | 11.96 | 12.33 | 13.07 |
| 22..... | 9.55 | 9.73 | 9.90 | 10.07 | 10.25 | 10.42 | 10.60 | 10.78 | 10.96 | 11.14 | 11.32 | 11.50 | 11.69 | 11.87 | 12.24 | 12.99 |
| 23..... | 9.44 | 9.62 | 9.79 | 9.97 | 10.15 | 10.33 | 10.51 | 10.69 | 10.87 | 11.05 | 11.23 | 11.42 | 11.60 | 11.79 | 12.16 | 12.92 |
| 24..... | 9.35 | 9.52 | 9.70 | 9.88 | 10.06 | 10.24 | 10.42 | 10.60 | 10.79 | 10.97 | 11.16 | 11.34 | 11.53 | 11.72 | 12.10 | 12.86 |
| 25..... | 9.26 | 9.44 | 9.62 | 9.80 | 9.98 | 10.16 | 10.35 | 10.53 | 10.72 | 10.90 | 11.09 | 11.28 | 11.47 | 11.66 | 12.04 | 12.81 |
| 26..... | 9.19 | 9.37 | 9.55 | 9.73 | 9.91 | 10.10 | 10.28 | 10.47 | 10.66 | 10.84 | 11.03 | 11.22 | 11.41 | 11.60 | 11.99 | 12.76 |
| 27..... | 9.12 | 9.30 | 9.49 | 9.67 | 9.85 | 10.04 | 10.23 | 10.41 | 10.60 | 10.79 | 10.98 | 11.17 | 11.37 | 11.56 | 11.95 | 12.73 |
| 28..... | 9.06 | 9.25 | 9.43 | 9.61 | 9.80 | 9.99 | 10.18 | 10.37 | 10.56 | 10.75 | 10.94 | 11.13 | 11.32 | 11.52 | 11.91 | 12.70 |
| 29..... | 9.01 | 9.19 | 9.38 | 9.57 | 9.75 | 9.94 | 10.13 | 10.32 | 10.52 | 10.71 | 10.90 | 11.09 | 11.29 | 11.48 | 11.88 | 12.67 |
| 30..... | 8.96 | 9.15 | 9.33 | 9.52 | 9.71 | 9.90 | 10.09 | 10.29 | 10.48 | 10.67 | 10.87 | 11.06 | 11.26 | 11.45 | 11.85 | 12.64 |
| 35..... | 8.79 | 8.98 | 9.18 | 9.37 | 9.56 | 9.76 | 9.96 | 10.16 | 10.35 | 10.55 | 10.75 | 10.95 | 11.15 | 11.35 | 11.76 | 12.57 |
| 40..... | 8.69 | 8.89 | 9.08 | 9.28 | 9.48 | 9.68 | 9.88 | 10.09 | 10.29 | 10.49 | 10.69 | 10.90 | 11.10 | 11.30 | 11.71 | 12.53 |

# Notes

## CHECK QUESTIONS

1. Mortgages make certain property security for payment, but the loan is evidenced by:
   (A) A Trust Deed    (B) A note
   (C) An endorsement    (D) None of the above.   ( )  **N1**

2. A written promise to pay money to another at a certain time in the future is referred to as
   (A) A joint and several note    (B) A Due Course Note
   (C) A promissory note    (D) A Chattel note.   ( )  **N3**

3. The holder of a note who receives the payments is called:
   (A) The payee    (B) The payor
   (C) The Vendor    (D) Debtor.   ( )  **N4**

4. Under a joint and several note:
   (A) The makers can be sued separately
   (B) The makers must be sued jointly
   (C) A default is void
   (D) None of the above.   ( )  **N16**

5. An innocent purchaser of a negotiable note for value without knowledge of any defect is known as the:
   (A) Conveyancer    (B) Assignor
   (C) Holder in due course    (D) Endorser.   ( )  **N13**

6. A note that may be transferred from one person to another in the course of business is:
   (A) A Trade note    (B) A Warrant
   (C) A negotiable note    (D) A conveyance.   ( )  **N10**

7. When a note provides for the money to be paid in a lump sum instead of in installments it is known as:
   (A) A straight note    (B) A several note
   (C) A Principal Sum Note    (D) An installment note.   ( )  **N5**

8. If he does not guarantee the payment to future holders the endorser should use the words:
   (A) Endorsement in Blank    (B) Without recourse
   (C) Holder in due course    (D) None of the above.   ( )  **N18**

9. If the endorser of a note merely signs his name without any qualifications it is called an endorsement:
   (A) In due course          (B) Without recourse
   (C) In blank               (D) Sole.                    (   )  N17

10. To pay off a note of $2100 at the rate of $50 per month plus interest at 12%, it would take the following period of time:
    (A) 2 years, 3 months      (B) 5 years, 4 months
    (C) 3 years, 6 months      (D) 4 years, 4 months.      (   )  N9

11. An owner who deeds his property to a trustee to secure a loan is:
    (A) One who subordinates    (B) An easement holder
    (C) A tenant at sufferance  (D) An equitable owner.     (   )  N20

12. What monthly payment is required to fully amortize a $10,000 loan over 10 years at a 12.0% rate of interest? *
    (A) $123.50                 (B) $143.50
    (C) $150.00                 (D) $14.35.                 (   )  N25

13. What monthly payment is required to fully amortize a $100,000 loan over 30 years at a 13.0% interest rate?
    (A) $857.50                 (B) $1,052
    (C) $1,106                  (D) $952.                   (   )  N25

14. You have a level payment amortized loan on your apartment building. Upon each succeeding monthly payment:
    (A) The amount which goes to principal remains the same
    (B) More of the payment goes to interest
    (C) More of the payment goes to paying the principal
    (D) None of the above.                                 (   )  N7

* The amortization table on page 152 will help you in answering this question. First, go to the 12% column, and then come down to the 10 year line. There you will find the figure $14.35. This is the monthly amount to amortize $1,000. For the $10,000 loan, multiply the $14.35 by 10. The monthly payment for the $10,000, then, is $143.50.

# STATE & FEDERAL LOAN LAWS

**CHAPTER**

**P1**    In the first chapter we spoke of real estate loan activities for which a real estate license is required. (See A5). We also discussed Real Property Securities Dealers and how their real estate loan activities are strictly governed by the Department of Real Estate. (See A50) The State Real Estate Law contains a number of additional regulations pertaining to loan activities of licensees. In the following, some of the highlights of these will be covered. Also, some federal law which provides protection to borrowers will be discussed.

## STATE LAW PERTAINING TO LOANS

**P2**    In the real estate business, the term "trust deed" is commonly used to mean a note secured by a trust deed. We will use "trust deed" for this meaning from time to time in this text. Also, you should know that the term "mortgage" is commonly used to mean "trust deed." For example, you will hear that someone is shopping for a mortgage loan, when he is actually shopping for a trust deed loan. Also, companies that deal in trust deeds are known as mortgage loan companies.

**P4**    If the licensee agrees to service a trust deed or sales contract, he must have a written authorization from his principal which fully outlines the services to be performed. (Section 10233)

**P5**    If the licensee negotiates a trust deed loan, he must arrange to record the trust deed before the funds are disbursed, unless the lender gives his written consent for prior release. If funds are released on the lender's written authorization, the trust deed shall be recorded, or delivered to the lender with a written recommendation that it be recorded within ten days following release of the funds. (Section 10234)

**P6**    If the licensee negotiates the sale of an existing trust deed note or real property sales contract, he must see that the assignment is executed, and is recorded within 10 days after the close of escrow. Or, he may give a written recommendation to the principal that the document be recorded promptly. (Section 10234)

## STATE REAL PROPERTY LOAN LAW

**P7**    The Real Property Loan Law is commonly referred to as the Mortgage Loan Broker Law. It is found in Article 7 of the Real Estate Law in Sections 10240 to 10248. The purpose of this law is to regulate real estate brokers in their negotiations of certain loans secured directly or collaterally by liens on real property.

**P8**    These regulations do not apply to first loans of $30,000 or more, or junior loans of $20,000 or more. Various persons and institutions are exempt from its provisions, such as banks, savings and loan associations, insurance companies and their loan correspondents, etc. They do not apply to loans insured or guaranteed by an agency of the federal government, such as FHA or DVA. Purchase money trust deeds are also exempt from these regulations.

**P9**    This law requires certain things to be done to protect the borrower. First, at the time the loan application is made, the broker must give the prospective borrower a complete statement of the estimated costs of the loan, including such items as appraisal fee, escrow fee, recording and notary fee, commission and others. Other pertinent information such as the term of the note, interest rate, method of repayment, etc., must be included. The form used must be approved by the Commissioner. A suggested form has been approved by him, which sets forth in detail the items the borrower must pay, together with other information the law requires. A sample copy may be obtained at any office of the Department of Real Estate. This form is called a **Mortgage Loan Disclosure Statement**. It is also referred to as the **Mortgage Loan Broker's Statement**.

**P10**   The broker's loan statement must be signed by the borrower and the broker or his salesperson, and must state the broker's license number. The broker must keep a copy on file for four years for the Commissioner's inspection. This statement may not contain blank spaces to be filled in later. The broker must certify that he himself is not the lender. Interest on the loan may not start until the borrower has the money available, or at least until it is placed in escrow by the lender.

**P11**   Note that the Mortgage Loan Broker's Statement **is for the protection of a borrower who seeks a loan**, so he will know what the total costs will be along with other information about the loan. The Real Property Securities Broker Statement described in A54, is for the benefit of the investor in trust deeds or sales contracts, so he will have information on the property which secures his investment.

**P12**   If the licensee is negotiating a loan to be made by an institutional lender such as a bank, savings and loan association or insurance company, and the licensee will receive a commission from the borrower not to exceed 2 percent of the principal amount of the loan, a Mortgage Loan Disclosure Statement is not required.

**P13**   Maximum allowable processing costs and broker commission rates are also included in this law. Processing costs excluding title and recording fees **may not exceed 5%** of the loan amount, with an allowable **minimum of $390 and maximum of $700**, but the maximum amount shall not exceed actual costs. The broker's commission on a first loan for less than 3 years cannot exceed 5%, or 10% on a loan of 3 years or more. On second or other junior loans for less than 2 years, the maximum commission is 5%, from 2 to 3 years it is 10%, and for 3 years or more, 15%. The borrower may sue for treble the amount of any overcharge. (Section 10242)

**P14**   A **collateral loan** is one made to a borrower, who uses a trust deed note he owns as security for a loan. When a collateral loan is made on a first trust deed, the charges cannot exceed the maximum charges for making a first loan on real property. Also, maximum charges for loans with junior paper as security are the same as for junior loans on real property.

**P15**    The Mortgage Loan Broker Law requires substantially equal payments over the term of any new installment loan secured by a lien on real property when the term of the loan is less than 3 years. No installment, including the last installment, may be greater than twice the amount of the smallest installment. This eliminates any balloon payment at the end of a loan. For owner-occupied dwellings, this applies when the term of the loan is 6 years or less. (Sections 10244 and 10244.1)

**P16**    The purchase of credit life or disability insurance may not be required of the borrower as a condition of making a loan. Reasonable fire and hazard insurance on the property offered as security may be required. (Section 10241.1)

## DISCLOSURE ON PURCHASE MONEY LIEN ON RESIDENTIAL PROPERTY

**P17**    The Real Property Loan Law, just discussed, does not include purchase money trust deeds. A law effective July 1, 1983, (Sections 2956 through 2967 of the California Civil Code) entitled **Disclosure on Purchase Money Lien on Residential Property**, as the name implies, deals with purchase money liens where the seller extends credit to the buyer which is secured by a lien on the property he is selling. These liens include trust deeds, mortgages and sales contracts. In most cases they would be trust deeds.

**P18**    This law came about because of problems caused during a period in the 1980's of very tight and costly mortgage funds from institutional lenders. Many homes were sold with "creative financing", which in most cases involved the seller taking back a trust deed as part of the purchase price. This "creative financing" caused many problems to both buyers who gave the purchase money trust deeds, and to sellers as well. Surprise balloon payments were a big part of the problem for trustors (buyers).

**P19**    This law applies to one to four-family dwellings, whether owner-occupied or not. It applies to transactions where there is an **arranger of credit**, and the extension of credit by the seller. It requires written disclosures pertaining to the credit lien.

**P20**    In most cases the "arranger of credit" will be the real estate broker in the sale. If there is more than one broker, then the one who obtained the offer from the purchaser is considered to be the "arranger of credit."

**P21**    For a transaction to come under the purview of this law, the credit involved must either be subject to a finance charge, or be payable by written agreement in more than four installments.

**P22**    Both the buyer and the seller must be given written disclosure containing details pertaining to the financing. The purchaser must be provided with information by the broker and the seller. The seller (beneficiary under the trust deed) must be provided with information from the broker and the purchaser. The "arranger of credit" must provide information to the seller which was provided to him by the buyer, regarding the buyer's name, occupation, income, credit data, etc. The best way of providing this information is by use of forms which list the various information required.

**P23**    The disclosure statement provided by the seller to the buyer must contain the following required warning:

> "If any of the obligations secured by the property call for a balloon payment, then seller and buyer are aware that refinancing of the balloon payment at maturity may be difficult or impossible, depending on the conditions in the mortgage marketplace at that time. There are no assurances that new financing or a loan extension will be available when the balloon payment is due."

**P24**    Notes which are subject to this law must contain the following statement:

"This note is subject to Section 2966 of the Civil Code, which provides that the holder of this note shall give written notice to the trustor, or his successor in interest, of prescribed information at least 60 days and not more than 150 days before any balloon payment is due."

**P25**  Failure to notify the borrower as required postpones the due date on the note to 60 days from the date the notice is finally delivered. Interest on the loan balance continues, however.

**P26**  A balloon payment is defined as the balance due at the maturity of a note which is more than twice the amount of the smallest regularly scheduled payment.

## MORE LAW ON BALLOON PAYMENTS

**P27**  Because of problems which can be caused by balloon payments, the legislature enacted additional law effective January 1, 1984 pertaining to them subsequent to the Disclosure on Purchase Money Lien on Residential Property law. The earlier law deals with seller financed "purchase money" liens on residential property. This newer law is applicable to other notes secured by real property containing one to four residential units, at least one of which is or will be occupied by the borrower. These notes must have a term in excess of one year. This is Section 2924(i) of the Civil Code.

**P28**  This law requires the holder of a balloon payment note which is secured by a property, to provide the obligor of the note with written notice at least 90 days, but not more than 150 days prior to the due date of the final/balloon payment on the loan.

**P29**  If the notice is not sent to the obligor in the required time, then the due date of the balloon payment is postponed for 90 days from the date of delivery of the required notice.

**P30**  This written notice must state the name and address of the person to whom the final payment is to be made, the date on which the final payment is due, and the exact amount of the final payment.

**P31** Notes subject to the Disclosure on Purchase Money Lien on Residential Property, and notes in connection with construction loans, need not comply with this law.

## USURY LAW

**P32** In 1979 new constitutional usury law was enacted by California voters. The maximum interest rate for consumer loans is 10%. The maximum interest rate for real estate loans is 10%, or 5% above the San Francisco Federal Reserve Bank discount rate, whichever is higher. Any loan made or arranged by a real estate broker and secured by real property is exempt from any interest rate limitation. Banks and savings and loan associations are also exempt. Loans directly from one private party to another are not exempt, except for purchase money trust deeds in most cases.

## FEDERAL LAW PERTAINING TO LOANS

**P33** The **Truth-in-Lending Law** affecting consumer credit is enforced by the Federal Trade Commission. It is commonly referred to as **Regulation Z**. Basically, it covers the advertising of credit terms, the delivery of a **Disclosure Statement** showing the total **Finance Charge** and the **Annual Percentage Rate (APR)**. It requires the conspicuous disclosure of the **Right of Rescission**. The law includes those who extend credit secured by a dwelling more than five times per year. Not included are industrial, commercial or apartment house property. It covers a borrower's dwelling. It also covers personal property loans to a maximum of $25,000. Real estate brokers are generally exempt from having to provide Truth-in-Lending disclosures.

**P34** Regulation Z does not limit the cost of a loan, but helps the borrower to know what he is paying for financing. It also helps him to compare various loan offerings subject to this Regulation, as the same information on each one will be provided on the same type of form.

**P35** The **Finance Charge** which must be disclosed, is the total cost of the loan over its entire life and includes the amount of interest, service charge, points, finder's fee, etc. The Finance Charge does not include: title insurance fees, escrow fees, appraisal fees, credit reports, notary fees, tax and insurance impounds, etc. The **Annual Percentage Rate** must appear as a percentage of the loan amount, and is the finance charge spread out as an annual percentage over the life of the loan. Under Regulation Z, there are many disclosures which may be required.

**P36** The Truth in Lending law's advertising regulations provide that if a down payment is stated, then you must also set forth the cash price, the number, amounts and due dates of all payments and the Annual Percentage Rate. Nothing prohibits advertising of general terms such as "liberal terms available," "desirable mortgage for assumption," "low monthly payments," or "FHA-VA financing available," etc.

**P37** Under the **Right of Rescission**, the borrower may cancel a loan on his principal residence no later than midnight of the third day following completion of the transaction or delivery of the Disclosure Statement. The borrower does not have the privilege of cancelling a loan transaction to finance acquisition of the borrower's principal dwelling and secured by that dwelling. First or junior trust deed loans for any other purpose will qualify as to the Right of Rescission.

**P38** A person giving false or inaccurate information, or failure to provide disclosure, or consistently understating the APR "shall be fined not more than $5,000, or imprisoned not more than one year, or both."

**P39** Another federal law is the **Real Estate Settlement Procedures Act (RESPA)**. RESPA requires that certain information regarding loan closing costs be provided to most **buyers of one to four dwelling unit properties. It pertains only to first liens.** It does not apply to refinancing, nor to any loan which is not used to finance the purchase of a property. This Act is applicable to all federally related mortgage loans. This includes loans made by banks and savings and loan associations with federally insured deposits, FHA and VA loans, etc.

**P40** RESPA requires that a **special information booklet** prescribed by the Secretary of HUD (Department of Housing and Urban Development), along with a **good faith estimate** of closing costs be given to every loan applicant who comes under the purview of this Act. **The booklet and good faith estimate must be provided within 3 days** after the loan application is received.

**P41** RESPA protects the borrower from any big surprises as to the amount of closing costs prior to the recording of a loan. It gives him a chance to question any of these costs, if necessary. The burden of complying with RESPA falls mainly on the lender, but the escrow officer may be involved also.

## State and Federal Loan Laws

## CHECK QUESTIONS

1. California law regulates interest rates on loans made by
   (A) Banks
   (B) Private individuals
   (C) Savings and Loan associations
   (D) None of the above.                              (   )   P32

2. Jones, as broker, arranged a $4000 second trust deed loan on Smith's home to run for two years. He made a charge of $400 for processing costs, such as appraisal fee, escrow fee, credit costs and others, in addition to his commission. This fee:
   (A) Is usurious              (B) Is permissible
   (C) Is an overcharge         (D) Is customary.       (   )   P13

3. For loans subject to the Mortgage Loan Broker Law, a new installment loan for less than three years must provide for:
   (A) Interest at 10 percent
   (B) Substantially equal payments
   (C) The maximum interest
   (D) The least costs.                                 (   )   P15

4. The Mortgage Loan Broker Law does not apply to first loans of:
   (A) $10,000 or more          (B) $15,000 or more
   (C) $30,000 or more          (D) None of the above.  (   )   P8

5. The commission on a second trust deed loan subject to the Mortgage Loan Broker Law to run for a period of two years and six months is limited by law to:
   (A) Five percent             (B) Ten percent
   (C) Fifteen percent          (D) Six percent.        (   )   P13

6. In arranging a new trust deed loan, a broker must:
   (A) Record the trust deed before funds are disbursed
   (B) If there is prior release, recommend that the trust deed be recorded within 30 days
   (C) Agree to service the loan
   (D) All of the above.                                (   )   P5

7. The broker loan statement required by the State Real Property Loan Law requires the following cost to be stated:
   (A) Notary fee               (B) Commission
   (C) Appraisal fee            (D) All of the above.   (   )   P9

8. Which of the following statements is false regarding the Broker Loan Statement of the State Real Property Loan Law:
   (A) It must include the broker's license number
   (B) It may contain blank spaces if they are filled in later.
   (C) It must be kept on file by the broker for 4 years
   (D) It must be signed by the broker and the borrower.          (  )  P10

9. A broker arranges a loan subject to the Real Property Loan Law on an existing first trust deed for $15,000 with a term of 5 years. What is the maximum commission he can legally charge?
   (A) $1,500                    (B) $3,000                         P13
   (C) $2,250                    (D) $1,250.               (  )  P14

10. The Real Property Loan Law does not apply to a loan when the loan:
    (A) Is more than $30,000
    (B) Is made by a savings and loan association
    (C) Is a purchase money trust deed
    (D) All of the above.                                   (  )  P8

11. Which of the following is subject to California usury law?
    (A) Licensed broker
    (B) Private party
    (C) Bank
    (D) Savings and loan association.                       (  )  P32

12. Regulation Z pertains to which of the following?
    (A) Shopping centers
    (B) Residential condominium
    (C) Industrial condominiums
    (D) All of the above.                                   (  )  P33

13. Under the Truth-in-Lending Law the borrower has how much time to exercise his right of rescission?
    (A) 24 hours                  (B) 5 days
    (C) 2 days                    (D) 3 days.               (  )  P37

14. One of the main purposes of the Federal Real Estate Settlement Procedures Act (RESPA) is to:
    (A) Place a limit on closing costs
    (B) Limit brokers' commissions
    (C) Advise buyers of 1 to 4 dwelling units of amounts of closing costs prior to the recording of loans.
    (D) Advise buyers of 1 to 4 dwelling units of the Annual Percentage Rate of their loans.                              P39
                                                           (  )  P41

15. The Special Information Booklet and Good Faith Estimate required by RESPA must be provided to the applicant within what period of time after the loan application is received?
    (A) 1 day                (B) 2 days
    (C) 3 days              (D) 4 days.              ( )   P40

16. Which of the following is not subject to the law entitled Disclosure on Purchase Money Lien on Residential Property:
    (A) A five unit residential building in which the owner occupies one of the units
    (B) An owner sells his home through a broker and takes back a 1st trust deed
    (C) An owner sells his home through a broker and takes back a 2nd trust deed.
    (D) None of the above.                             ( )   P19

17. Notes which are subject to the Disclosure on Purchase Money Lien on Residential Property, must state that the holder of the note must give written notice to the trustor containing prescribed information how many days before a balloon payment is due?
    (A) Between 60 and 150      (B) Between 10 and 30
    (C) Between 60 and 90       (D) Between 30 and 60.    ( )   P24

18. Which one of the following would be in violation of the Truth in Lending Law's advertising regulations?
    (A) 4 bedroom, 2 bath home - liberal terms available
    (B) 3 bedroom home on lake - desirable mortgage for assumption
    (C) Two bedroom house, FHA-VA financing available
    (D) Two bedroom house - $5,000 cash down payment.      ( )   P36

# GOVERNMENT HOME FINANCING AGENCIES & CONVENTIONAL MORTGAGE LENDERS

## GOVERNMENT HOME FINANCING AGENCIES

**Q1**    In recent years the part played by the various governmental agencies which make real estate loans, or insure loans made by approved private lenders, has been an important consideration in the real estate business. These agencies, both State and federal, have been set up for the purpose of aiding private builders to meet housing shortages, encourage home ownership, and assist veterans to acquire homes. Their efforts have been very successful.

**Q2**    Some reference is made to the operations of these agencies in license examinations, but to date questions have been of a fairly general nature and have not required detailed knowledge of the applicant. There is no question that a new licensee would be handicapped if he were not somewhat acquainted with these agencies and their functions, and therefore a reasonably good understanding of the following information is important.

**Q3**    Bear in mind that the rules and policies of these government finance agencies may change from time to time. All of the figures stated in this chapter were checked with the various government agencies shortly before going to press, however, they are subject to change.

## DEPARTMENT OF HOUSING AND URBAN DEVELOPMENT

**Q4**    When the **U.S. Department of Housing and Urban Development (HUD)** was created, it brought together under one authority several already existing federal agencies. Among the most important agencies in the Department are the Federal Housing Administration (FHA), and the Government National Mortgage Association (GNMA - Ginnie Mae).

## HUD/FEDERAL HOUSING ADMINISTRATION

**Q5** When the **Federal Housing Administration (FHA)** was created in 1934, it caused a great change in home mortgage lending. The object of its sponsors was to improve housing standards and living conditions by providing for a system to insure home loans. **HUD/FHA does not make loans, but insures loans** made by lending institutions such as banks, savings and loan associations, credit unions, mortgage companies, etc. This permits these lenders to make larger loans on more favorable terms than would otherwise be possible for many residential properties. FHA formerly maintained its own property standards, but it now accepts the standards of local building codes.

**Q6** The Federal Housing Administration's authority extends over 11 main subdivisions of the 1934 Housing Act. Three of these subdivisions, known as titles, are of greatest interest to real estate agents. These are:

Title I. Property improvement and mobilehome loans
Title II. Home mortgage insurance
Title III. National Mortgage Associations

### FHA Title I

**Q7** **Title I loans, property improvement and mobilehome loans,** are made by banks and other financial institutions which are Title I approved lenders. Title I loans are not only for the repair or alteration of individual homes, but also for improvements to apartment buildings and non-residential structures.

**Q8** **Title I loans are made on the borrower's first or junior trust deed note** to a bank or other lending institution. He must have a good credit record and adequate income.

**Q9** The maximum insured loan for home repairs, and for building a small non-residential structure, is $17,500. Under Title I, loans may be insured for improvement of multiple dwelling units to a maximum amount of $43,750, limited to $8,750 per family dwelling unit. In all cases the borrower must own the property, be buying on contract, or have a valid lease which does not expire until at least 6 months beyond the term of the loan.

**Q10** FHA charges an annual insurance premium on Title I loans of 1/2 of 1% of the loan amount. Interest rates on these loans are usually relatively high.

## FHA Title II

**Q11** Title II is one of the most important activities of the FHA, and a Title that you should be generally familiar with. Below are a few of the sections under this Title:

1. **Section 203.** Insures loans for financing one to four-family dwellings, the main concern of the average broker.

2. **Section 207.** This provides for insurance of loans for the construction or rehabilitation of multiple-family rental housing, and for mobilehome parks.

3. **Section 213.** Insures loans for the construction of non-profit "cooperative" apartment buildings. This section is widely used in connection with "senior citizen" projects where stock is bought in a corporation with the right to occupy a certain apartment. Individual apartment loans may be insured under this section.

4. **Section 221.** Insures loans for financing rental or cooperative multiple-family housing for moderate income households, and increases homeownership opportunities for low and moderate income families.

5. **Section 231.** Insures loans for building rental projects for elderly persons.

6. **Section 234.** Insures loans for the construction and purchase of condominium dwelling units.

**Q12** While there is no limit as to the price a buyer may pay in the purchase of a home, there is a limit on the amount of a home loan which FHA will insure under Section 203B of Title II. As of 1992 the maximum insurable mortgage amount is $124,875 for a single-family dwelling; $140,600 for a two-family dwelling; $170,200 for a three-family dwelling and $197,950 for a four-family dwelling. These amounts will change for some areas. Bear in mind that these are presently the maximum limits which FHA will insure, and that the loan amount on a particular property is also determined by the appraisal of the property. The lender also has the right to limit the amount that he is willing to lend, and for what length of time. The maximum term permitted by FHA for these insured loans is 30 years. Only owner-occupant purchases are allowed to be made with these loans.

**Q13** The minimum down payment permitted in the purchase of one to four family dwellings is 3% of the first $25,000, and 5% of the balance of the FHA appraisal amount. **No junior financing is allowed at the outset of a purchase as part of the purchase price**. Owners are required to have higher equities if FHA insured loans are used for refinancing.

**Q14** If the purchase price exceeds the FHA appraised value, additional cash is required. **An FHA appraisal is valid for a period of 6 months on existing construction, and 12 months on proposed construction.**

**Q15** Since December 1, 1983, **HUD/FHA no longer sets interest rates for FHA insured loans. They are negotiated between the borrower and the lender**. The maximum loan fee which the lender may charge the borrower is one percent of the loan amount. In addition to the loan fee, if the current market interest rate is higher than the negotiated rate, the lender may charge discount points on the loan. Discount points are a one-time fee to compensate for the difference in the two rates. Points may be paid by either buyer or seller. On Title II insured loans, interest is paid only on the reduced unpaid principal balance.

**Q16** A one-time mortgage insurance premium may be paid to HUD/FHA, or for a slightly higher premium it may be added to the loan amount. As of the time of this writing, the premium structure is undergoing a change, and is to be phased in over the next few years. The agent should contact the lender regarding the premium on a particular loan. This insurance protects the lender against loss he might incur on an FHA mortgage.

**Q17** These fully amortized FHA loans on dwellings require monthly payments which include principal and interest and impounds. Impounds are monies placed in trust with the lender for the payment of real estate taxes, property insurance, and FHA mortgage insurance premiums. Loans may be paid before maturity. **The trustor (borrower) may make as many multiple payments as he wishes, with no penalty.**

**Q18** Applicants for insured loans must show satisfactory credit standing, and have a reasonably assured, adequate income to meet the payments. FHA insures loans in all geographical areas. Each application is considered on an individual basis.

**Q19** If a home with an FHA mortgage is sold and the buyer wants to assume it, the owner (seller) is relieved of liability for the loan if the buyer meets FHA requirements and a substitution of liability is made. FHA does not permit home loans to be assumed by investors.

**Q20 FHA will also insure Graduated Payment Mortgages (GPM) and Adjustable Rate Mortgages (ARM).** Graduated Payment loans are designed to assist buyers whose incomes are expected to increase as time progresses. In an Adjustable Rate Mortgage, the interest rate starts out generally lower than the current rate of a fixed rate FHA loan, and is adjusted upward or downward annually based upon the average yield of 1-year U.S. Treasury securities. Changes in the interest rate may not increase or decrease more than 1% in any one year, or more than 5% over the entire period of the loan.

**Q21   There is also an FHA Home Mortgage Insurance Program for veterans**. Section 203B2. These home loans require less down payment than under other FHA programs. Vets discharged under other than dishonorable conditions with at least 90 days of service prior to September 8, 1980, or at least 24 months of service after that date are eligible for the FHA Home Mortgage Insurance Program. Under the HUD/FHA program, veterans are not required to make any down payment on the first $25,000 of the FHA appraised value, but must pay 5% on the balance.

## FHA Title III

**Q22   Title III provides for the establishment of the federal government's National Mortgage Association (GNMA or Ginny Mae)**. Ginny Mae provides a means of channeling funds from the nation's securities markets into the residential mortgage market. The program's purpose is to attract investors into the residential mortgage market by offering them high yield, government guaranteed securities (backed by VA and FHA mortgages) with none of the servicing obligations associated with a mortgage loan portfolio.

**Q23   The Federal National Mortgage Association (FNMA - Fannie Mae)**, was divided in 1968 into two associations - Fannie Mae and Ginny Mae. Ginny Mae remained a federal government agency, but Fannie Mae became a private corporation. Fannie Mae buys and sells existing mortgages in what is termed the **secondary mortgage market**. Fannie Mae deals in VA, FHA and conventional mortgage loans.

**Q23.1** There is another association, known as the **Federal Home Loan Mortgage Corporation (FHLMC - Freddie Mac)**, which is a subsidiary of the Federal Home Loan Banks. Freddie Mac's major function is to provide a secondary mortgage market for these savings and loan lenders and other financial institutions whose deposits are insured by the federal government. Freddie

Mac deals with conventional (not government guaranteed) residential mortgage loans. It sells securities, known as participation securities to private investors to acquire funds for its operation.

**Q23.2** Fannie Mae and Freddie Mac, the two government-sponsored institutions, do not receive any federal funds. However, their quasi-governmental status allows them to borrow funds on markets at reduced rates, which has lowered the cost of mortgage money to consumers by a half percentage point or more. The interest rate advantage derives from what the financial world has decided is an implicit guarantee that the federal government would cover any losses in the event either company goes under.

## DEPARTMENT OF VETERANS AFFAIRS

**Q24** Veterans of the armed services during World War II, the Korean conflict and Vietnam are assisted by the government's Department of Veterans Affairs (DVA) in the purchase of a home if they have had at least 90 days total service. Also eligible are peacetime veterans with 181 continuous days or more of active duty, any part of which occurred after July 25, 1947 to September 6, 1980, for enlisted persons and to October 17, 1981 for officers. Enlisted veterans who began their service after September 6, 1980 and officers after October 16, 1981, are eligible if they have completed 24 months of continuous active duty.

**Q25** Veterans must have been discharged under conditions other than dishonorable. Vets disabled in the line of duty are eligible despite length of time served. The DVA provides for **partial guarantees of loans** to veterans in connection with the purchase of a home up to a maximum of $46,000. On mobilehomes and lot loans, the maximum guaranteed amount is $20,000. The veteran is charged a funding fee of 0.625% of the loan amount by the lender when the loan closes. The lender then turns this fee amount over to the DVA. While the amount of the guarantee is limited, there is no maximum loan amount set by the DVA. That is the responsibility of the lender.

**Q26**   To get a partial DVA loan guarantee, the law requires that the veteran must either occupy or intend to occupy the home within a reasonable period of time after the closing of the loan. One must have good credit and enough income to meet the mortgage payments along with other obligations. There is no time limit for obtaining a loan by a veteran. Veterans who used up their entitlement prior to October 1, 1980 can qualify for an additional entitlement. The maximum home loan guarantee has been raised from $4,000 in 1944 to $46,000 currently. The amount of the additional entitlement would be the difference between the $46,000 and the amount used on prior DVA loans.

**Q27**   Partial guarantees may also be obtained on loans to repair, improve or refinance an existing home to be occupied by a veteran; or to buy a lot on which to place a mobilehome owned and occupied by a veteran.

**Q28**   The DVA establishes maximum interest rates which may be charged. These vary with changes in the money market. The length of the loan is subject to negotiation between the veteran and the lender, but the repayment period cannot exceed 30 years. The DVA does not usually require a down payment, however the lender may require one. A down payment is required by the DVA when the purchase price exceeds the property's appraised value. If the latter is the case, the veteran must certify that the difference is being paid in cash without the help of additional loans. The maximum amount of the mortgage the DVA will guarantee is determined by a DVA appraisal. There is no ceiling on the amount the veteran can borrow, but the amount of the guarantee is limited. No prepayment penalty is permitted on DVA loans.

**Q29**   As stated previously, the DVA does not make loans directly, but only partially guarantees loans. An exception is that in some instances the DVA will provide a grant to enable a disabled veteran to acquire a specially adapted home. This is for certain eligible veterans who have permanent and total service connected disabilities.

**Q30** The FHA entered into a veterans' loan program under provisions of the Housing and Urban Development Act of 1965. This is not a DVA program, and those eligible need merely to have been in the armed forces for a certain period of time without any war service. See Q21 for more details.

**Q31** Should the government have a loss as the result of any guarantee, the veteran is responsible for it, and is obliged to repay the government.

**Q32** The procedure for applying for a DVA guaranteed loan is quite simple. The veteran finds the property he wants. He then goes to the private lending agency with his discharge papers and applies for the loan.

**Q33** The property is then appraised by an approved DVA appraiser. **A CRV (Certificate of Reasonable Value) is issued**. This is used to determine loan amount that the DVA will guarantee.

## CAL-VET LOANS FOR CALIFORNIA VETERANS

**Q34** The State of California Department of Veterans Affairs has provided a Cal-Vet loan program for assisting its veterans to acquire homes or farms on a favorable financing plan. **Loan funds for this program are obtained through the issuance and sale of bonds by the State government**. There are no direct costs to the taxpayers because these bonds are repaid by the veterans participating in the program. The State Department of Veterans Affairs purchases the property from the seller. Having taken title to the property, they in turn sell it to the veteran on a purchase contract. Until the loan is fully repaid, the Department holds legal title, but the veteran, who holds **equitable title**, has full use of the property.

**Q35** The veteran must have been born in California or have been a bona fide resident of the State at the time of entering the armed services. The applicant must have had at least 90 consecutive days on active duty and a minimum of one day of service during either World War I, World War II, or the Korean, Vietnam or Persian Gulf hostilities. Under certain conditions a vet may be eligible during a peacetime period. A discharge under honorable conditions is required.

**Q36** **Application for Cal-Vet benefits must be made within 30 years from the date of release from active duty,** except under State law, veterans who were wounded or disabled as a result of their war service or who were prisoners of war have an unlimited time after release from active duty in which to apply for Cal-Vet benefits.

**Q37** A completed Cal-Vet loan application must be received in the State Department of Veterans affairs before the veteran completes his purchase of the property he intends to finance with a Cal-Vet loan.

**Q38** The loan amount, which is provided by the State, is limited by law. $125,000 is the maximum amount the Department will provide on the purchase of a single-family home, townhouse or condominium. $125,000 is the maximum on mobilehomes on land owned by the borrower, and $70,000 on mobilehomes in an approved mobilehome park. $200,000 is the maximum on working farms with sufficient income to provide for loan and tax payments. As much as 95% of the Cal-Vet appraisal may be borrowed on farms. A home must be appraised for at least the purchase price. On homes, the Department may loan 97% of the first $35,000 of appraised value, and 95% of additional value.

**Q39** Secondary financing may be permissible under the Cal-Vet loan program at the time of purchase of the property. A veteran in some cases may obtain a second loan from another lender to increase his total loan amount, but the combined financing of both loans cannot exceed 90% of the Department's appraised value of the property. A Subordination Agreement must be obtained from the lender under the second trust deed note.

**Q40**   A very favorable interest rate of 8% is currently being charged by the Department on all new loans, except for mobilehomes in mobilehome parks where the rate is 9%. The rate may vary over the period of the loan. The interest rate is based upon the continuing costs of bonds sold to support the program and is reviewed each year. Any increase or decrease in bond rates will affect existing loan contracts, and will result in a change in monthly payments. There is a maximum repayment period of 30 years on all loans, except for mobilehomes in mobilehome parks, which have a repayment period of 15 to 20 years. A loan origination fee of $430 is currently being charged on all Cal-Vet loans plus an appraisal fee.

**Q41**   Loan payments are made to the State Department of Veterans Affairs. There may be a prepayment penalty if the veteran prepays his loan in whole or in part within 2 years from the time it is started. The charge is equal to the payment of six months advance interest on the amount prepaid in excess of 20% of the original loan amount.

**Q42**   The veteran, or a member of the veteran's family, must live on the property within 60 days after signing the contract, and he must continue to keep it as his principal residence until the loan is fully repaid. There are few exceptions. If good cause is shown, the Department may give permission to the veteran to rent the property. However, the property may be rented for only a maximum period of four years during the term of the contract.

**Q43**   The Department of Veterans Affairs does not make construction loans. If a veteran wants to have a home constructed on a building site of his choice, he must first apply to the Department for approval of the site and to verify his eligibility. After obtaining approval, the State will issue a commitment for a Cal-Vet loan allowing 12 months for construction to be completed. The veteran then gets a construction loan from a bank or other private lender. When the property is ready for occupancy, the Department will then refinance the construction loan with a permanent loan which is known as a take-out loan.

**Q44** All Cal-Vet purchasers are responsible for maintaining fire and hazard insurance and life insurance. The life insurance policy pays off the unpaid contract balance in case of the death of the insured, and his survivors secure clear title without further payments. Disability insurance is required for veterans under the age of 62 who are fully employed and in good health.

## CONVENTIONAL MORTGAGE LENDERS

**Q45** Briefly, a **conventional loan** is one which is not guaranteed, insured, or carried by a state or federal governmental agency. So-called conventional loans are made by individual lenders and various kinds of lending institutions, such as banks, insurance companies, savings and loan associations, and privately owned mortgage companies.

## LIFE INSURANCE COMPANIES AND PENSION FUNDS

**Q46** In general, these lenders prefer to make large real estate loans on properties such as commercial and office building complexes, shopping centers, industrial properties, and apartment buildings. They generally do not make loans on single-family dwellings.

**Q47** Unlike savings and loan associations and banks which make loans directly to borrowers, insurance companies and pension funds usually lend their money through local mortgage companies, or mortgage brokers. Mortgage companies both originate and service loans for these types of lenders.

**Q48** While the terms of the loans are not regulated by law, these companies, as a general rule, prefer fixed-rate loans with a term of five to ten years. However, they will lend up to 30 years on adjustable rate mortgages. Life insurance companies are governed by the laws of the state in which they are incorporated, as well as the laws of the state where they operate.

# COMMERCIAL BANKS

**Q49** Commercial banks are "general purpose" lenders. They are either chartered or licensed by the State, or federal government. Banks make loans on improved properties such as single-family dwellings, apartments, industrial and commercial buildings, etc., and also on properties to be constructed. They also make home improvement loans. Banks may loan as much as 90% of the appraised value of the property, and these loans may run for as long as 30 years. If the loan to value ratio exceeds 80%, private mortgage insurance is required. Private mortgage insurance guarantees the lender against loss because of default. The activities of state-chartered banks are covered by the Banking Law, while those of national banks come under the National Bank Act. All national banks are required to be members of the Federal Reserve System. State banks are members by their own choice. All commercial banks in California are insured by the Federal Deposit Insurance Corporation (FDIC) under which each depositor is insured up to $100,000.

## SAVINGS AND LOAN ASSOCIATIONS

**Q50** Here again we have two kinds, those chartered by the State and those chartered by the federal government. The federal savings and loan associations are governed by the Office of Thrift Supervision, while the State-chartered savings and loans are governed by the Savings and Loan Commissioner of California. All State and federal chartered associations are members of the Federal Home Loan Bank System which provides credit to these institutions. Deposits in both State and federal chartered institutions are insured up to $100,000 by the Association Insurance Fund, which is a division of the FDIC.

**Q51** Savings and loan associations are the greatest source of money for home financing. Their funds are derived from many sources, including savings accounts invested in by the public which are, in turn, reinvested in real estate loans. However, they are not limited solely to single-family residential properties. Some make loans on apartment buildings, commercial and industrial properties, however, many S & L's have had problems with these types of loans in recent years and are no longer making them. They also make home improvement loans.

**Q52** Savings and loan associations are permitted to make conventional home loans for as much as 90% to 95% of the appraised value of a property. The amortization period for home loans is usually in a range of 15 to 30 years. On commercial loans, the maximum is 80% of the appraised value, and the term of the loan is usually in a 5 to 10 year range.

## MORTGAGE COMPANIES

**Q53** These are privately owned companies which lend their own money, or that of their clients. They are not regulated as to the term and loan-to-value ratios of their loans. Some specialize in making second or other junior loans. Those which use their own funds usually sell the loans to buyers at a profit, so as to keep their funds liquid to make further loans. Some firms act as lending agents for insurance companies, pension funds and other loan sources. When a mortgage company represents a life insurance company, pension fund, etc., it is known as a **mortgage loan correspondent**. Loan correspondents originate loans, and then service them for some lenders.

## INDIVIDUALS

**Q54** **Private lenders** also are not regulated as to the type of loan they may make. They make their loans directly or obtain them through private mortgage companies or real estate brokers.

**Q55** Private lenders must comply with California's usury law when making direct real estate loans without the help of a real estate broker. This is to say that the interest rate charged by a private lender must not be higher than the maximum rate stipulated by law. The term of the loan will vary with each individual lender and the particular loan, but it is usually fairly short term.

## MORTGAGE MARKETS

**Q56 Mortgage Markets** are termed **"primary"** and **"secondary"** markets. The primary market deals with original loans made directly to borrowers. The secondary market has to do with existing mortgages that are purchased, sold or borrowed against. For example, these could be first trust deeds sold to the Federal National Mortgage Association.

## SOFT AND HARD MONEY LOANS

**Q57** When a seller takes back a note and trust deed as part of the purchase price, it is referred to as a **soft money loan**. A **hard money loan** is one where actual cash is given to a borrower who provides his real property as security for the loan.

## SAVINGS AND LOAN AND BANK PROBLEMS

**Q58** The problems that the savings and loan industry has experienced during the past few years has been well publicized. Hundreds of them have become bankrupt due to unwise lending practices and other factors. Bad commercial property and construction loans have been a big part of the problem. The federal government has been greatly affected, since it guarantees depositors accounts up to $100,000. The Federal Savings and Loan Insurance Corporation (FSLIC) for many years protected depositors. However, not only were its reserves exhausted, but probably well over one hundred and fifty billion dollars will ultimately be required of the government to straighten out this huge financial disaster. Some troubled S&L 's have been taken over by healthy ones. Others have been dissolved, and their assets sold off. The Resolution Trust Corporation was formed by the government to dispose of seized assets of defunct S&L's. The FSLIC has been replaced by the Association Insurance Fund, a division of the Federal Deposit Insurance Corporation (FDIC), which insures the accounts of bank depositors. However, many banks have either gone bankrupt, or are experiencing financial problems for some of the same reasons which affected the S&L's. As of the time of this writing, the FDIC is asking the government for additional billions of dollars to replenish its reserves.

# Government Home Financing Agencies and Conventional Mortgage Lenders

## CHECK QUESTIONS

1. The main function of the Federal National Mortgage Association (FNMA) is:
   (A) Originate loans on apartment buildings
   (B) Buy and sell mortgages in the secondary market
   (C) Insure home mortgages
   (D) Insure loans for "senior citizen" housing.     ( )   Q23

2. The maximum advance on a dwelling under the Cal-Vet program amounts to:
   (A) $70,000        (B) $125,000
   (C) $15,000        (D) $40,000.     ( )   Q38

3. The amount which an approved lending institution may loan to a qualified veteran on a VA guaranteed loan is based on:
   (A) The assessed value of the property
   (B) The purchase price
   (C) An amount determined solely by the lender
   (D) The amount shown on the Certificate of Reasonable Value (CRV).     ( )   Q25

4. Under the Cal-Vet loan plan the veteran's interest in the property is termed:
   (A) Leasehold interest        (B) Fee simple title
   (C) Equitable title        (D) Squatters rights.     ( )   Q34

5. The money advanced on Cal-Vet financing comes from:
   (A) State Legislature
   (B) Federal Land Grants
   (C) Private lending institutions
   (D) State bond issues.     ( )   Q34

6. If a borrower defaults on an FHA insured loan, any losses sustained by the lender by foreclosure are made up through:
   (A) An attachment lien against the borrower
   (B) An assessment against the lending institution
   (C) HUD/FHA mortgage insurance
   (D) The Federal Treasury.     ( )   Q16

7. Payments made by veterans on Cal-Vet financing are made to:
   (A) The lending institution
   (B) The beneficiary
   (C) The State Department of Veterans Affairs
   (D) The Veterans Administration.     ( )   Q41

8. An FHA appraisal is valid for which period of time on existing construction:
   (A) One month      (B) Six months
   (C) Nine months      (D) One year.      ( ) Q14

9. FHA Title I loans:
   (A) Are for home purchase only
   (B) Are the same form of financing as Title II
   (C) Can be used for any form of lot improvement
   (D) Are used for home improvements.      ( ) Q7

10. Under FHA, if the borrower decides to sell the property later on:
    (A) The note becomes immediately due and payable and new buyer must secure new financing
    (B) The buyer cannot assume the FHA Loan but must buy the property subject to the loan
    (C) The buyer may assume the FHA loan and relieve the original mortgager of liability, but he must meet FHA requirements
    (D) The sale must be for all cash to the amount of the FHA loan as no secondary financing is permitted.      ( ) Q19

11. You have negotiated the sale of a 50 story downtown office building. What type of lender would be most interested in a loan on this type of property?
    (A) Savings and loan.
    (B) Federal bank
    (C) State bank
    (D) Life insurance company.      ( ) Q46

12. The best source for a conventional home loan would probably be:
    (A) Pension fund      (B) Mortgage company
    (C) Savings and loan      (D) Private individual.      ( ) Q51

13. A California savings and loan association sells a block of 1st trust deeds which it has originated to a S and L in New Jersey. The market for such sales is called:
    (A) Resale market
    (B) Secondary market
    (C) FNMA market
    (D) Savings and loan exchange.      ( ) Q56

14. An FHA home loan would most likely be secured through:
    (A) A bank or savings and loan association
    (B) A life insurance company
    (C) The local HUD/FHA office
    (D) A pension fund.      ( ) Q5

This page intentionally left blank.

# LEASES

**R1**　Unless an industrial, retail commercial or other type of building or land is occupied by the owner, it is usually leased to one or more tenants for the income it will provide. Some agents devote a good portion of their time to the leasing of real estate, and this can be a very financially rewarding activity.

**R2**　Having a property well leased is, of course, important in providing the owner with income. It is also very important to the market value and salability of a property. "Well leased" means having desirable tenants on well written leases at rents which are in line with the market or better. Experienced owners of income producing properties well recognize and appreciate the services of professional leasing agents in helping them to achieve this.

**R3**　A lease is a contract between owner and tenant, which sets forth the conditions upon which the tenant may occupy and use a property. It states the agreed-upon rent, length of the lease, and various other conditions and obligations of the parties.

**R4**　The landlord or owner is called the **lessor**. The renter is called the **lessee**.

**R5**　The interest which the lessee holds in a real property is termed a **leasehold interest** or **leasehold estate**. Leasehold interest basically refers to the right of exclusive possession and use of real property for a period of time by the lessee.

**R6**　The interest which the owner of the fee simple estate has in a property when he leases it, is termed the **leased fee estate**. The holder of the leased fee estate, the landlord, has the right to receive **rent payments** according to the terms of the lease and the return of the possession and full use of the real estate at the expiration of the lease. This is called the **reversion**.

**R7**     There are three types of leasehold estates which the student should be familiar with. These are classified according to their duration:

**R8     Estate for years.** An estate for years is one which is to continue for a definite period of time as fixed by the lease agreement. Even though it is termed an estate for years, the period may be for less than one year.

**R9     Estate from period to period.** This is also referred to as periodic tenancy. It is one which continues from period to period automatically until it is cancelled. A month-to-month tenancy is the most common example of this.

**R10     Estate at sufferance.** One where the lessee has had possession of the property under a lease, and after the expiration of the lease he is still in possession of the property for a period of time until a new lease is agreed-upon or the tenant is asked to vacate the premises.

**R11     Leases for one year or less do not have to be in writing,** although it is a good idea to have any agreement in writing to prevent misunderstanding. Oral leases in most cases are considered to be on a month-to-month basis. The Statute of Frauds requires that **any lease which is longer than one year must be in writing** in order to be enforced by law.

**R12     A written lease must be signed by the lessor. It is not essential that the lessee sign the lease.** If a copy of the lease is delivered to the lessee, and the lessee occupies the premises and pays rent, this is sufficient to signify his acceptance of the lease.

**R13**     The terms of a written lease can only be changed or modified by another agreement in writing. Oral agreements to modify a written lease are not enforceable.

**R14**     Some written leases are quite brief, while others can be extremely lengthy in covering many possible contingencies. Some written leases are on standardized forms obtained at stationary stores. Important and complex leases are best drawn by an attorney specializing in this area of the law.

**R15**   A lease document does not need to be drawn in any particular form. It should include as a minimum the following:

1. Names of the lessor and lessee.

2. Description of the premises. An exhibit (drawing) is often included for clarification.

3. Commencement and termination dates of the lease.

4. Amount of the rent, and when and where it is to be paid.

5. The type of use permitted the lessee.

6. Who is responsible for paying various property expenses such as taxes, insurance, building maintenance, etc.

7. Liability of lessor and lessee for injuries resulting from the condition of the premises.

8. The assigning or subletting of the lease.

9. Positions of lessor and lessee in the event of damage to the property by fire or earthquake, etc.

10. The right of the landlord to enter and inspect the property under certain conditions.

11. The right of a lessee to remove fixtures which might be considered a part of the real property because of the way they are affixed. Ordinarily trade fixtures may be removed, but an agreement is desirable.

**R16**   The law provides a time limit for leases on various kinds of property. Property located in a city or town cannot be leased for longer than 99 years. Oil and gas leases also cannot be for more than 99 years. Agricultural property cannot be leased for a period longer than 51 years, except in special cases as a city leasing it for sewage disposal purposes.

**R17**   Lease agreements for some retail businesses, hotels, restaurants, etc., often call for the lessee to pay **percentage rent**. Usually, the tenant pays a fixed minimum monthly rental amount. He then pays an additional amount based on a percentage of his gross sales less the amount of the minimum rent. The percentage figure varies a great deal depending on the type of business the lessee operates.

**R18**  A **step-up** lease usually calls for a fixed dollar amount annual rent increase. This can be beneficial to a new business in helping it get started with a relatively low rent. It would then pay higher rents each year as it becomes more established.

**R19**  More common than step-up rent is the **cost of living adjustment clause**. In this, the amount of rent is changed in accordance with changes in the cost of living as indicated by the Consumer's Price Index for a certain area. This type of rent adjustment is important to property owners during periods of high inflation. Lessees usually require a "cap" on the maximum amount that the increase can be for any period; for example a 6% maximum increase for any one year period. Lessors often require that the rental amount may not decrease below a certain amount.

**R20**  Whether the lessor or lessee pays the various property expenses is a matter of agreement as spelled out in the lease. In a **net lease** (often referred to as **triple net**) the lessee (tenant) pays all of the expenses. In a **gross lease** the lessor (landlord) pays all of the expenses. In a **modified-gross lease** the lessor pays certain of the expenses such as taxes, insurance and exterior building maintenance, and the lessee may pay utilities, janitorial service and interior building maintenance. These will vary according to the agreement of the parties as expressed in the lease.

**R21**  Unless the provisions of the lease prohibit, a property can be **sublet** by the renter (lessee), or he can **assign** the lease. There is a distinct difference. If the lessee sublets, he is still in the position of the lessee. If he assigns, he transfers his rights and responsibilities to the new renter (assignee). Even if the lessor did consent to the assignment, the lessee is almost always secondarily responsible if the assignee does not perform according to the terms of the lease. However, the lessor may specifically release the lessee from further liability should he wish to do so.

**R22**  A lessee who sublets is still responsible (liable) under the original lease. He may sublet all or a part of the property. Sometimes property is sublet two or three times, each time usually at a different rental.

**R23** Some lessees make a substantial profit by subletting. Should a lessee sublet a property, he is said to hold a **sandwich lease**, as he is sandwiched between the lessor and the sublessee.

**R24** When a lease is **renewed**, an entirely new lease document should be drawn-up and executed. If a lease is **extended**, the tenant remains in possession of the property under the terms of the old lease.

**R25** The renter of a residential dwelling is required to take reasonable care of the premises. He must keep the part of the premises which he occupies clean and sanitary, and properly dispose of garbage and rubbish.

**R26** The tenant of a residential dwelling may expect the landlord to make necessary repairs to keep the property habitable. If the landlord does not, the tenant may make necessary repairs at a cost of not more than one month's rent, or abandon and break the lease. The amount paid by the tenant for such repairs may be deducted from the rent when due. However, the tenant is required to give the landlord adequate written or oral notice, and sufficient time to make the repairs, before doing either. If the lessee is not in default as to the payment of his rent, the landlord may not take retaliatory action against him through eviction, decreasing services or raising his rent for a period of 180 days. This remedy shall not be available to the tenant more than twice in any 12-month period. The law covering this is fairly lengthy with a number of fine points and exceptions.

**R27** If a lessee fails to pay the rent as agreed, or otherwise breaks any of the provisions of the lease, the landlord may take steps to recover possession by legal process. He must serve the tenant with a **"three day notice to cure default or quit,"** stating the nature of the default.

**R28** If the tenant (lessee) fails to remedy the default within the three days, he is guilty of **unlawful detainer,** and may be sued for **treble** the amount of the back rent, or for the rent and damages. The three day notice must be served personally upon the delinquent tenant, or in other manner provided by law. Such a suit is called an unlawful detainer suit.

**R29**   As a result of such a suit, the court may give a judgment for the sums sued for, and order eviction of the tenant from the premises.

**R30**   The landlord can require a tenant on a month-to-month tenancy to vacate even though the tenant is not in default, but he must give him at least a thirty-day advance written notice to do so. A month-to-month tenant who plans to vacate must give the landlord at least a thirty day advance notice that he is going to vacate. If the tenant fails to do so, he may be liable for additional rent.

**R31**   If a tenant abandons a property during the term of a lease, it does not relieve him from paying rent. The owner may sue for the amounts as they become due. Or, after notifying the tenant, he may re-rent the property to another. If he must accept a lower rental in order to lease the property, he can sue the original lessee for the difference.

**R32**   Payments made to landlords as **security deposits**, to assure that the tenant will not abandon the property or fail to pay rent, are trust funds and cannot be spent by the landlord for improvements or other purposes. If they are specified as paying rent for a certain period, such as the last month of the lease, they may be used in such specified way.

**R33**   The death of either lessor or lessee does not usually cancel the lease. The usual lease binds the "heirs and administrators, successors and assigns." If the lessee dies, the lessor should file his rent claim against the estate.

**R34**   The rent for most commercial and industrial properties is computed on a dollar amount per square foot of building area. For instance, a space in an office building could be offered at $1.25 per square foot per month on a triple net basis.

**R35**   A **sale and leaseback** is a financial arrangement where at the time of sale the seller retains occupancy by concurrently agreeing to lease the property from the purchaser. The seller receives cash while the buyer is assured a tenant for the property.

# Leases

## CHECK QUESTIONS

1. If a lessee assigns a lease he:
   (A) Is usually still secondarily responsible
   (B) Has no responsibility under any circumstances
   (C) Becomes a sub-lessee
   (D) Signs a new lease with the lessor.                    (  )  R21

2. A residential tenant under a one year written lease may break the lease if:
   (A) The property is uninhabitable
   (B) The property is destroyed
   (C) Lessor does not comply with the lease provisions
   (D) Any of the above.                                     (  )  R26

3. The law which states that leases of real property for a period of more than one year must be in writing is known as:
   (A) The Statute of Limitations
   (B) The Statute of Frauds
   (C) The Real Estate Law
   (D) The Business and Professions Code.                    (  )  R11

4. Before a lease can be recorded there must be an acknowledgment of the signature of the:
   (A) Notary Public              (B) Lessee
   (C) Lessor                     (D) Tenant.                (  )  R12

5. Landlord and new tenant agree on the terms of a 5 year lease. Lessor has signed, but lessee has not, even though lease had been delivered to him for signature. The tenant moved in and paid rent, but in two months he moved out, claiming the lease is invalid because he had not signed. On the basis of the facts given, the lease was:
   (A) Valid, as any lease needs only the lessor's signature
   (B) Valid, because the lessor signed the lease and the lessee indicated acceptance by his actions
   (C) Invalid because not signed by the lessee
   (D) Invalid because tenant served notice he would not sign the lease by his moving out of the building.              (  )  R12

6. If a tenant retains possession of the premises after a default under the terms of his lease, he is guilty of:
   (A) Perjury                    (B) Unlawful detainer
   (C) Adverse possession         (D) Lis pendens.           (  )  R28

7. Farmland leases in California usually may be made for a period not to exceed:
   (A) 10 years          (B) 15 years
   (C) 99 years          (D) 51 years.      ( )   R16

8. The interest which a lessee holds in a real property is called:
   (A) Leasehold estate       (B) Tenant's equity
   (C) Leased fee estate       (D) Security interest.      ( )   R5

9. The owner of the leased fee estate is entitled to:
   (A) Return of possession of the property at the termination of the lease
   (B) Rent payments
   (C) Reversion of the property
   (D) All of the above.      ( )   R6

10. A lease is signed by the property owner and the tenant for a fixed term of six months. Which type of leasehold estate is this?
    (A) Estate for months
    (B) Estate from period to period
    (C) Estate for years
    (D) Estate at sufferance.      ( )   R8

11. Which of the following does not have to be included in a lease?
    (A) Uses to which the property may be put
    (B) Name of the lessee
    (C) Name of the mortgagee
    (D) Which party pays for the painting of the building.
         ( )   R15

12. A landlord may enjoy rent increases under a lease when the lease contains:
    (A) A step-up clause
    (B) A clause providing for cost of living adjustments      R17
    (C) A clause providing for percentage rent      R18
    (D) All of the above.      ( )   R19

13. In a lease where the landlord pays all of the property expenses, it is which type of lease?
    (A) Gross lease          (B) Net lease
    (C) Modified gross lease     (D) Triple net lease.      ( )   R20

14. When a tenant who is in default is served a notice to "pay rent or quit" by the landlord, how many days does the tenant have to pay his rent?
    (A) 5 days          (B) 30 days
    (C) 3 days          (D) None of the above.      ( )   R27

# JUDGMENTS

**S1** A **judgment** is the final order of a court as a result of a lawsuit. It is a determination of the rights of the parties to the suit.

**S2** An award of a judgment requiring the payment of money by one party to another is called a **money judgment**.

**S3** Judgments are not final until the period in which parties to the suit have the right to appeal has elapsed.

**S4** When a certified abstract of the judgment is recorded with the county recorder, the judgment becomes a lien on all nonexempt property of the judgment debtor (loser of the suit) that he owns in that county or may acquire while the judgment is good. Recording is necessary to make it a lien. The abstract of judgment may be recorded in any California county where it is believed the debtor has property.

**S5** A judgment lien normally continues to be good for a period of **10 years** after it is entered. Steps may be taken to secure an order of the court, during this period, to enforce collection of the debt.

**S6** If the judgment is not paid, the judgment creditor (to whom money is owed) may take steps by a court action to have the debtor's property sold to pay the debt. He may secure a **writ of execution**, which is an order of the court to the sheriff to sell the debtor's property to satisfy the judgment.

**S7**    If the debtor pays the judgment amount before the property is sold, the creditor causes the lien to be removed from the property by providing the debtor a **satisfaction of judgment** which the debtor records.

**S8**    If the creditor who has brought suit fears that the party sued may dispose of his property, he may take steps to attach the property. A **prejudgment attachment** is the legal seizure of property to be retained by the court as security for a judgment in case one is obtained. These may be obtained only when the debtor is engaged in a profession, business or trade, and the debt is in connection with a contract.

**S9**    An attachment is a lien and is effective for **three years** after it is secured, although the court in some cases may extend it.

**S10**    An attachment may be released in various ways. If the judgment is paid, the person who held the judgment, or his attorney, prepares a release which is acknowledged and recorded. The court may release the attachment if bond is posted in an amount determined by the court. This is often done when the attachment interferes with a person's business.

**S11**    Certain property is exempt from execution for payment of a judgment providing a proper claim is made for exemption. Tools with which one makes his living, household effects, wearing apparel, pensions, life insurance (to a certain limit), etc., are exempt. The most important exemption is the "homestead", which will be discussed in the next chapter.

**S12**    If a person expects to secure relief by some court action, he cannot wait an unreasonable time to start his suit. The law sets certain time limits. If an action is not started within the time provided by law, the matter **outlaws**. These legal time limits vary in length from 90 days to ten years. The law specifying the time limits is called the **Statute of Limitations**.

**S13**   A **lis pendens** is a notice recorded for the purpose of warning all persons that the title or right to certain real property is in litigation, or that a lawsuit is pending, and that should a judgment be obtained, it will have priority as of the date of the lis pendens.

**S14**   Generally speaking, a misdemeanor is a minor offense for which the offender may be sentenced to the city or county jail. Felonies are major crimes for which the offender may be sentenced to a state prison.

**S15**   If a person commits a misdemeanor, he must be prosecuted within one year, otherwise he is free from prosecution.

**S16**   **Small Claims Courts**. These courts are now permitted to handle suits for amounts up to $5,000 maximum. No attorney is required and court costs are low. Such suits are often brought by owners to collect rents, and by brokers to obtain payment of commissions, etc.

**S17**   **Moratorium**. A moratorium is a law which stops or delays an action. During the depression of the 1930's the State passed several moratorium acts to stop foreclosures and give distressed property owners additional time to meet their obligations. In some communities there have been moratoriums on new construction because of lack of sewer capacity, or for some other reason.

# Judgments

## CHECK QUESTIONS

1. The final order of a court as the result of a lawsuit is known as a:
   (A) Lis pendens        (B) Attachment
   (C) Section        (D) Judgment.      ( )  S1

2. On an unpaid judgment, the judgment creditor may take steps by a court action to have the debtor's property sold to pay the debt by securing:
   (A) Writ of attachment        (B) Writ of execution
   (C) Writ of limitations        (D) A lis pendens.      ( )  S6

3. Legal seizure of property to be retained by the court pending the outcome of a suit to enforce collection, is:
   (A) A writ of execution
   (B) A prejudgment attachment
   (C) An abstract of judgment
   (D) Impounds.      ( )  S8

4. An attachment lien is normally valid for a period of:
   (A) One year        (B) Two years
   (C) Three years        (D) Four years.      ( )  S9

5. The law sets certain periods of time during which a person must start to secure relief by court action as set forth in the:
   (A) Statute of Frauds        (B) Ninety Days Law
   (C) Statute of Limitations        (D) Real Estate Law.      ( )  S12

6. After it is entered, a judgment lien normally continues to be good for a period of:
   (A) Five years        (B) Ten years
   (C) Fifteen years        (D) None of the above.      ( )  S5

# HOMESTEADS & FAIR HOUSING

**CHAPTER**

**T1**     Because of the importance of the home to the welfare of both the family and the State, our lawmakers have passed laws which give special protection to home owners against loss of their homes because of debt owed to **unsecured creditors**.

**T2**     Ordinarily, if one has debts and does not pay them, and the creditors sue and obtain court judgments, the court may issue a writ of execution whereby his property is sold to raise money to satisfy the debts.

**T3**     So that the home, the center of family life, may be given some protection from such an action, the law provides that a person may protect his home by **recording a declaration of homestead** in the county where the dwelling is located. The law even affords some protection to homeowner debtors who meet all of the homestead requirements, except for recording the declaration. The following pertains to the recording of the declaration, followed by comments on the non-filing of the declaration of homestead.

**T4**     The homestead must be the principal place where a person actually resides, and may be any one of several types of dwellings, which include a detached single-family dwelling, condominium, mobilehome, a boat and others. Multiple family dwellings qualify providing the homesteader occupies one of the units. It even includes a leasehold interest in one of the above, providing that the remaining term of the lease is at least two years. Only one homestead may be held at a time.

**T5**     Persons who may file a declaration of homestead include: the declared homestead owner (this may be both husband and wife), the spouse of the declared homestead owner, or the guardian or conservator of these persons. Where unmarried persons hold interests in the same dwelling, each must record a separate homestead declaration.

**T6** There are certain items of information which must appear in the declaration. These include:

1. The name of the declared homestead owner.

2. A description of the declared homestead.

3. A statement that the declared homestead is the principal dwelling of the declared homestead owner or such person's spouse, and that the declared homestead owner or spouse is residing in the homestead on the date the homestead declaration is recorded.

**T7** Untrue statements in the declaration make the homestead voidable.

**T8** A homestead cannot legally be declared after the homeowner files a petition for bankruptcy.

**T9** The amount of the homestead exemption is based on the debtor's status at the time the creditor's lien is established. The amount is one of the following: (CC 704.730)

1. $75,000, if the judgment debtor or his/her spouse is a member of a "family unit." The judgment debtor and the judgment debtor's spouse, if residing together in the homestead, are a "family unit." There are also many other combinations that will qualify as a "family unit." For example, a judgment debtor and his minor child, or minor grandchild, or father or mother, etc., whom the judgment debtor cares for in the homestead.

2. $100,000, if the debtor or the debtor's spouse who resides with the debtor on the homestead premises is 65 years or older or is unable to engage in substantial gainful employment because of a physical or mental disability. This exemption amount also applies to a judgment debtor 55 years of age or older if that person's gross annual income is not more than $15,000 ($20,000 if married).

**T10** The amount of the exemption is $50,000 for persons who do not qualify for the larger exemptions.

**T11**    The court will only issue an order for the sale of a property on which a declaration of homestead has been filed if it determines that there is sufficient value in the property. The value must be more than enough to satisfy the cost of the sale plus any secured liens on the property, such as tax liens, mechanic's liens and trust deed notes - plus the amount of the homesteader exemption. If the market value of the property is equal to or less than the total of these, then there is nothing left for the unsecured creditors, and there is no point in having the sale. Therefore, the court will not order it. If the amount of these items is less than the property's market value, then the property is sold, and after satisfying them, the unsecured creditors are paid. After paying off the unsecured creditors in full, any remaining amount then goes to the homesteader. The property may not be sold for an amount less than the minimum bid amount set by the court.

**T12**    Should the property be sold at an "execution sale," the exemption amount which the debtor receives is protected against action taken by creditors for a period of **six months**. This gives the owner the opportunity to purchase another home upon which he can record a new declaration of homestead within the six month period.

**T13**    The homestead does not protect against judgments which were of record before the homestead was recorded, nor against tax liens, mechanics' liens, or mortgages placed upon the property before the recording of the declaration of homestead. It does protect against judgment liens which become effective after recording the homestead.

**T14**    Once the declaration of homestead is recorded, the homestead is not broken by moving out of the property. To break the homestead (abandon it), an **Abandonment of Homestead** may be prepared and recorded. It is also broken if the property is sold to others.

**T15**    Forms for declaring a homestead are available at stationary stores, but it is far better to have an attorney attend to the filing, as there are many items to get correct, and any errors or omissions may make the declaration void. Signatures to the declaration must be acknowledged.

**T16**    It should be stressed that a little knowledge of homesteads is dangerous. Sometimes, well-meaning but uninformed persons advise others to file declarations when it may work to their disadvantage. Anyway, there is no need to seek this protection until it is needed. There is plenty of time after a suit is started, if one should ever be sued. Premature filings may injure credit and cause title complications.

**T17**    As of July 1983, new law provides homestead exemption in some cases for those who do not file a declaration of homestead, but meet all of the other requirements for entitlement to an exemption that one who files a declaration must meet. Certain legal procedures must be followed to qualify. The exemption amounts are the same as for those who do record a declaration of homestead.

**Note:** The State law permitting filing a declaration of homestead should not be confused with "taking-up", or homesteading public lands by settling thereon and making certain improvements. That is entirely a different operation.

## Fair Housing

### STATE LAW

### Discrimination Prohibited In General

**T18**    The **Unruh Civil Rights Act** (Civil Code Section 51, et seq.) states: "All persons within the jurisdiction of this State are free and equal, and no matter what their sex, race, color, religion, ancestry, or national origin, are entitled to the full and equal accommodations, advantages, facilities, privileges, or services in all business establishments of every kind whatsoever." This Act applies to real estate activities. Thus, real estate brokers who unlawfully deny full and equal accommodations, advantages, facilities, privileges and services of their business establishment on grounds of race or color, are in violation of this Act.

**T19** This Act further states, "Whoever denies, or who aids, or incites such denial, or whoever makes any discrimination, distinction or restriction on account of sex, color, race, religion, ancestry, or national origin is liable for each and every such offense for the actual damages, and two hundred fifty dollars ($250) in addition thereto, suffered by any person denied the rights provided in this code."

**T20** The California Supreme Court has held that age discrimination (primarily against children in apartments, condominium developments, etc.) is illegal under the Unruh Civil Rights Act. In 1984 the Legislature enacted some of the court's age discrimination rulings into law, but exempted certain housing for senior citizens which was designed to meet their particular physical and social needs.

## Housing Discrimination Prohibited

**T21** The **Fair Employment and Housing Act** applies to owners of specified types of property, to real estate brokers and salespersons, and to financial institutions. Portions of this Act specifically cover housing discrimination This Act expands upon the Rumford Act of 1963.

**T22** The law prohibits discrimination in supplying housing accommodations because of race, color, religion, sex, marital status, national origin, or ancestry. Housing accommodations as used in the law means real property used or intended to be used by the owner for residential purposes, and which consists of **not more than four dwelling units**. It forbids such discrimination in the sale, rental, lease or financing of practically all categories of housing, and establishes methods of investigating, preventing and remedying violations.

**T23** Housing discrimination complaints made to the Department of Fair Employment and Housing are investigated by its staff. If the department decides that the law has been violated, and if the person accused of violating the law cannot be persuaded to correct the violation, the Department may file an accusation, or bring an action in the Superior Court for an injunction. If the Commission of Fair Employment and Housing, after a hearing, finds a violation of the law, it may order the sale or rental of the accommodation or like accommodations, if available. It may order financial assistance terms, conditions or privileges previously denied. In addition, it may order payment of punitive damages. The Department is required to follow up on the case to determine whether its order is being carried out.

T24    The term "discrimination" includes refusal to sell, rent, or lease housing, including misrepresentation as to availability, inferior terms, cancellations, etc. For sale or rent advertisements containing discriminatory information are prohibited.

## Discrimination in Financing of Housing Prohibited

T25    The **Housing Financial Discrimination Act of 1977** prohibits financial institutions (banks, savings and loan associations, or other financial institutions, including mortgage loan brokers, mortgage bankers and public agencies) which regularly make, arrange, or purchase loans for the purchase, construction, rehabilitation, improvement, or refinancing of housing accommodations (real property used as an owner-occupied residence of **not more than four dwelling units**) from engaging in discriminatory loan practices.

T26    A financial institution cannot discriminate in its financial lending on the basis of race, color, religion, sex, marital status, national origin, or ancestry. Nor may it consider the racial, ethnic, religious or national origin composition, or trends in a neighborhood or geographic areas surrounding a housing accommodation. The foregoing permits the lender to demonstrate that such consideration in a particular case is required to avoid an unsound business practice.

**T27** The Secretary of the Business, Transportation and Housing Agency has issued regulations for enforcement of the Act and is empowered to investigate lending patterns and practices, and to attempt to conciliate complaints. Investigation of complaints has been delegated to the State agency which regulates the particular financial institution involved. If a violation of the Act is found to have occurred, the Secretary can order that the loan be made on non-discriminatory terms, or impose a fine of up to $1,000. Financial institutions are required to notify loan applicants of the existence of the Act.

**T28** This law makes **redlining** illegal in California. Redlining is the policy of a lender of not making real estate loans in delineated older urban areas, usually with large minority populations, because of supposed higher lending risks, without giving due consideration to the creditworthiness of the individual loan applicant.

## Real Estate Commissioner's Regulations

**T29** The Commissioner's Regulations set forth in great detail many acts of discrimination which if practiced by real estate licensees, will be the basis for disciplinary action. (Regulations 2780, 2781 & 2782)

**T30** One of the things covered is **inducement of panic selling.** This is the instilling of fear in the minds of residential property owners to induce the sale, lease, or the listing for sale or lease of their property on the grounds of loss of value, increase in crime, or decline in the quality of the schools due to the presence or prospective entry into the neighborhood of persons of another race, color, religion, ancestry or national origin.

**T31** Regulation 2782 requires that a broker licensee shall take reasonable steps to become aware of and to be familiar with, and to familiarize his or her salespersons with the requirements of federal and State laws and regulations relating to the prohibition of discrimination in the sale, rental or financing of the purchase of real property.

## FEDERAL LAW

**T32** **Title VIII of the Civil Rights Act of 1968** (42 U.S.C. 3601-3619) made it unlawful to discriminate in any aspect relating to the sale, rental or financing of dwellings, or in the provision of brokerage services or facilities in connection with the sale or rental of a dwelling because of race, color, religion, sex, or national origin. Under the provisions of Title VIII, persons who believed that they had been subjected to, or were about to be subjected to, a discriminatory housing practice could file a complaint with the Secretary of Housing and Urban Development (HUD). Title VIII required the Department of Housing and Urban Development to investigate each complaint, and where the Department determined to resolve the matters raised in a complaint, to engage in informal efforts to conciliate the issues in the complaint.

**T33** However, where these informal efforts to conciliate a case were unsuccessful, Title VIII did not provide the Secretary with any administrative mechanism for redressing acts of discrimination against an individual. In addition, while the Secretary could refer a case involving a pattern or practice of discrimination to the Attorney General for the initiation of a civil action, Federal courts did not award individual relief to the victims of discrimination in such cases.

**T34** According to a California official of HUD, although the 1968 Civil Rights Act contained provisions against housing discrimination, little had been done in 21 years to enforce them. This changed with the **Fair Housing Amendments Act of 1988**. This new law provides HUD with some strong enforcement powers, including the levying of fines up to $50,000.

**T35** The provisions in the Fair Housing Amendments Act describing the nature of conduct which constitutes a discriminatory housing practice have been revised to extend protection to persons with handicaps and to families with children. The Act prohibits discrimination in any activities relating to the sale or rental of dwellings, in the availability of residential real estate-related transactions, or in the provision of services and facilities in connection therewith because of race, color, religion, sex, handicap, familial status, or national origin.

**T36**   The Fair Housing Amendments Act also makes it unlawful to refuse to permit, at the expense of a handicapped person, reasonable modifications to existing premises occupied or to be occupied by such a person, if such modifications are necessary to afford such person full enjoyment of the premises. With respect to rental housing, the Act provides that a landlord may, where reasonable, condition permission for a modification on the renter's agreeing to restore the interior of the premises to the condition that existed before the modification, reasonable wear and tear excepted. The Act also makes it unlawful to refuse to make reasonable accommodations in rules, policies, practices, or services to afford a handicapped person equal opportunity to use and enjoy a dwelling.

**T37**   Further, the Fair Housing Amendments Act makes it unlawful to design and construct certain multifamily dwellings for first occupancy after March 13, 1991, in a manner that makes them inaccessible to persons with handicaps. All premises within such dwelling also are specifically required to contain several features of adaptive design so that the dwelling is readily accessible to, and usable by, persons with handicaps.

**T38**   With respect to the new protection for families with children, this Act prohibits discrimination because of familial status (generally, the presence of children under age 18 in a family) in the sale or rental of housing. However, the Act provides an exemption from this prohibition for housing which qualifies as "housing for older persons".

**T39**   A new federal law known as the **Americans with Disabilities Act** went into effect on January 26, 1992. It requires improved handicapped access in existing buildings frequented by the public and prohibits physical barriers in newly built or remodeled commercial structures. Anywhere the general public is asked in, the invitation must also extend to the blind, deaf, mobility impaired and those with manual dexterity problems. California's accessibility law is considered among the most advanced in the country, but the federal mandate goes further by applying to all public accomodations, not just new ones. Existing buildings subject to this new law include stores, many office buildings, restaurants, bars, hotels, airports, gas stations, sports and entertainment facilities, doctors' offices, libraries, day care centers, private schools and parks. Warehouses and office buildings not open to the public must provide accessibility when built new or altered, although existing buildings need not undergo modification. Only private clubs, facilities run by religious organizations and personal residences are exempt.

**T40** The law calls for increased accessibility in all existing business facilities in little more than a year's time, provided removal of barriers is **easily accomplished at a low cost**. That could include, for instance, the addition of curb cuts and ramps, substitution of offset door hinges to widen passageways and installation of lower shelves and grab bars in lavatories. Larger businesses must modify their premises by January 26, 1992. Small businesses of 25 or fewer employees and gross receipts of under $1 million can avoid legal entanglementsfor an additional six months. Still smaller concerns with 10 or fewer employees and gross receipts of under $500,000 can wait until January 26, 1993 to complete alterations. The design of any newly built or altered building first occupied after January 26, 1993 cannot present any physical impediments under the new law.

**T41** The law is vague about exactly what must be done to comply, requiring removal of physical barriers where **readily achievable** and providing auxillary aids such as telecommunication devices for deaf people when it won't present an **undue burden**. But, unlike many earlier laws, this one has teeth: Disabled people and federal agencies can begin taking businesses and governments to court if they feel the law is not being obeyed. Ultimately, courts could order compliance in new and altered buildings that fail to meet requirements. Fines for violating this law can be as high as $100,000. The sale of an older hotel in San Diego fell through when the buyer became aware of this law and didn't want to "chance it." The broker in the transaction talked to a government official involved in the enforcement of this law for thirty minutes on the telephone, and could not get satisfactory answers for his buyer as to what changes would probably have to be made in the building.

# Homesteads/Fair Housing

## CHECK QUESTIONS

1. A recorded declaration of homestead can give protection against:
   (A) Unsecured creditors      (B) Secured creditors
   (C) Mortgages                (D) Lien holders.                    (  )   T1

2. A declaration of homestead may be filed on a home by a:
   (A) Beneficiary              (B) Attorney
   (C) Promisor                 (D) None of the above.              (  )   T5

3. For the purpose of recording a Declaration of Homestead, the homestead declarant could be:
   (A) The spouse of the declared homestead owner
   (B) The guardian of the declared homestead owner
   (C) Two unmarried persons each having an interest in the same home
   (D) Any of the above.                                            (  )   T5

4. Under the protection of a recorded declaration of homestead, a fifty year old single person without dependents is entitled to an exemption amounting to:
   (A) $5000                    (B) $7500                                   T9
   (C) $50,000                  (D) $20,000.                        (  )   T10

5. A declaration of homestead may not be filed legally on a property which:
   (A) Is already encumbered by a trust deed or mortgage
   (B) Has a value in excess of $45,000
   (C) Is not community property
   (D) Is not the principle place where the declarant actually resides.
                                                                    (  )   T4

6. Which of the following **is not** required in a declaration of homestead:
   (A) A statement that the declarant is residing on the premises and claims it as a homestead
   (B) A statement of the cost of the property when it was purchased
   (C) A description of the declared homestead
   (D) The name of the declared homestead owner.                   (  )   T6

7. A homestead is terminated by:
   (A) Moving from the property
   (B) Renting the home to others
   (C) Selling the property
   (D) Moving to another state.                                    (  )   T14

8. If a homestead property is sold by the order of a court for more than the liens secured by the property plus the homeowner's exemption and costs of the sale, the owner must be paid the amount of:
(A) His exemption only
(B) His equity
(C) His exemption plus any amount remaining after the required payments are made
(D) None of the above.                                      (  )  T11

9. A declaration of homestead, properly filed:
(A) Protects anyone, regardless of the value of his property, from forced sale to pay an existing mortgage or trust deed
(B) Gives the claimant the rights to title by adverse possession after a period of five years use and occupancy
(C) Protects the claimant against subsequent judgment liens up to the amount of his classification exemption
(D) Invalidates all subsequent unsecured liens.             (  )  T11

10. After receiving a check from the court-ordered sale for the amount of the exemption, the homestead owner has how much time to purchase another home with these funds and record another declaration of homestead.
(A) Six months            (B) Six years
(C) One year              (D) None of the above.            (  )  T12

11. The Unruh Civil Rights Act applies to:
(A) Dentists              (B) Grocery stores
(C) Real estate brokers   (D) All of the above.             (  )  T18

12. The penalty for violation of the rights of a person under the Unruh Civil Rights Act is:
(A) $1,000
(B) $5,000
(C) $250 plus actual damages
(D) Actual damages only.                                    (  )  T19

13. The Fair Employment and Housing Act applies to:
(A) Hotels
(B) Duplexes
(C) Apartment buildings containing 25 units or more
(D) Apartment buildings containing 8 units or more.         (  )  T22

14. The Housing Financial Discrimination Act of 1977 is administered by which agency:
(A) Business, Transportation and Housing
(B) HUD
(C) Department of Real Estate
(D) Federal Housing Administration.                         (  )  T27

15. The Fair Housing Amendments Act of 1988 provides amendments to, and tools for enforcing which one of the following:
    (A) The Unruh Civil Rights Act
    (B) Fair Employment and Housing Act
    (C) The Housing Financial Discrimination Act of 1977
    (D) The Civil Rights Act of 1968.                        (  )  T34

16. Real estate licensees who unlawfully deny full and equal housing accommodations under the Unruh Civil Rights Act, because of a person's race, are subject to which of the following damages:
    (A) $50,000
    (B) $250
    (C) Actual damages
    (D) Actual damages plus $250.                           (  )  T19

17. A housing discrimination complaint under California law should be filed with which one of the following agencies:
    (A) Attorney General's office
    (B) Department of Fair Employment and Housing
    (C) The Civil Rights Agency
    (D) Department of Equal Housing.                        (  )  T23

18. The term "redlining" pertains to:
    (A) Land descriptions
    (B) Delineation of areas by lenders where they will not make real estate loans
    (C) Appraising
    (D) None of the above.                                  (  )  T28

19. The Fair Employment and Housing Act as to housing accommodations pertains to:
    (A) Misrepresentation of availability
    (B) Refusal to rent or sell
    (C) Advertisements containing discriminatory information
    (D) All of the above.                                   (  )  T24

20. It is unlawful to refuse to permit, at the expense of a handicapped person, reasonable modifications to existing premises occupied or to be occupied by such a person if such modifications are necessary to afford such person full enjoyment of the premises. What is the law that provides for this?:
    (A) The Fair Employment and Housing Act
    (B) The Fair Housing Amendments Act of 1988
    (C) The Unruh Civil Rights Act
    (D) The Housing Financial Discrimination Act of 1977.   (  )  T36

This page intentionally left blank.

# GOVERNMENT LAND USE PLANNING & CONTROLS

**CHAPTER**

**U1**     Older sections of many of California's cities often show the lack of good planning as evidenced by congestion, incompatible uses located near each other, lack of public facilities, lack of parks, poor traffic circulation, etc. Most newly developing urban areas in this State are now being well planned by the city or county governments which have jurisdiction over them. As a result, these communities are generally more attractive, and more pleasant to live and work in than are the older communities. Further, they should not see the same degree of decline in desirability and property values which has been true of many of our older communities.

**U2**     Long term land planning by cities and counties is now required in California by State law. They are required to adopt a comprehensive, long term **general plan** to guide future development under their jurisdictions. Each general plan must include at least nine elements, or areas of concern, including land use, circulation, housing, open space, conservation, safety, seismic (earthquake) safety, noise, and scenic highway. The general plan may also include other elements such as recreation, historic preservation, and public services. Depending on the community's location, its general plan may also have to include special consideration and policies for coastal development, protection of mineral and forestry resources and other special areas of concern.

**U3**     State law also requires that zoning, subdivision approvals and public works projects must be consistent with the adopted general plan. Copies of general plans, including the text and maps are available from the various cities and counties.

**U4**     While a general plan, as the name implies, is "general" in character, **zoning** spells out specific controls on the uses to which each individual property may be put. The **police power** of the State permits this on the grounds that zoning is for the good of the public welfare.

**U5** Zoning symbols vary from community to community. Some of the basic symbols that are frequently used are **R** for residential, **C** for commercial and **M** for industrial. From these there can be several sub-designations. **R-1-5**, for example, is for a single-family dwelling with a minimum lot area of 5,000 square feet.

**U6** Some of the still-existing zoning designations that were placed on land many years ago may simply state the uses the property may be put to, and the minimum lot size and building setback requirements. Over the years, more and more restrictions and requirements have been included in zoning designations. These often cover such things as maximum permitted building area and height, landscaping, on-site parking, fencing, signs, and more.

**U7** It's convenient to have a zoning manual and map in the broker's office for handy reference. However, zoning designations on properties are sometimes changed (rezoned), as well as the particulars of certain zoning designations. Therefore, when it's important that zoning information be exactly correct, check with the zoning department to make sure you have the latest information.

**U8** When a city or county has a complete adopted general plan, State law permits the formulation of **specific plans** within the general plan area. A specific plan may be used in lieu of zoning for an area which is to be developed.

**U9** A specific plan may be formulated for an entire tract of land, showing the locations of streets, which portions will be for various uses, such as residential, commercial, schools, open space, etc. It addresses the requirements for such things as public facilities, transportation, social needs, environmental matters, landscaping, building design, grading of the land, etc.

It is enough to remember that the specific plan includes just about "everything" to do with the development of a tract of land. The land may include one or several ownerships. A specific plan is usually formulated by a private planning firm under the guidance of local government planning department staff members, and in conjunction with a citizens' advisory committee. The city council or board of supervisors must give final approval to the plan.

U10  The specific plan process can result in excellent planning which is very beneficial to the community. It also benefits the land owner/developer, because after the plan is approved he knows how his land can be utilized without having to go back time after time for approval of the use of various portions of the land.

U11  A local government may grant **variances** to the development standards in a zoning ordinance under special circumstances. For example, a property's zoning requires a 25 foot building setback from the front property line, but because of special circumstances a variance might be approved to permit a 15 foot setback. State law provides that a variance may be granted where "the strict application of the zoning ordinance deprives such property of privileges enjoyed by other property in the vicinity and under identical zoning classification."

U12  A **conditional use permit (CUP)** is sometimes given to permit a use that the zoning of a property does not include. An example is a nursery school on a lot which is zoned for residential use. The permittee/owner must sign the permit and agree to comply with all of its provisions and conditions. Before issuing a **CUP**, the local government must conclude that the proposed use will not adversely affect the neighborhood or the intent of the general plan.

U13  **Rezoning**, as the name implies, is changing the zoning. After the requirement came into effect for local governments to formulate general plans for their areas, and to have zoning consistent with a general plan, much rezoning of areas was required to accomplish this consistency. Often included in this was downzoning, where the number of dwelling units which could be built per acre of land was reduced. Individuals also seek rezoning for their individual properties.

**U14** Most communities have a **planning department** staffed with professional planners. Planning departments in larger cities may have several divisions such as current planning, long-range planning, and environmental quality. The planning department makes studies, reviews applications, assists the public in various ways, and makes recommendations to the planning commission, and to the city council or board of supervisors.

**U15** Every incorporated city and county in California is required to have a **planning commission**. The planning commission consists of citizens appointed by the city council or board of supervisors. It holds hearings and decides on matters of specific plans, subdivisions, rezonings, variances, etc. Property owners have the **right to appeal** its decisions. State law specifically charges the planning commission with major responsibility in the preparation and adoption of the general plan, and for its implementation and amendment. However, all final decisions on planning and zoning matters are made by the elected officials of the city council or board of supervisors.

# Government Land Use
# Planning and Controls

## CHECK QUESTIONS

1.  An officially appointed group which makes decisions on zoning matters is called:
    (A) City Growth Board       (B) Master Zoning Board
    (C) City Policy Commission  (D) Planning Commission.    (   ) U15

2.  The control which designates what use an individual property can be put to is known as:
    (A) Planning    (B) Set-back
    (C) Zoning      (D) Conservation.    (   ) U4

3.  A long range program for the guidance of the growth of a community is called a:
    (A) Zoning plan     (B) Area plan
    (C) General plan    (D) Long range plan.    (   ) U2

4.  State law requires which of the following to conform to an adopted general plan:
    (A) Zoning                   (B) Subdivision approvals       U3
    (C) Conditional use permit   (D) All of the above.    (   ) U12

5.  The control of the use of real estate is permitted by the State's:
    (A) Police power     (B) Legislature
    (C) Planning power   (D) Department of Real Estate. (   )   U4

6.  A Specific Plan does not include which one of the following:
    (A) Transportation          (B) Social needs
    (C) Environmental concerns  (D) Property value.    (   )   U9

7.  A property owner makes application to the city for a greater height on a building he wishes to construct than is permitted by the property's zoning. What he is asking for is a:
    (A) Conditional use permit   (B) Rezoning
    (C) Variance                 (D) Specific use change.    (   ) U11

8.  Which of the following is not a function of a city's planning department:
    (A) Environmental quality
    (B) Final decisions on rezoning requests
    (C) Long range planning                               U14
    (D) Directly assisting the public.    (   ) U15

9.  Which of the following does zoning not ever pertain to:
    (A) Landscaping   (B) Parking
    (C) Signs         (D) None of the above.    (   )   U6

This page intentionally left blank.

# HOME CONSTRUCTION
# TERMITES

**V1**   Questions have appeared in real estate license examinations relative to the construction of homes and other residential units. So far, these have been rather elementary. No doubt a broker or salesperson presenting a home for sale should be able to refer to the different parts of the construction within reason. Almost everyone knows the roof, walls and foundation. However, many don't know a floor joist from a header.

**V2**   On the following page is a drawing showing the usual construction parts of a house, with the names of the various pieces of lumber, timbers, concrete, etc.

**V3**   The average dwelling has one of two types of floor structure. One has a standard concrete foundation which supports horizontal timbers called floor joists, and upon them is a board or plywood subfloor. The other uses a concrete "slab" floor. Upon these the wall framing is erected, usually with lumber 2 inches by 4 inches, called studs. These are capped by a plate. They rest on 2" x 4" lumber nailed or anchored to the floor called the "sole." As a picture of this sort of thing is worth a thousand words, refer to the illustration. The wall studs usually must be not more than 16 inches from center to center. Standard floors must have at least 18 inches clearance to bottom of floor joists from the ground level. This area under a house is called the "crawl space."

**V4**   The **Uniform Building Code**, which applies to homes in areas where there are not equal or more strict local ordinances, provides many minimum requirements. For instance, ceilings must be at least 7 ft., 6 in. high, except that kitchen and bathroom ceilings may be a minimum of 7 feet high. One room must have a minimum of 120 square feet of area, and the others, excepting the kitchen and bathrooms, must have at least 70 square feet of area. Sizes of bathroom windows and vents from these rooms are also regulated. Local requirements are usually more demanding. Building permits must be obtained from the building department of the city or county which enforces the State and local requirements.

**V5**

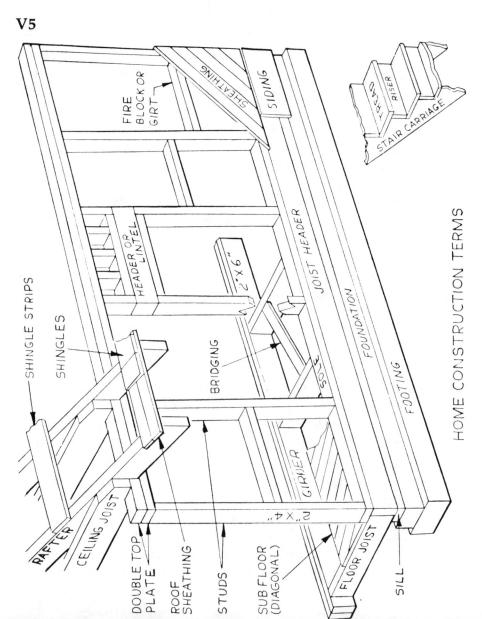

HOME CONSTRUCTION TERMS

# COMMON CONSTRUCTION DEFINITIONS

**V6**    **Anchor bolt**

Bolt embedded in masonry, such as the foundation, to fasten the sill (plank or timbers).

**Batten**

Narrow strips of wood to cover joints of outside wall boards.

**Board**

Lumber less than 2 inches thick is usually termed board. If thicker, they are called planks or timbers.

**Board feet**

Measurement used in lumber business. Unit is 1 foot square by one inch thick.

**Bridging**

Two inch planking nailed between joists to give lateral support. (See illustration).

**Casement window**

One which opens on hinges.

**Casing**

Trim of finished lumber around door or window openings.

**Crawl space**

Air space between ground and lower floor.

**Drywall Construction**

This term usually refers to a gypsum board interior wall and ceiling cover which has largely taken the place of plaster.

**Eaves**

Overhang of roof beyond outer walls.

**Fire blocking (girt)**

Short pieces of 2" x 4" lumber braced horizontally between wall studding. Serves two purposes; reinforces studs and stops draft in wall in case of fire.

**Flashing**

Material (usually sheet metal) inserted in roof troughs and around chimneys, etc. to make them watertight.

**Floor joists**

These are timbers which support the floor boards or heavy plywood with a standard foundation.

**Footing**

Heavy masonry or concrete courses placed in ground, upon which the masonry or concrete foundation is set. (See illustration).

**Foundation**

Masonry or concrete courses which rest on the footing, and upon which the sill is laid, usually with anchor bolts.

**Furring**

Narrow wooden strips nailed onto framing to even it out for the purpose of leveling it for plastering, etc.

**Gambrel roof**

One which has two pitches, Dutch style. Popular for barns.

**Girder**

Heavy plank for support of joists, wall beams, etc.

**Header or lintel**

Rather heavy joist across top of opening for door, window or passageway. Size of lumber depends on span of opening.

**Hip roof**

Roof that slopes up to the ridge from all sides.

**Jamb (door)**

Framing for a door or opening.

**Joists (ceiling and floor)**

These are rather heavy timber (2" x 6" and greater) which support the flooring or ceiling, spaced to meet requirements.

**Joist header**

Timber placed on edge, resting on sill to box-in floor joists. Usually a 2" x 6" timber.

**Lath**

Small strips of board nailed to studs for the application of plaster. These are now obsolete, and sheets of composition or gypsum lath board are now used. They are easily applied to walls - much faster and cheaper. They hold the plaster well.

**Membrane**

To keep moisture from seeping through a concrete slab floor, a membrane is laid between layers of concrete. A plastic material is used.

**Pier**

A concrete block placed in the ground to support floor joists within the confines of the foundation. They are spaced at various distances, depending on type of construction and subflooring used.

**Ridge board**

Board along peak of roof to which rafters are nailed.

**Shakes**

Heavy thick shingles, usually cut to look "hand hewn".

**Sheathing**

Boards, usually 1 inch thick, used to close in the sides and roof of a house. Solid side sheathing is not used too much in California, as it is not too necessary for insulation, and it increases costs. Spaced strips (shingle strips) are commonly used on roof rafters instead of solid sheathing.

**Shingle strips**

Strips, usually one inch boards, nailed across rafters and spaced to take the shingles. Used instead of solid sheathing on the roof.

**Siding (wood)**

Finished boards applied to outside walls of a home and painted or stained. Many homes have stucco instead, but some partially use board siding or masonry for decorative effect.

**Sill**

This is the timber which is bolted to the foundation and which is the basis for the higher construction timbers. These timbers for average homes are 2" x 6" or 2" x 8" planks. They are required to be dry rot and termite resistant, either treated with chemicals or of redwood. They were called "mud sills" in the days when masonry foundations were not required and they rested directly on the ground.

**Sole (bottom plate)**

Plank nailed on flooring to which studding is erected.

**Span**

The distance a board or timber must bridge between supporting posts. The greater the span, the greater the dimensions must be for the supporting timber over a doorway or window, or for rafters, ceiling joists, etc.

**Stairs**

Note names of parts in illustration.

**Studding (studs)**

Lumber, usually 2 x 4's, used in framing of house walls. Usually required to be spaced on 16 inch centers.

**Subfloor**

Formerly 1 x 6 inch boards laid diagonally across the floor joists upon which hardwood flooring was laid. Today it is common to substitute heavy plywood, saving time and labor, especially when wall-to-wall carpeting is to be used.

**Timbers**

Heavier lumber for posts, headers, etc. Probably lumber greater than 4 x 4 inches. In some beamed ceilings they run up to 8" x 16" or larger.

Hundreds of other terms for materials and construction features are used in the building trades. It would take another text to describe them fully. However, the above should reasonably cover questions asked in a real estate exam.

# TERMITES

**V7**    Termites are ant-like insects which infest lumber. They gnaw tunnels in it and breed. Their community life and habits make an interesting story. From a real estate standpoint however, we are merely interested in their destructiveness to buildings.

**V8**    There are two types which are often encountered. One is the subterranean type which works between the ground under buildings and the structure above, the floor, sills and studding. The other, a flying variety, lodges in the roof or walls. Both devour the wood and sometimes cause damage necessitating expensive repairs. Substantial damage is more likely to be found in older buildings. However, the fresh wood used in new buildings is especially tempting to termites, and therefore preventive measures should be started early

**V9**    There is also a fungus which causes dry rot of wooden structures. All of these perhaps have been overemphasized at times, and buyers have become unnecessarily wary of them, although sometimes with good cause. Certain lumber such as redwood, is more resistant to termites and fungus than others. Also, lumber used for house sills is now impregnated with chemicals to resist these pests.

**V10**    Pest control operators are in business to examine buildings, make reports of termite and dry rot conditions, estimate cost of repairs, and even contract to do the repair work. These operators are licensed by the State.

**V11**    The law requires pest control operators to make **structural pest control certification reports** on a prescribed standard form, and in each case to deliver a copy promptly to the **State Structural Pest Control Board** when the report is delivered to the person requesting the inspection, or to his agent. Any person may request copies of these reports from the State Structural Pest Control Board.

**V12**   While State law does not require these reports, some buyers require that the seller deliver a building free of all termite infestation, dry rot and fungus in accessible areas, as well as being free from damage from these causes. It is usually the buyer who selects the inspection company, and pays for the service. **The transferor or real estate broker, when acting as agent in a transaction, is required to effect delivery of the inspection report, certification, and the notice of work completed, if any, to the buyer when the purchase contract calls for these documents. This is to be done as soon as practical before transfer of title**. Many lending institutions also require these reports. (CC1099 and Regulation 2905)

**V13**   When there is a possibility that a building to be sold has damage from these pests, the prudent seller will get a report before putting the property on the market and agreeing to deliver it free from termites, fungus and dry rot damage. The cost of repairs could be far higher than expected, and the seller would be in a better position to act in his best interest if he had this information before being locked into a transaction with limited time before the closing of the sale. This would allow him time to get several bids to have any damage repaired, or he might opt for only selling the property with the buyer being responsible for any repairs the buyer might wish to make.

# Home Construction - Termites

## CHECK QUESTIONS

1. The document given, to the effect that a structure upon careful inspection showed no visible signs of termite infestation, is known as:
   (A) A zoning report
   (B) Building inspection report
   (C) A Termite report
   (D) Structural pest control certification report.　　　( )　V11

2. The sole supports:
   (A) Shingles　　　　　　　　(B) Bridging　　　　　　　　V3
   (C) The sill　　　　　　　　(D) The studs.　　　　( )　V5

3. The "crawl space" is an area:
   (A) For the ceiling furnace
   (B) For spiders
   (C) In the attic
   (D) Between floor and ground
   (E) Between the studs.　　　　　　　　　　　　( )　V3

4. The Uniform Building Code requires that at least one room in a dwelling contains a minimum of:
   (A) 150 square feet　　　　　(B) 170 square feet
   (C) 200 square feet　　　　　(D) 100 square feet.　　( )　V4

5. Shingle strips rest on which structural members:
   (A) Ceiling joist　　　　　　(B) Rafters
   (C) Girder　　　　　　　　　(D) Double top plate.　　( )　V5

6. The Uniform Building Code requires that bathrooms have a minimum ceiling height of:
   (A) 7 ft., 0 in.　　　　　　　(B) 7 ft., 6 in.
   (C) 8 ft., 0 in.　　　　　　　(D) 6 ft., 7 in.　　　　( )　V4

7. Which kind of wood is most resistant to termite and fungus infestation:
   (A) Cedar　　　　　　　　　(B) Birch
   (C) Redwood　　　　　　　　(D) Spruce.　　　　　( )　V9

8. Copies of structural pest control certification reports may be secured by:
   (A) The broker　　　　　　　(B) The buyer
   (C) Anyone　　　　　　　　　(D) The seller.　　　　( )　V11

**NOTE:** Study the drawing "Home Construction Terms" (V5) very well. Know the relationships of the various building components.

# APPRAISING

CHAPTER

**W1** It is essential for the real estate broker and salesperson to have an understanding of the principles and methods of appraising. The purpose of this chapter is to give the student an overview of the subject. An agent who specializes in single family homes would do well to take a basic course in the principles of appraising. An agent who deals in income producing property, in addition should take one or more courses in appraising this type of property.

**W2** **An appraisal is an estimate or opinion of value.** It may be communicated orally, or as a written report. If written, it may be in narrative style, or on an appraisal form. An agent who deals in single family dwellings in a particular neighborhood, and is familiar with the various home sales which have recently occurred, may be able to quickly appraise a property and communicate his opinion of value orally to his client. It should be noted here, that any oral opinion of the value of real property should be supported by a written backup memorandum in the broker's file which includes market data and his valuation analysis. On the other hand, professional appraisers sometimes spend several weeks in appraising unique and complicated properties. In doing these, they usually interview many people, collect volumes of data and do extensive analyses. These appraisals are usually communicated in the form of lengthy narrative reports. Both the agent and the appraiser made an appraisal and communicated it, though the appraisals and methods of communication are quite different in character.

**W3** A good appraisal, that is, one which provides a reliable **estimate of value**, requires having all the facts on the property being appraised, having accurate market data (comparable sales, listings, rental information, etc. on similar properties); having knowledge of the market for the type of property being appraised, and the mortgage market; making use of the proper method or methods of valuation; and having good, unbiased judgment on the part of the appraiser. When an appraiser has all of this, his appraisal is still an estimate of value. Several experienced appraisers appraising the same property and meeting the above requirements, will all probably have somewhat different opinions of value. These opinions however, should be fairly close, unless the property is a difficult one to appraise.

**W4** The various rights in a parcel of real property are referred to as a **bundle of rights**. They include all of the legal rights incident to ownership of property including rights of use, possession, encumbering, and disposition. The appraiser must be knowledgable regarding the various rights which are held in the property he is appraising. Any one of these rights can be valued, such as an easement, or a leasehold interest. Most appraisals are of the fee simple estate interest. In appraising the value of the fee simple estate, the appraiser must consider the effect of other rights in the property by lessees, holders of easements, etc. If there is any question about the various rights held in a property, it's a good idea to order a title report which would show these.

**W5** In order for anything to have value, it must meet four requirements. These are referred to as the **underlying factors of value**. This of course includes real estate. It must have:

- **Utility-** It must be of some use to someone. Who could make use of an acre of land at the north pole?
- **Demand-** Someone must have the desire to possess it. If no one wants it, it has no value. On the other hand, the more with adequate financial means who want it, the greater its value.
- **Scarcity-** The less there is of a commodity, provided there is demand for it, the higher the value goes. Beach frontage near populated centers illustrates this. There is a limited amount with many who desire to own it - therefore it commands a relatively high value.
- **Transferability-** Ownership must be capable of being transferred to a buyer for the commodity to have value on the market. These underlying factors of value are also called "characteristics of value" and "elements of value." They may be referred to as such in examinations.

**W6**    There are, of course, hundreds of things which influence value. These vary depending upon the type of property and its potential uses. Location is an important one. It is so important that there is a saying in the real estate business that the three most important property qualities are location, location, location. Building quality, condition, design and esthetic appeal are important. Such things as availability and cost of financing, income tax shelter, and potential for value appreciation have been important factors in recent years.

**W7**    In the real estate business the type of value most often required is fair market value, which is usually referred to as **market value**. One definition of market value is: "the highest price in terms of money on the date of valuation, which a property would bring in a competitive market, with adequate exposure to the market, and with both buyer and seller under no urgent necessity for entering into a particular transaction, and with both parties acting prudently and knowledgeably."

**W8**    Sellers want the highest possible price, and buyers want the lowest. Sales data from a competitive market indicates the price levels at which the two are having meetings of the minds for different types of properties, and these indicate "highest price" in the above definition of market value. The "most probable price" is sometimes used instead of "highest price." The two have the same meaning as defined above.

**W9**    As everyone knows, real estate values change with the passing of time, so it is necessary to estimate the value of a property as of a certain date. This date of valuation should always be stated in the appraisal report.

**W10**    The term "market value" pertains to an open market situation where the buyer has the choice of all of the properties on the market, and the seller exposes his property to all of the buyers in the market. Sometimes a buyer will pay twice market value, or more, when he requires a specific property and none other will do. An example of this would be a very successful business needing an adjacent lot to expand its facilities. This type of sale would not qualify under the definition of market value, and would not be used as a "comparable sale" in helping to estimate the market value of another property.

**W11**  The definition of market value calls for both buyer and seller to act prudently and knowledgeably. The author once spoke with a buyer of an industrial site who, after the purchase, discovered that the property had an unsatisfactory subsoil condition. It cost him as much to cure this problem as he had paid for the property. This buyer certainly was not knowledgable, nor was he prudent. If he were prudent he would have had engineering soil testing done prior to the purchase. Buyers sometimes pay more than they should because they are not sufficiently knowledgeable about a property, and occasionally sellers sell too low for the same reason, or because they are not sufficiently aware of market conditions and values.

**W12**  The first thing a person should do in appraising a property is to get all of the facts concerning it. Some of these facts could have to do with the zoning, availability of utilities, earthquake faults, flood conditions, soil condition, lot and building sizes, building condition, encumbrances against the property, etc. These of course, will vary a good deal depending on the type of property being appraised. Some city and county offices will provide information on zoning, utilities, streets, locations of earthquake faults and earth slide areas, flood conditions, environmental problems, etc.

**W13**  After becoming familiar with the property, the neighborhood in which it is located, and the local real estate market, the appraiser makes a determination of the highest and best use of the property. The **highest and best use** of a property is, "that reasonable legal use of a property which will cause it to have its highest value as of the date of the valuation."

**W14**  The highest and best use of a property may be very obvious. An example of this would be a fine single family home in a neighborhood of similar properties, and where the zoning permits only that use. On the other hand it may require a lengthy study to make a highest and best determination as to whether or not an old commercial building should be kept for that use, or if it should be razed and the site put to use for a new building. A common example of achieving the highest and best use of a property is the conversion of apartment buildings to condominiums. Some substantial profits have been made by means of these conversions.

**W15** Next, the appraiser must determine which of the **three basic approaches to value** to use in the appraisal. At times only one approach applies to an appraisal problem, and other times two, or all three will apply. Each approach used provides a **value indication** for a property. Each of the three approaches is known by different names, however the following are perhaps the most commonly used today.

1. The **cost approach** to value.
2. The **income approach** to value.
3. The **sales comparison** approach to value.

**W16** After determining which valuation approaches to use, the appraiser makes an investigation of the market, and collects appropriate data that would bear on the particular valuation. These may include sales of similar lots which are unimproved, sales of similar improved properties, rental rates, rates of return on investments buyers are requiring, building cost data, and a number of other things depending on the type of property being appraised.

## THE COST APPROACH TO VALUE

**W17** The **cost approach** considers the amount it would cost to construct an equally desirable building, less any accrued depreciation, on an equally desirable lot to the property being appraised. The theory being that an informed buyer is not going to pay more for a property than the amount for which he can acquire an equally desirable property by constructing it. See paragraph W48 in which the Principle of Substitution is defined.

**W18** In using the cost approach, the appraiser estimates the cost of replacing the improvements as new, and from this figure subtracts any depreciation. He first estimates the **direct costs**, which have to do with the physical aspects of construction. He then estimates the **indirect costs** which include any of a number of things such as the architect's fee, soil engineering, building permit, cost of construction financing, etc.

**W19** If the appraiser finds that it is warranted, an amount should be included in the cost approach for a **developer's profit**, which the developer earns by making a feasibility study of the project, finding and purchasing the site, employing the architect and general contractor, getting the project financed, and taking the risk in putting all of this together successfully. The land value is estimated by comparison with sales of similar vacant sites.

**W20** A simplified example of the cost approach is as follows. This is summarized from an actual appraisal of a new motel property. Since it was a new, well designed and a proper improvement for the location, there was no depreciation in the improvements.

**W21  Cost Approach - Motel:**

| | |
|---|---:|
| Building: 39,057 sq. ft. @ $46.00 per sq. ft. | $1,796,622 |
| Yard improvements including paving, fencing, landscaping, swimming pool, etc. | 150,000 |
| Total direct costs of the improvements | 1,946,622 |
| Indirect costs | 291,993 |
| Total construction cost | 2,238,615 |
| Total accrued depreciation | - 0 - |
| Depreciated replacement cost | 2,238,615 |
| Developer's profit | 386,385 |
| Total replacement cost new of the improvements plus developer's profit | 2,625,000 |
| Land value by comparison, 39,000 sq. ft. @ $25/sq. ft. | 975,000 |
| Indicated value by the cost approach | **$3,600,000** |

**W22** In this case, the actual building contract amount was available to the appraiser. The reasonableness of this figure was confirmed by use of a construction cost manual. Several services publish information on building costs which appraisers use. A more accurate estimate can be gotten by employing a building cost estimator, or by getting recent actual cost of construction figures of similar buildings, and comparing them on a square foot basis. The land value was estimated by comparison with sales of similar vacant properties.

**W23** The cost approach is most applicable to well designed newer buildings. This is because older buildings and buildings of poor design usually have accrued a good deal of depreciation, and depreciation is one of the most difficult things for an appraiser to measure. The student should be familiar with the following terms regarding depreciation:

**W24** **Book depreciation** refers to the owner's mathematically calculated depreciation for accounting records. It is not a measure of actual depreciation, and it has nothing to do with the cost approach.

**W25** **Total accrued depreciation** refers to actual loss in value to the improvements from all causes. This can be broken down into physical deterioration and obsolescence. Depreciation always pertains to improvements, never to land.

**W26** **Physical deterioration** can result from the normal aging of improvements, wear and tear from use, damage by dry rot, termites, etc. Physical deterioration can be **curable** or **incurable**. Termite damage to inaccessible structural members in a building which cannot be cured economically is an example of incurable physical deterioration. The replacing of a wooden stairway, which is unsafe because of severe termite damage is an example of curable physical deterioration. Physical deterioration in building components which can be cured, such as a furnace which does not work, painting which needs to be done, a roof cover which is leaking and needs to be replaced, is referred to as **deferred maintenance**. This is not difficult to estimate, as estimates can be gotten for having the work done. The measure of this form of depreciation is called **cost-to-cure**.

**W27**  There are two forms of **obsolescence**; obsolescence within a building, and obsolescence external to a building. Obsolescence within a building is called **functional obsolescence**. This may be curable or incurable. If a room arrangement is very bad, but it can be made satisfactory by rearranging interior walls, then the functional obsolescence is **curable**. The amount of this form of depreciation is measured by the **cost-to-cure**. If some of these walls are structurally supporting walls and cannot be moved and the floor plan cannot be improved, then this is **incurable functional obsolescence**. It may be difficult to accurately estimate an amount for this. In most cases it would be based on the appaiser's judgment.

**W28**  **External obsolescence** is loss in value to a building because of causes external to the property. Two examples of the many forms this type of depreciation may take, are odors from a meat packing plant, and a change in zoning which permits inharmonious nearby uses. Changing the zoning in a single family dwelling neighborhood to permit the construction of apartments is an example of this. This form of depreciation, of course, is not curable.

**W29**  Sometimes the **age-life method** of measuring depreciation is used. This method considers the relationship of the present age of a building, or other type of improvement, to its total anticipated life span. Say a building is expected to have a total life of 50 years, and 25 years have expired. The amount of depreciation by the age-life method is then 50%. However, a building with an actual age of 25 years, because of excellent maintenance and perhaps some remodeling, could be the equivalent of a 15 year old building. Fifteen years would then be used instead of 25 years as the building's age. The 15 years is called the **effective age** of the building.

**W30**  The age-life method usually assumes **straight-line depreciation**. In straight line depreciation an equal amount of depreciation is considered to occur annually.

# THE INCOME APPROACH TO VALUE

**W31** Apartment houses, shopping centers, office buildings, warehouses and many other types of income properties are purchased for the financial benefits they provide the owner. In times past, purchases of these properties were essentially for the income they would provide from rents. Today, income tax shelter, and the possibility of a property increasing in value (appreciation) to provide a hedge against inflation are also considerations in most purchases of this category of property.

**W32** There are several techniques available for use in the income approach. We are going to discuss just one of these in this text. This is the use of an **overall capitalization rate**, the technique which is used most often today in California. If used properly and with good judgment, it provides a good indication of an income producing property's market value. It involves dividing a property's **annual net income** by an overall capitalization rate. The use of this technique is explained in the following.

**W33** A **capitalized value** is an estimate of value which results from a capitalization process. It is the present worth of anticipated future money benefits.

**W34** To estimate an overall capitalization rate for a property being appraised, the appraiser finds sales of similar properties. For each sale property he acquires information as to the date of sale, the price, gross scheduled income, expenses, vacancy, financing, quality of construction, age and condition of the improvements, desirability of the location, etc. From the above information, he estimates a sale property's annual net income (before mortgage payments) and divides this by the sale price. The result is the overall capitalization rate at which the property sold. For example, say a property's net income is $287,000, and it sold for $3,000,000. Then, $287,000 divided by $3,000,000 equals 0.0957, or 9.57%, the overall capitalization rate.

**W35**  The appraiser if possible, should obtain several sales of similar properties. Then in consideration of the qualities of each of these properties, the overall "cap" rates at which they sold, and the qualities of the property being appraised, the appraiser selects a rate which in his opinion is the most applicable to it. It is not usually easy to get reliable information on sales for use in this technique. An agent who specializes in a certain type of income property has an advantage in this respect. The following is a simplified example of the use of the overall capitalization rate. It is from the same appraisal of a motel which was used in the cost approach to value.

### W36  Income Approach - Motel:

Estimated annual gross income at market rates:
81 rooms @ $40 per day average x 365 days = .......... $1,182,600

Estimated vacancy - 35%............................... (413,910)

Effective annual gross income ........................... 768,690

Estimated annual expenses
(Itemized in actual appraisal - Mortgage payments
and depreciation are not expenses) ................................ (407,406)

Estimated annual net income ........................ $361,284

Capitalization:

$\dfrac{\$361{,}284 \text{ (net annual income)}}{0.10 \text{ (overall cap rate)}}$ = .................................... $3,612,840

Indicated value by the income approach, (Rounded) ...... **$3,600,00**

## SALES COMPARISON APPROACH TO VALUE

**W37**  In the sales comparison approach, properties similar to the property being appraised which have sold, are compared to the property being appraised. Adjustments to the sales prices are made for differences in the properties, such as desirability of the locations, building size and condition, view, etc. This is usually the best approach in appraising single family dwellings.

**W38**  It is also the most commonly used approach for valuing land. Large parcels are most often valued on a per acre basis, and smaller parcels by the square foot. Again, adjustments are made for the various differences between sale properties and the property being valued.

**W39**  Retail, industrial and office buildings may be compared on a square foot basis of rentable area. Apartments can be compared on a square foot basis, by the room, or by the apartment.

**W40**  Another means of comparison is the **gross rent multiplier (GRM).** The GRM is simply the number of times a property's annual gross rent it sold for, or at which it is valued. The gross rent refers to the **scheduled annual gross rent,** which is the total rent as if the building were fully rented for a year. Sometimes the actual, or scheduled rent, is below the market level rent which a buyer anticipates receiving. Then the gross annual rent must be adjusted to the market rent level. For example, a building sold for $900,000 and its annual scheduled gross income was $90,000. Its gross rent multiplier then was 10.0. The GRM is frequently used in connection with apartment houses. It is fairly simple to use, but does not provide the accuracy of the income approach which utilizes the net income. Expenses and vacancy can vary a good deal from property to property, and the gross rent multiplier does not properly reflect this. This technique is the most reliable when the property being appraised, and the comparable sale properties from which the GRM is derived, are highly similar to one another.

### W41  Sales Comparison Approach - Motel:

The sales comparison approach was used in the appraisal of the motel by comparing it with four sales of similar motels on the basis of sale price per motel room. The result was as follows:

> Subject motel 81 rooms times
> $43,000 per room ............................................................. $3,483,000
>
> Indicated value by the
> sales comparison approach (Rounded) ......................... **$3,500,000**

**W42** The final step in an appraisal where more than one approach to value is used, is the **reconciliation** of the value indications by the approaches used into a final opinion of value. More weight is given to the approach, or approaches, which the appraiser believes most reliably indicate a property's market value.

**W43** In the motel appraisal example, the income approach was considered to be the most reliable, as good data was available for its use, and it is the approach which a buyer (the market) would place the most reliance upon. It indicated a market value of the property in the amount of $3,600,000. The sales comparison approach indicated a value of $3,500,000. This approach is not as reliable as the income approach in this appraisal, yet it is fairly close to the indicated value by the income approach, and therefore lends support to the validity of the value indicated by the income approach. Based on these two approaches the appraiser arrived at a final opinion of value of $3,600,000.

**W44** The estimated cost of replacing the property by constructing an equally desirable substitute property as indicated by the cost approach, was $3,213,615 (Improvements: $2,238,615 and Land: $975,000). With the market value of the completed property at $3,600,000, the developer (entrepreneur) has earned a profit of $386,385 less sales expense, were he to sell the property. Knowledgeable buyers should be satisfied that this is a reasonable profit in relation to the cost of the land and improvements, the skill, time, and effort required to put the development together, and the risk involved. Therefore, the cost approach also indicates the reasonableness of the $3,600,000 market value when the developer's profit is included.

## FINAL COMMENTS ON APPRAISING

**W45** The appraiser should understand that sellers and buyers are the ones who make values in real estate markets. The appraiser's job is to reflect what the market is indicating for the property he is valuing. The appraiser should look at value through the eyes of sellers and buyers, and use the same valuation methods that they are using for a particular kind of property, so far as is practicable.

**W46** The term price is often wrongly used for the term value. **Value** refers to the worth of something. A lot may have a market value of $50,000. **Price** is the amount asked for or paid for something. The listing price of the lot was $75,000, and it sold for $40,000, making its sale price $40,000. It sold for $10,000 below its value.

**W47** Also, the terms **cost** and **value** are sometimes confused. A building may cost $1,000,000 to build, but its market value after completion may be only $600,000 due to bad design, or to having been constructed in the wrong location. Another oft-cited example of this is a well that cost $50,000 to drill, but since there was no water to be had, its value was zero.

**W48** **The Principle of Substitution**. This principle affirms that when a property is replaceable, its value tends to be set by the cost of acquisition of an equally desirable substitute property. The Principle of Substitution is the primary basis for the three approaches to value.

**W49** **Plottage** is the increase in value to a parcel of land by increasing its utility by joining it with an adjoining parcel or parcels.

**W50** The **economic life** of improvements is the period over which the improvements add value to the land. For instance, a commercial building may be in quite good condition physically, but it may not provide nearly as high a net income as would the leasing of the land if it were vacant. In this case the economic life of the improvements is over. It is not uncommon to see attractive buildings being razed to make way for more profitable structures.

# Appraising

## CHECK QUESTIONS

1. An appraisal may be communicated:
   (A) On a form        (B) Orally
   (C) Narrative style     (D) All of the above.     ( )   **W2**

2. Which of the following is not included in a real property's bundle of rights?
   (A) An easement
   (B) A sandwich lease
   (C) The furniture
   (D) All of the above.                    ( )   **W4**

3. In the appraisal of real property, which of the following would be classified as external obsolescence:
   (A) Termite damage
   (B) Peeling paint on the exterior of a house
   (C) Normal wear and tear
   (D) Odors from a fish cannery.            ( )   **W28**

4. The sum of money at which a property is offered for sale is the:
   (A) Value        (B) Warranted value
   (C) Price         (D) Market value.     ( )   **W46**

5. Functional obsolescence is a loss of value due to:
   (A) Physical deterioration
   (B) Adverse zoning in the area
   (C) Bad floor plan
   (D) Lack of maintenance.               ( )   **W27**

6. The accumulation of several contiguous properties under one ownership, thus creating a large parcel of proportionately greater value, involves a factor of value called:
   (A) Depreciation      (B) Plottage
   (C) Corner influence   (D) Zoning value.     ( )   **W49**

7. Which of the following is not an underlying factor of value?
   (A) Depreciation      (B) Demand
   (C) Utility          (D) Scarcity.        ( )   **W5**

8. The definition of market value includes which of the following?
   (A) Amortization     (B) Highest price
   (C) Depreciation      (D) Demand.         ( )   **W7**

9. Which of the following would an appraiser be concerned with in appraising a property?
(A) Earthquake faults      (B) Utilities
(C) Zoning      (D) All of the above.     ( ) W12

10. The highest and best use of a property is:
(A) The highest use permitted by zoning
(B) The most predominant use in a neighborhood
(C) The most profitable use
(D) The reconciled value.     ( ) W13

11. Which of the following does not have to do with the cost approach to value?
(A) Vacancy factor      (B) Architect's fee     W18
(C) Soil engineering      (D) Developer's profit.     ( ) W19

12. The cost of replacing improvements can be estimated by:
(A) A building cost estimator
(B) Use of a building cost manual
(C) Comparing actual costs of similar improvements
(D) All of the above.     ( ) W22

13. The cost approach is most applicable to:
(A) A farm      (B) A motel
(C) A new building      (D) An old building.     ( ) W23

14. A building's roof cover is in bad condition. This is:
(A) Physical deterioration
(B) Deferred maintenance
(C) Depreciation     W25
(D) All of the above.     ( ) W26

15. A building is 50 years old. However, it has been completely rehabilitated, and now has modern fixtures, etc. An appraiser feels that it now has an effective age of only 30 years, and that the total life for this type of building is 60 years. The age-life method would indicate how much depreciation for this building?
(A) 25%      (B) 50%
(C) 40%      (D) None of the above.     ( ) W29

16. The overall capitalization rate method:
(A) Is outdated
(B) Makes use of the effective gross income
(C) Requires a property's net income
(D) Is used in the sales comparison approach.     ( ) W32

17. Usually the best approach in appraising single family dwellings is the:
    (A) Sales comparison approach
    (B) Cost less depreciation
    (C) Cost comparison approach
    (D) Income approach.                                    (  ) W37

18. A property sold for $450,000. We are certain that the amount it sold for was its:
    (A) Market value              (B) Assessed value
    (C) Price                     (D) Fair value.           (  ) W46

19. You are appraising a small, 5-year old neighborhood shopping center. You estimate the value of the land at $1,000,000 by comparisons with sales of similar sites. You estimate the direct building cost of the 20,000 square foot building at $800,000, the indirect costs at $300,000, a total of $50,000 actual depreciation, and a developer's profit of $400,000. Using these figures, what is the indicated value of the property by the cost approach?
    (A) $2,450,000               (B) $1,950,000                      W18
    (C) $2,650,000               (D) $2,200,000.                     W19
                                                            (  ) W21

20. The shopping center in the previous question has 18,000 square feet of rentable area. It is presently fully leased at an average of $1.25 per square foot per month to eight tenants. The leases are all on a net rent basis to the owner. A potential buyer of the property considers that if he is able to acquire it, he would probably hold it for a 5 year period. He estimates that the property would probably experience an average annual vacancy of 5% over the 5 years, and that while the rents would be net to him, he would still have some expenses. These would be the expense of professional management of the property, possible legal fees, the share of the center's expenses for any vacant space, the cost of refurbishing vacant stores for new tenants, and leasing commissions. He estimates that these expenses will run $16,500 per year. He knows that similar centers have been selling at an overall capitalization rate of 10%. Based on this information, what is the indicated value of this property by the income approach?
    (A) $2,200,000               (B) $2,400,000                      W34
    (C) $2,500,000               (D) $2,450,000              (  ) W36

21. The potential buyer in the previous question was aware of three very similar shopping centers which had recently sold on the basis of approximately $130 per square foot of their rentable area. If he were to use this rate for the center he is considering purchasing, what would be the property's indicated value by the sales comparison approach?
    (A) $1,800,000               (B) $2,200,000                      W37
    (C) $2,340,000               (D) $1,900,000.             (  ) W39

22. The income approach would probably not be used in valuing:
    (A) Apartments                 (B) Single family dwellings
    (C) Office buildings           (D) Warehouses.              (  ) W31

23. You have sales data which indicates that the apartment complexes
    similar to the one you are appraising have been selling at a gross rent
    multiple of 8.0. The property you are appraising has a scheduled annual
    gross income of $150,000 and a vacancy factor of 7.5% What is the
    indication of the property's value using the GRM?
    (A) $1,000,000                 (B) $1,500,000
    (C) $1,200,000                 (D) $825,000.                (  ) W40

24. In estimating the net income of a property for use in the income
    approach, the appraiser would not include as an expense:
    (A) Management fee             (B) Taxes
    (C) Insurance                  (D) Actual depreciation.     (  ) W36

25. One of the most difficult things for an appraiser to measure is:
    (A) Gross income               (B) Depreciation
    (C) Land area                  (D) The building.            (  ) W23

This page intentionally left blank.

# LAND DESCRIPTIONS

**X1**    It is necessary to give a definite description of land, recognized by law, in various documents used in the real estate business, such as deeds, land leases, easements, rights-of-way, and others. Such a land description is called a **legal description**. Certain methods have been devised which are accurate and convenient to provide such a description.

**X2**    A legal description may be:
1. By reference to a recorded map.
2. By metes and bounds.
3. By U. S. Government survey, that is, reference to section, township and range.

**X3**    **Recorded subdivision maps** were discussed under the heading of subdivisions. Briefly, they are maps prepared by surveyors or civil engineers containing numbered lots, which are recorded with the county recorder after approval by a board of supervisors or city council. They are based upon (tied into) points established by government surveys. Merely the lot number and tract name or number need to be referred to in the land description. In large tracts, blocks are also included, usually being designated by a letter. Thus a deed bearing a description "Lot 1, Block B in Tract 5750, as per map recorded on pages 93 and 94, official map records of Blank County" is a legal description. Various dimensions, angles, etc, need not be given, as these are shown on the recorded map and need not be repeated.

**X4**    **Metes and bounds descriptions** are descriptions usually prepared by professionals, and are often long and highly involved. Various distances, angles, objects and monuments are mentioned. They are used to describe irregularly shaped parcels when there is no recorded subdivision map, and when government surveys cannot be referred to conveniently except to establish a starting point.

# CITY LOT PROBLEMS

Here are a couple of simple city lot problems which the student should be familiar with. All necessary dimensions are given in the problems. Sometimes you have to deduct certain distances from the total to get the distance you are looking for. A good thing to remember is that the area of a triangle is one half the area of a rectangle with the same base (parcel with opposite sides parallel and corners forming 90° angles).

Refer to the two plats on the opposite page, numbered 1 and 2. They represent portions of recorded city subdivision maps showing the bounding streets, with lot numbers and dimensions. Engineers and surveyors write fifty feet as 50', in case you haven't had experience with maps. Maps are usually prepared so that the top indicates NORTH, unless an arrow indicates otherwise. Instead of asking for a direct answer, we will put the questions in multiple-choice form, as this is usually done in license tests.

**Questions on Plat No. 1**

1. If the lots in the shaded area fronting on White Street and on Brown Street brought $95.50 per front foot, what would the total price be?
   (A) $24,340    (B) $30,160    (C) $28,650    (D) $27,140.    ( )
2. Which group of lots or partial lots in the shaded area have frontages on streets?
   (A) 7, 8, 9, 23, 24, 25   (B) 8, 24   (C) 23, 24, 25    (D) 8, 23, 24, 25. ( )
3. What is the area in square feet on the portion of Lots 9 and 25 in the shaded area?
   (A) 1,875    (B) 6,250    (C) 937.5    (D) 3,200.    ( )
4. What is the total area of the shaded portion in square feet?
   (A) 1,875    (B) 12,500    (C) 18,750    (D) None of these. ( )

**Questions on Plat No. 2**

1. The portion in the shaded area sold for $75 per running foot for the frontage on Second Street. What total price did it bring?
   (A) $5,063    (B) $20,250    (C) $8,475    (D) $10,125.    ( )
2. What is the total number of square feet in the shaded area, excluding that portion in Lot 10?
   (A) 15,300    (B) 11,475    (C) 7,650    (D) 8,360.    ( )
3. Excluding the shaded area, what is the number of square feet in the balance of the block?
   (A) 11,250    (B) 27,000    (C) 14,850    (D) 24,750.    ( )

**Answers**
Plat 1:    1. (C)    2. (D)    3. (B)    4. None of these. (ANS: 37,500 SQ. FT.)
Plat 2:    1. (D)    2. (C)    3. (D)

# CITY LOT PROBLEMS

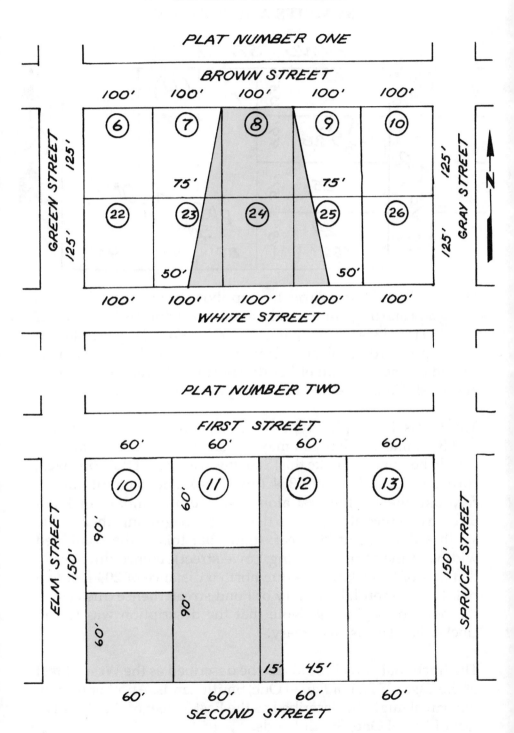

## DESCRIBING A PARCEL OF LAND
## BY METES AND BOUNDS

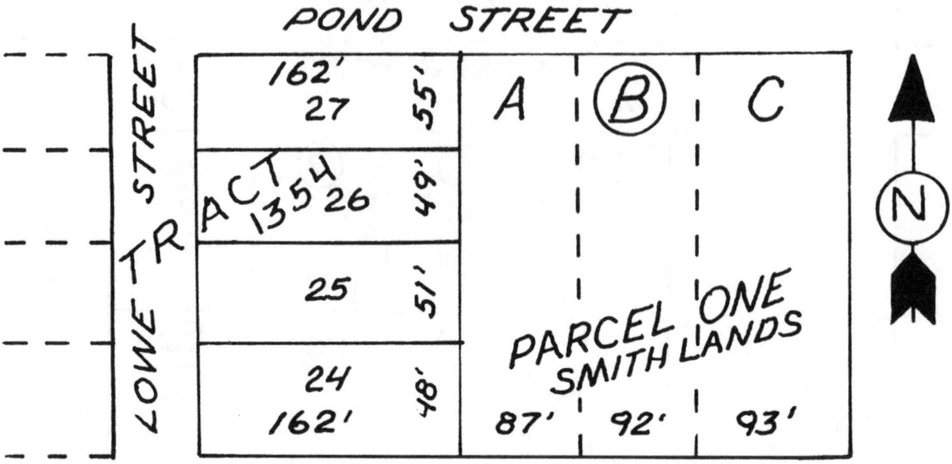

POND STREET

LOWE STREET

TRACT 1354

162'
27    55'

A  (B)  C

26  49'

25  51'

24  48'
162'

PARCEL ONE
SMITH LANDS

87'  92'  93'

N

Describe Parcel B shown on the map above by metes and bounds, using as a starting point a stake at the exact northwest corner of Lot 27, Tract 1354, as per map recorded in Book 17, pages 45 and 46, Map records of Pacific County. All parcel boundary lines shown on the map run either due north and south, or due east and west. Consequently, all lot angles are right angles (90°).

This forms the simplest type of a metes and bounds description, and is similar to what you may be asked to solve. Your answer should be somewhat like this: Starting at a stake at the northwest corner of Lot 27, Tract 1354 (give book and page of county records); thence due east along the south boundary of Pond Street a distance of 341 feet to the point of beginning; thence due south a distance of 203 feet; (note that this is the combined widths of the four lots facing Lowe street); thence due west a distance of 92 feet; thence due north a distance of 203 feet to a point on the south boundary of Pond street; thence due east to the point of beginning. Note that the description was traced clock-wise. This is customary.

The fractional parcel could also be described as the West 92 feet of the East 185 feet of Parcel One, Smith Lands. Another option: the parcel might be described as the East 92 feet of the West 179 feet of Parcel One, Smith Lands.

# GOVERNMENT SURVEY

**X5**     The Federal Government surveyed California many years ago. The land was mapped into squares 6 miles on edge, called **townships**. To do this, lines were run east and west and were spaced 6 miles apart, called **township lines**, and other lines run north and south, called **ranges**. Certain east-west lines from which others are numbered are called **base lines**, while certain north-south lines from which others are numbered are called **principal meridians**.

**X6**     As California is irregular in shape and extends in a northwest-southeast direction, three base lines and principal meridians were necessary. The ones from which land in the southern part of California is measured are called the San Bernardino Base and Meridian (abbreviated S.B.B.&M.). The ones for the central part of the State and most of the northern section are called the Mt. Diablo Base and Meridian (abbreviated M.D.B.&M.), and those in the northwestern section are called the Humboldt Base and Meridian (H.B.& M.).

**X7**     Townships are located by reference to a base line and principal meridian. Thus the township located in the third tier north of the San Bernardino Base line and the fourth tier (range) east of the San Bernardino Principal Meridian would be located along the west edge of the Mojave Desert. It is usually written, T 3 N, R 4 E, S.B.B.& M.

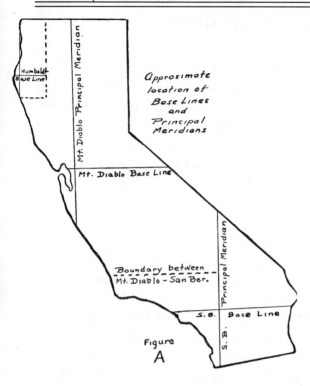

Figure
A

## BASE LINES
## PRINCIPAL MERIDIANS

If all range and township lines were drawn in this map, it would show the State covered with small squares (townships). They are numbered east and west from the principal meridians shown on the map, and north and south from the base lines. Thus each is definitely located.

Dotted lines show where different numbering systems come together. If California were square like New Mexico, only one base line and principal meridian would be needed.

## A SECTION

This is one of the 36 sections taken from the township in figure C. It happens to be Section 1, taken from the northeast corner.

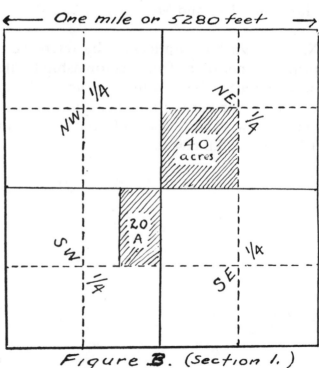

Figure B. (Section 1.)

**X8**    In order that smaller parcels of land may be described, townships are divided into 36 sections containing 640 acres each. These in turn may be broken down into fractional sections, such as the northeast quarter, the southwest quarter, etc., each quarter section containing 160 acres. When a quarter section is divided again into quarters, these smaller parts contain 40 acres. By further quartering they can be divided into pieces containing 10 acres, 2 1/2 acres, 5/8 acre, etc.

**X9**    The 36 sections in a township are always located in the same order and numbered in the same manner. See **Figure C**. The top of the map is always the north, the bottom south, etc.

**X10**    **Figure B** shows Section 1 lifted from the township in **Figure C**. In it we have located the southwest quarter of the northeast quarter, and the east half of the northeast quarter of the southwest quarter. The first contains 40 acres and the second 20 acres. Can you figure this out?

**X11**    Instead of writing out the quarters such as "southwest quarter," it is usually written SW1/4. Thus the first of the above descriptions would be written: SW1/4 of the NE1/4 of Sec. 1. The second would be written: E1/2 of the NE1/4 of the SW1/4 of Sec. 1.

**X12**    Can you locate the SW1/4 of the SE1/4 of Sec. 1 in figure B? The NW1/4 of the NW1/4 of the NW1/4 of Sec. 1?

**X13**    Have you noticed that in locating these tracts you need to start with the largest quarter (160 acres), then the next largest quarter (40 acres), etc. In other words, you need to **work backwards** from the section number. That is the secret of locating land in a section from given descriptions.

**X14**    Sometimes the location of a tract of land requires two or three of these descriptions. They may be connected by the word "and", or merely a semi-colon. The SW1/4 of the SW1/4 and the SE1/4 of the SW1/4 of Section 8, is also written the SW1/4 of the SW1/4; the SE1/4 of the SW1/4 of Section 8.

**X15**    Computing the number of acres in any described tract is simple. Any standard section contains 640 acres, a quarter section 160 acres, a quarter of a quarter section 40 acres, etc. Most sections illustrated in examinations are divided into 16 forty-acre parcels by dotted lines.

**X16**    Each of the 36 large numbered squares in a township (See Figure C) is a section containing 640 acres. Note that each of the sections is divided into 16 smaller squares containing 40 acres each. Sections in a standard township are always numbered the same way, Section 1 being in the northeast corner. They are then numbered to the left to number 6, then back and forth until number 36 is reached in the southeast corner. A section is 1 mile on edge, a sixteenth section (the small square) is 1/4 mile on edge. A mile is 5,280 feet.

## Figure C
### Township showing 36 sections

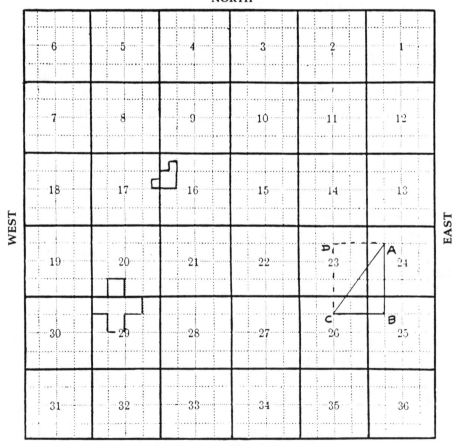

# DESCRIPTION PROBLEMS
## (See Figure C)

**X17**    The SE1/4 of the SW1/4 of Sec. 20; the NW1/4 of the NE1/4 and the NW1/4 (excepting therefrom the SW1/4) of Sec. 29. This tract forms a cross and contains 200 acres.

**X18**    The SE1/4 of the NW1/4 of the NW1/4; the SW1/4 of the NW1/4 of Sec. 16, and the SE1/4 of the SE1/4 of the NE1/4 of Section 17. (60 acres).

**X19**    Beginning at the NW corner of the SE1/4 of the NW1/4 of Section 24, thence due south one mile; thence due west 3/4 mile, thence to point of beginning, (240 acres). To find area, square out to rectangle A-B-C-D and divide by 2 to get area of triangle A-B-C. The rectangle contains twelve 40-acre tracts. The triangular tract contains one-half this number, or the equivalent of six 40-acre tracts.

**X20**    For more practice, draw the following: Beginning at the SW corner of the SE1/4 of Sec. 4, thence to the NE corner of said quarter section, thence to the SE corner of the SW 1/4 of Section 3, thence to the SW corner of the NW1/4 of Section 10, thence to the point of beginning. This tract forms a square equivalent to a 1/2 section, or 320 acres. Always trace from one point to another in a **straight line**.

**X21**    Here is another one for you to draw: Starting at the NW corner of the SE1/4 of the NW1/4 of Section 8, thence due east 2640 ft. (1/2 mile or half a section wide), thence due south to the SE corner of the SW1/4 of the SE1/4 of Section 8, thence to the point of beginning. It will form a triangle. Its area will be one-half that of six 40-acre squares, or 120 acres. Always square out triangular parcels and divide the area of the rectangle by 2.

**X22**    The SW1/4 of the SW1/4 of the SW1/4 of Section 8 contains 10 acres.
The SW1/4 of the SW1/4 of Section 8 contains 40 acres.
The SW1/4 of Section 8 contains 160 acres.

**X23**    Important figures to remember: 1 mile equals 5280 ft.; 1 section contains 640 acres; 1 acre contains 43,560 square feet.

## Figure D

NORTH

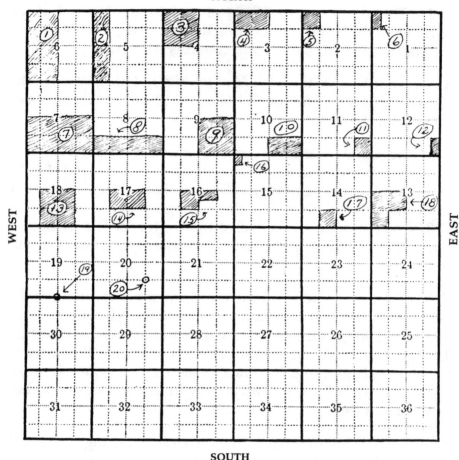

SOUTH

WEST

EAST

## Practice Descriptions

In the event the student has not yet become adept at describing fractional sections, perhaps a study of the following descriptions in Figure D will help. Each problem is set out on the plat with number corresponding to number of the description. Take them in order. Note that the longer the description, the smaller the parcel, and to locate them you start with the section number and work backwards.

(1)  W1/2 of Sec. 6.
(2)  W1/2 of W1/2 of Sec. 5.
(3)  NW1/4 of Sec. 4.
(4)  N1/2 of NW1/4 of Sec. 3.
(5)  NW1/4 of NW1/4 of Sec. 2.
(6)  W1/2 of NW1/4 of NW1/4 of Sec. 1.
(7)  S1/2 of Sec. 7.
(8)  S1/2 of S1/2 of Sec. 8.
(9)  SE1/4 of Sec. 9.
(10)  S1/2 of SE1/4 of Sec. 10
(11)  SE1/4 of SE1/4 of Sec. 11
(12)  E1/2 of SE1/4 of SE1/4 of Sec. 12.
(13)  E1/2 of SW1/4, and W1/2 of SE1/4 of Sec. 18.
(14)  NE1/4 of SW1/4 and NW1/4 of SE1/4 of Sec. 17.
(15)  NE1/4 of SW1/4, and N1/2 of NW1/4 of SE1/4 of Sec. 16.
(16)  NW1/4 of NW1/4 of NW1/4 of Sec. 15.
(17)  SE1/4 of SW1/4 of Sec. 14.
(18)  SW1/4 of Sec. 13, excepting therefrom the SE1/4 of the SW1/4 of Sec. 13.
(19)  SE Corner of SW1/4 of Sec. 19.
(20)  SE Corner of NW1/4 of SE1/4 of Sec. 20.

This page intentionally left blank.

# TAXES

## CALIFORNIA REAL ESTATE TAXES

**Y1**    The taxing of real estate is one of the oldest forms of taxation. Before industry became one of the greatest sources of wealth, a person's wealth was measured largely by the land he owned. As a result, the taxing powers chose land as the best source of tax revenue, as the amount of land owned by anyone indicated his ability to pay taxes.

**Y2**    Other forms of taxation have come into being, such as income and sales taxes. Real estate however, remains the main source of tax revenue for city and county governments. Although the State of California is permitted by its constitution to tax real estate directly, it does not do so, and probably will not except in an emergency.

**Y3**    Cities and counties place a value on all real estate as a basis of levying a tax. The placing of value for tax purposes is called **assessing**. The official charged with this duty is the city or county assessor. The tax rates for the various districts within a county are calculated by the county's tax collector. Most cities arrange with the county to assess property and collect taxes for them.

**Y4**    Real estate taxes are **ad valorem taxes**. The Latin term ad valorem means "according to value."

**Y5**    In 1978 the citizens of California voted overwhelmingly in favor of **Proposition 13**, a constitutional amendment which places limits on real property taxes in California. This Amendment limits the tax of a property to **1% of its full cash value (market value), plus an additional percentage to pay the property's share of bonded indebtedness approved by the voters**. The full cash value of a property was established to be the value as shown on the tax roll as of **March 1, 1975**. An annual increase to this value for increase in the cost of living is allowed, **but this may not exceed 2% per year**.

**Y6**    When the ownership of a property changes, a new full cash value is established. This is based on a new assessor's appraisal. This is effective **as of the date of change of ownership**. Taxes on a property may increase enormously because of this. For example, a property which had a market value of $50,000 in 1975 could have a value of $200,000 in 1992 because of inflation and other factors. Two similar properties, side by side, may be paying extremely different tax amounts. There are those who claim that this inequity is unconstitutional, and as of this writing (January, 1992) they have a case before the U.S. Supreme Court. Again, each year after the transfer, the assessed value may be increased an amount not to exceed 2% annually, and the property's share of voter approved bonded indebtedness may be added to the 1% tax rate.

**Y6.1** Transfers between spouses are exempt from being reassessed, and certain transfers between parents and children are exempt. Also, homeowners at least 55 years old may transfer their current low property tax assessment to another home of equal or lesser value in any county in California providing the board of supervisors in the new county has approved this for their county. For married couples, only one spouse need be 55 years or older. The replacement property must be purchased within two years of the sale of the original property. Both the original and the replacement dwellings must be the owner's principal place of residence. Seniors may take advantage of this only one time. Your county assessor will give you more details on this program.

**Y7** If you construct a major improvement on an unimproved vacant lot that you have owned, for example an office building, a new "full cash value" will be established for the property. This would consist of the already existing assessed value on the lot, plus the assessed value of the new improvements as of the date of their completion.

**Y8** If an existing major improvement is further improved, for example a room is added, the property keeps the same value for the major improvement, plus an additional value amount for the addition. If it is replacement construction (such as a new roof), a reappraisal by the assessor is not required.

**Y9** The following illustration is given to clarify the above information regarding changes in assessed values.

**Year 1985 - 1986**
$400,000 - full cash value. (A property was purchased in 1985 for $400,000, and the county assessor estimated its full cash value at the same amount.)

**Year 1986 - 1987**
$400,000 x 1.02 = $408,000 - full cash value - same owner. (The 1.02 factor increases the assessed value by 2%, which is permitted if the cost of living increased during the past year by at least that amount.)

**Year 1987 - 1988**
$408,000 x 1.02 = $416,160 - full cash value - same owner.

**Year 1988 - 1989**
The property is sold at market value for $480,000. The assessor's full cash value is then $480,000.

**Year 1989 - 1990**
$480,000 x 1.02 = $489,600 - full cash value - same owner as previous year.

**Year 1990 - 1991**
The building is improved by adding an air-conditioned office, which added $30,000 to its value.
Then: $489,600 x 1.02 = $499,392, plus $30,000 = $529,392 - full cash value - same owner.

**Year 1991 - 1992**
$529,392 x 1.02 = $539,980 - full cash value - same owner.

**Y10**   As shown in the above illustration, the full cash values were increased by the maximum permittable annual increase of 2% since inflation was above that figure during those years.

**Y11**   The additional tax amount permitted for voter-approved bonded indebtedness is not figured in the assessed value, but is included in the tax rate. For example, the base tax rate is 1%, and say 0.08% is required to cover the voter approved debt in a certain district. Then, the total tax rate would be 1.08%. At this rate, the 1991-92 tax in the above illustration would be the full cash value of $539,980 x 1.08%, or $5,831.78.

**Y12**   The fiscal year for real property taxes in California begins on July 1 and ends on the following June 30th. The lien date, or the date that real property becomes a security for payment of taxes, is March 1 preceding the fiscal tax year. The fiscal tax year 1991-92 begins on July 1, 1991 and ends on June 30, 1992. The lien date for that fiscal year is March 1, 1991.

**Y13**   There are properties that are partially or totally tax-exempt. Some of the latter are churches, cemeteries, orphanages, non-profit colleges, fruit and nut trees less than four years old, grapevines less than three years old and date palms under eight years old. All growing crops are exempt.

**Y14**   All **owner-occupied** residential property, which is the principal place of residence, including a condominium, an owner-occupied unit in a multiple residential property, etc., is entitled to a $7,000 exemption which is deducted from the full cash value of the property. Once granted, the exemption remains in effect until the owner no longer qualifies for the exemption. A 25% penalty is assessed if the owner fails to notify the assessor of the termination of the right to the exemption.

**Y15**   Veterans living in California who have served in the military during war times are entitled to a $4,000 exemption of full cash value, if the veteran qualifies. This may be applied to any type of property owned by the veteran, and does not have to be his place of residence. A veteran cannot use both the veteran's exemption and the homeowner's exemption on the same property.

**Y16** State law permits "senior citizens" (persons 62 years of age or older), and blind and disabled persons, to defer payment of taxes on their residences. To qualify, an individual must own and occupy the home, have at least a 20% equity in the property (using the assessor's full cash value as the standard), and have a yearly total household income of $24,000 or less. If married, only one spouse need qualify.

In applying the law, a lien in favor of the State of California is placed against the property, and an interest rate determined by the rate earned by the Pooled Money Investment Fund is charged. The postponed taxes and interest run for an indefinite period. They are not recovered until the property is sold, the claimant no longer occupies the property, or he does not meet the terms of the program.

Complete information about the deferral program and claim forms are available from the State Controller's Office at P.O. Box 953, Sacramento, CA 95814. Or you may telephone: 1-(800)-952-5661.

**Y17** What can the property owner do if he believes the assessor has placed too high a value on his property? He can appeal the assessment. There are strict rules of both procedure and time limitations to be followed in connection with assessment appeals. Your county assessor's office will provide you with information on this. The owner and the assessor's appraiser testify before an assessment appeals board made up of citizens appointed by the county's board of supervisors. The owner must be able to justify the value he places on the property. Most often he does this by comparing properties similar to his, which have sold, to his property. Or he may employ an independent appraiser to appraise the property and testify for him. He may also have an attorney represent him. The author is familiar with cases in which property owners have been successful in getting their taxes lowered substantially by means of the appeal process.

**Y18** **One-half the tax is due on November 1**, and is **payable without penalty until December 10**. The **second half is due on February 1**, and is **delinquent if not paid by April 10**. A **10% penalty** applies to an installment that becomes delinquent.

**Y19** **Supplemental Property Tax**. Legislation entitled "Change in Ownership and New Construction After the Lien Date," which has been added to the Revenue and Taxation Code, accelerates the collection of property taxes, and affects taxpayers acquiring property on or after July 1, 1983. Generally, property will be reappraised immediately upon transfer of ownership or completion of construction, with a supplemental tax bill issued several months later reflecting the new assessment. This bill will be in addition to the regular tax bill based on the prior assessment as of March 1. It will reflect the difference in the previous assessed value and the new assessed value, and will be a prorated amount based on the number of months remaining in the fiscal year ending June 30.

**Y20** For example, if you purchased a property in September 1991 which had a market value of $150,000, and the previous assessed value of that property was $100,000, you would receive a supplemental assessment on the difference ($50,000) for the remainder of the fiscal year (from October through the following June). The amount of supplemental property tax to be paid would be the tax rate times the increase in value of $50,000, prorated for the remaining months of the fiscal year. This supplemental tax bill would be in addition to the regular tax bill.

**Y21** A major exception to the supplemental assessment is the **"Builder's Inventory Exclusion"**. Under this, any property on which new construction is completed, shall not receive a supplemental assessment until such time as the property changes ownership, or is rented or leased, providing the owner notifies the Assessor in writing prior to, or within 30 days after the start of construction, and states that the property is intended for resale. Other new construction will be billed as discussed in Y19. The regular assessment will not be affected by the "Builder's Exclusion".

**Y22**    What happens to the owner who doesn't pay his taxes? In June the tax collector publishes an "intent to sell" the property in a local newspaper. The "intent to sell" states that the property is going to be sold to the State of California because of unpaid taxes. After the property is sold to the State, the property owner still holds title and remains in possession of the property, and a **5 year redemption period** begins.

**Y23**    The property may be redeemed by full payment of taxes, interest, costs and redemption penalties. This may be done in 5 annual installments, providing the current taxes are paid. The redemption payment is made to the county tax collector, who issues a "certificate of redemption" as evidence of payment in full.

**Y24**    If the delinquent property is not redeemed at the end of 5 years, it is subsequently sold by the county tax collector. The tax collector must sell the property within a 2 year period. He may sell it directly to certain public agencies or non-profit organizations, or may sell it at public auction to any person. Payment by the highest bidder at auction must be in cash. Upon completion of the sale the buyer receives a **tax deed**.

**Y26**    The personal property taxes of a real estate owner become a lien on his real estate. All personal property taxes, such as taxes on a person's business furniture, fixtures and stock, etc., are due and payable in full with the **first** real estate tax installment in most cities and counties, although some permit payment in two installments. Household furnishings and personal effects are tax exempt.

**Y27**    Mortgage and trust deed notes on real estate are not taxed in California. Shares of stock are also exempt.

**Y28**    When property is sold, the taxes are divided between buyer and seller in accordance with what the fair share of each would be. As the tax year starts on July 1st, taxes are divided (prorated) between buyer and seller with reference to July 1st.

**Y29** Prorations of taxes and insurance are usually made from the close of escrow, and not the day the sale agreement is made. This is fair, as the seller usually collects rent or occupies the property until the escrow is closed, and the buyer should not be liable for the taxes and insurance until title to the property is transferred to him.

**Y30** The lien created by unpaid taxes comes ahead of (has priority over) any trust deeds on a property. That is why there is a provision in standard trust deeds that failure to pay taxes when due defaults the trust deed, and gives grounds to start foreclosure.

## CALIFORNIA ESTATE TAX

**Y31** Both California's inheritance and gift tax laws were repealed as the result of the passage of Proposition 6 in 1982. Proposition 6 also enacted the **California estate tax**. The purpose of this tax is to take advantage of a provision in the federal law, which allows the estate to claim a credit against the federal estate tax for death taxes paid to the State. The tax is fixed in the maximum amount that the federal government will allow as a credit against the federal estate tax for death taxes paid to the State. This tax does not cost the estate any additional amount, due to the fact that if the amount were not paid to the State, it would have to be paid to the federal government.

## DOCUMENTARY TRANSFER TAX

**Y32** State law allows a county or city to adopt a **documentary transfer tax** to apply on all transfers of real property within their jurisdictions.

**Y33** The tax is computed at the **rate of 55 cents for each $500 of the transfer value of the property (usually the sale price) or fraction thereof. The amounts of liens which remain on the property are excluded from the tax.** For example, a property sells for $100,000. The buyer puts $30,000 cash in escrow and the balance of the purchase price is provided by a new trust deed note. Then, the tax must be paid on the full $100,000, and the tax would be $110. If the $70,000 trust deed was an existing trust deed which the buyer purchased the property subject to, then the transfer tax would be $33.

**Y34**  Notice of payment of the transfer tax must be entered on the face of the deed, or on a separate paper filed with the deed. Also, there must be a declaration as to whether the value on which the tax was computed was on the full value of the property conveyed, or the full value less liens remaining at time of sale. An agent or appraiser sometimes finds it helpful to know the transfer tax amount on a deed where it is computed on the full amount, as it may give him a clue as to the approximate price at which a property sold.

## SPECIAL ASSESSMENTS

**Y35**  Special assessments are taxes on particular properties which are benefited by public improvements for which the taxes are levied. The more common improvements are street paving, storm drains, sewer installations, street lights, etc.

**Y36**  **Vrooman Street Act.** This was the original act passed for street improvements. It permits cities to improve streets and install public sewers. Bonds may be voted to cover costs, and be retired by a tax levy on each property benefitted. Public utilities may also be acquired in this way. This act, passed in 1885, can be used by either cities or counties.

**Y37**  **Street Opening Act of 1903.** This Act applies to both cities and counties. It permits authorities to build new streets or highways, and to acquire property for this purpose. The funds may also be spent to straighten and improve streets or highways. Surrounding property owners are assessed according to the benefits they receive from the improvements, and must pay their share (assessment) within thirty days after they are notified, or let the sum go to bond.

**Y38   Street Improvement Act of 1911.** This law is frequently used to finance street and highway improvements. Again, property owners are charged with a share of the costs, the amount depending upon how much they are benefitted. They can pay the contractor within 30 days after the work is done, or let the sum go to bond. They are then taxed each year to retire the bonds. Bonds cannot run over 15 years.

**Y38.1** The California legislature passed the **Mello-Roos Community Facilities Act of 1982.** This act allows local governments to establish a Mello-Roos special tax assessment district in a developing area to finance specific public facilities and services needed by that particular area. The formation of a Mello-Roos Community Facilities District (CFD) has to be approved by two-thirds of the eligible voters or land owners in the proposed district. If less than 12 registered voters reside within the proposed district, the vote is by the land owners only, with each land owner having one vote per acre owned.

**Y38.2** Mello-Roos bonds can only be used to finance new or additional facilities and services. The services and facilities that can be financed by a Mello-Roos CFD are: elementary and secondary schools, police protection including criminal justice facilities, fire protection including ambulance and paramedic facilities, flood and storm protection, libraries, natural gas pipelines, electrical transmission lines and facilities and any other government facility which is owned and operated by the local government. Financing existing facilities and services is not allowed by this Act.

**Y38.3** Once established, the Mello-Roos district has bonding and taxing authority. It can issue bonds to finance the designated public facilities and services, which are then repaid by a special tax levied by the Mello-Roos district. This special tax is collected by the County Tax Collector. Although the Act does not specify how the special tax should be allocated, most districts apply it according to the benefit received by the parcel (i.e., square footage of new homes is commonly used for schools, and frontage is used for new roads.)

The agent must be sure to advise a buyer that the Mello-Roos tax will be in addition to the 1% tax allowed by Proposition 13. The buyer must be informed as to both the amount and the number of years that he/she will be obligated for this special assessment tax. Buyers, of course, should be informed by the agent of all special assessment liens, even though the preliminary title report would show them as "exceptions." See F6 and F12.

## BOARD OF EQUALIZATION

**Y39** The Board of Equalization is a State agency, with members elected by districts. This agency has important duties in connection with real estate. It assesses the properties of public utilities, such as land, buildings, power lines, gas lines, etc. This is on the theory that it is better equipped to do this job, and can do it more uniformly state-wide than local assessors can do. The assessed values are turned over to cities and counties as a basis for local taxation.

**Y40** Another important function of this Board is to keep the assessed values of various cities and counties more or less uniform. Under the law it has the power to reassess properties within any city or county if they get too much out of line. This power is used sparingly however, and the Board prefers to work with local officials rather than make an issue of their assessments. It is generally known that the Board has many other duties including the collecting of sales taxes.

## REAL ESTATE OWNERSHIP AND INCOME TAXES

**Y41** The subject of income tax advantages in the ownership of real estate is vast, complicated in many respects, and is ever-changing as new legislation is frequently passed. A special course in this subject for the real estate agent is advised. The counsel of tax accountants and attorneys is often well advised when making real estate decisions which include income tax considerations. It is our intention here to only mention briefly some of the advantages of real estate ownership in relation to income taxes.

**Y42**    The California State income tax law parallels the federal system in many respects, however there are some differences. The following comments pertain to the federal income tax.

**Y43**    There are important **federal** income tax benefits in the ownership of a primary home and a second home. While there are some exceptions, the following information is basic. This applies only to owner-occupied dwellings. Both mortgage loan interest and real estate taxes are deductible from personal income with some limitations on interest depending on the amount of the mortgage. The homeowner is not taxed on the gain from the sale of his home, providing he purchases another home within two years at a price which is equal to or higher than the sale price of his original home, less the cost of the sale and expenses incurred in preparing the home for sale. He may do this any number of times. Homeowners 55 years and older may sell their home and pay no income tax on the profit from the sale up to $125,000. The home must have been the primary residence for at least three of the preceding five years. This may be done just once in a lifetime. If the amount of the profit is less than $125,000, the portion not used may not be used later. Ownership and occupancy requirements must be met by the homeowner.

**Y44**    Income producing properties such as apartments, commercial and industrial buildings are purchased by investors partly for the income tax shelter that these properties provide. This shelter is provided by an annual depreciation amount on the improvements which the law allows to be deducted from the owner's gross income. Land, of course, may not be depreciated. Depreciation may be taken on the improvements even though the property's value is actually increasing each year. When the depreciation period runs out, the owner in some cases exchanges the property for another, and providing certain requirements of the law are met in the exchange, the new property may be depreciated for tax shelter. However, the federal Tax-Reform Act of 1986 has greatly reduced the income tax advantages of owning income producing improved real estate. The depreciation period has been lengthened to 27.5 years for residential income properties and 31.5 years for commercial and industrial properties, and permits only straight line depreciation. Annual operating losses from rental properties are limited in offsetting income from other sources up to $25,000 with certain exceptions; and capital gains upon sale no longer receive special treatment, but are taxed as ordinary income.

**Y45**  The annual depreciation permitted to be taken for income tax purposes is based on the cost of the building at the time it is acquired, plus the cost of any subsequent major improvements. This cost of the building is called the owner's **basis**. Each year the depreciation is taken, it is subtracted from the previous basis, causing the property to have a new and lower basis. Then, when the property is sold, the gain between the basis at that time and the sale price is taxed as capital gain (with some exceptions). This assumes that the property is sold at a sufficiently high price to have a gain. The following example illustrates how this works.

**Y45.1**  Say an apartment building is purchased for $1,250,000, and the land is valued at $425,000. The owners basis for the building, then, is $825,000. The building may be depreciated over 27.5 years on a straight line basis. The depreciation allowance is then $825,000 divided by 27.5, or $30,000 per year. If the property is sold after five years, $150,000 in depreciation has been taken, lowering the basis to $675,000. Then, if the property is sold for, say, $1,400,000, the gain would be $725,000.

**Y45.2**  If one of the parties in an exchange of properties gives the other additional compensation in the form of cash or something else of value to make up for the difference in the values of the properties, the additional compensation is known as **boot**.

## Taxes

# CHECK QUESTIONS

1. The real estate tax is which of the following:
   (A) A prescriptive tax          (B) An ad valorem tax
   (C) A priority tax          (D) None of the above.          (  )    Y4

2. The tax on real property in California may not exceed:
   (A) 1% of its full cash value
   (B) 2% of its full cash value
   (C) 1% of its full cash value plus an additional percentage to cover
       bonded indebtedness
   (D) None of the above.          (  )    Y5

3. Which one of the following properties is tax exempt:
   (A) A college operated for profit
   (B) A mortuary
   (C) A five year old orange grove
   (D) Two year old grapevines.          (  )    Y13

4. You construct a regional shopping center on land you have owned for
   several years. The assessor's full cash value is established:
   (A) As of the date of completion of the improvements
   (B) As of March 1 following the date of completion of the improvements
   (C) As of the date the building permit was approved
   (D) By using the existing assessed value on the lot plus the assessed
       value of the improvements as of the date of their completion.
                                                                 (  )    Y7

5. The fiscal year for real property taxes in California begins on which date:
   (A) July 1          (B) June 30
   (C) January 1          (D) March 1.          (  )    Y12

6. When real property remains under the same ownership and no
   improvements are made to it, the most the assessor may increase its full
   cash value annually is:
   (A) 2.5%
   (B) 2%
   (C) 2% plus an amount to cover bonded indebtedness
   (D) 1%.          (  )    Y5

7. An owner-occupied dwelling enjoys an exemption from its full cash value in the amount of:
   (A) $7,000
   (B) $5,000
   (C) $10,000
   (D) None of the above. ( ) **Y14**

8. For senior citizens in California to enjoy deferment of property taxes they must:
   (A) Be at least 60 years of age
   (B) Have an equity in the home of at least 10% of its full cash value
   (C) Have a total household annual income of $24,000 or less
   (D) All of the above. ( ) **Y16**

9. If an owner feels that the assessor has placed too high a value on his dwelling, he should take his case to:
   (A) The Board of Equalization
   (B) The tax collector
   (C) Assessment Appeals Board
   (D) The assessor. ( ) **Y17**

10. One-half of real estate taxes are each due on:
    (A) November 1 and February 1
    (B) December 10 and April 10
    (C) December 1 and April 1
    (D) July 1 and June 30. ( ) **Y18**

11. After a property is sold to the State for non-payment of taxes, the owner has how many years to make up the unpaid taxes in order to redeem the property?
    (A) 1 year
    (B) 3 years
    (C) 5 years
    (D) 4 years. ( ) **Y22**

12. Which one of the following taxes must be paid in California?
    (A) Gift tax
    (B) Estate tax
    (C) Inheritance tax
    (D) None of the above. ( ) **Y31**

13. The amount of the documentary transfer tax for each $500 of transfer value or fraction thereof is:
    (A) 65 cents
    (B) 75 cents
    (C) 50 cents
    (D) 55 cents. ( ) **Y33**

14. 1911 Improvement Act bonds cannot run longer than:
    (A) 5 years
    (B) 11 years
    (C) 15 years
    (D) 25 years. ( ) **Y38**

This page intentionally left blank.

**CHAPTER**

# BUSINESS OPPORTUNITIES

**Z1**    In 1966, the Department of Real Estate eliminated the requirement of a special license for those engaged in the business of brokering "**business opportunities**." Since then, only a real estate license has been required. Because of this, business opportunity questions are included in the real estate license examinations.

**Z2**    As in the case of real estate, certain persons are not required to have a real estate license to sell business opportunities. The list given in A10 applies. Corporation officers who deal with their firm's property without special compensation are exempt.

All penalties for acting under a license in connection with real estate transactions also apply to business opportunities, such as the penalty for paying commissions to unlicensed persons.

**Z3**    A business opportunity is the sale, lease, rent or exchange of a business, which may also include the "**goodwill**" of the enterprise. Goodwill is the reasonable expectation of continued patronage by those who have been customers in the past. Business opportunities usually involve the sale of personal property. Personal property is defined as property that is movable, or that which is immovable but which is not real property. Examples of such businesses are: grocery stores, barber shops, machine shops, auto repair shops, bars, restaurants, drugstores, etc.

## BUSINESS OPPORTUNITY PRACTICES

**Z4**    If a buyer of a business also purchases the building that houses the business, the sale of the business and the sale of the building are considered as two separate and concurrent transactions, and the transfers are completed through two separate and concurrent escrows.

**Z5**    Business opportunity brokers sometimes give prospective buyers a list of businesses to visit by themselves. The broker will have the person sign a customer registration form which states that the prospective purchaser must either deal with him if he purchases any of the properties on the list, or must pay him a commission if he buys directly from an owner or through another agent. Before providing such a list and getting the prospective buyer to sign such an agreement, the broker must obtain written authorizations to sell from the business owners. Failure to do so is grounds for revoking or suspending a real estate license. (Sec. 10176{J})

**Z6**    The laws of agency require the licensee to exercise good faith, loyalty and honesty in all relationships with his principal, and at the same time to deal fairly and honestly with the buyer. This is very important, because the buyer is often investing a substantial amount of his life savings, and must be made well aware of all of the material aspects and liabilities affecting the business, since he will end up being responsible for them. He must be knowledgeable about the past, present and future potential (with good management) of the income of the business, and the probable future risks involved in ownership of the business.

**Z7**    When taking a listing, the licensee should get as much information as possible about the business. The agent is responsible for accurately detailing all information provided by the seller. It is the seller's responsibility to accurately present all material facts pertaining to the business. Not to do so constitutes fraud. "Padding", or the distortion or manipulation of the records by the seller also constitutes fraud.

**Z8**   When preparing a listing, an exclusive authorization to sell form should be used. A detailed listing of all inventory and fixtures, as well as their condition should be included. The broker must do his best to independently verify all listing information provided by the seller. If the broker cannot do so, he must state "not verified by agent" on the listing form.

**Z9**   There are important details that a broker must attend to for the protection of the buyer. These include:

- A complete inventory of the stock, fixtures and equipment. Both buyer and seller should sign as to their approval of this.

- Terms of the property lease, if there is one. These of course, would be provided in a copy of the lease.

- Confirmation with the planning department as to the conformity of the business to zoning regulations, and as to the probable continuance of such conformity.

- Matters relating to the transfer of necessary licenses, if license transfers are a part of the transaction.

- Determination as to who is liable for any unpaid sales taxes.

- Assurance of continuance of the business license by local authorities.

- A hundred other details could be given in the sale of specialized businesses, e.g., smog control, sign permits, etc.

**Z10**   All of the above items may be incorporated in the sales agreement (deposit receipt), or by a separate document placed in escrow. Although the broker is the agent of the seller if he was given a listing, in business opportunity transactions the buyer is in greatest jeopardy, and the broker is duty bound to give him reasonable protection.

**Z11**   The seller is responsible for transferring all required licenses and permits, and seeing that clearances from governmental agencies are secured. An escrow holder is usually instructed to take care of these matters, however. The use of an escrow is considered of utmost importance for most business opportunity transactions because of the many requirements and complexities of this type of transaction. The escrow helps to assure that all requirements are met. However, an escrow is not mandatory, unless an Alcoholic Beverage license is to be transferred. The escrow holder is liable for damages if proved negligent. The escrow fee is usually split between the two parties on a fifty-fifty basis.

**Z12**  It is important that a buyer have access to the books and accounts of the business after he has signed an agreement to purchase or lease. It is well to have the sales agreement provide for this, and make the transaction subject to the buyer's approval of these records. This of course, is to help make sure that the business operation is as represented.

**Z13**  The services of an attorney who has expertise in this type of transaction, preferably early in the negotiations, may be advisable. ·

**Z14**  **"Advance fee operators"** have devoted much of their efforts to collecting fees in advance for the advertising and circulation of information regarding businesses for sale. They are strictly regulated in the use of contracts, handling of the fees they collect and in other respects. See paragraphs A60-A62 in the first chapter for more details.

## CHATTELS

**Z15**  **Chattel** is another name for an interest in personal property, that is, anything that is not real property.

**Z16**  Because of the movable nature of most personal property, the law has set up certain regulations governing its sale in order to prevent fraud. Creditors especially need to be protected.

**Z17**  Business opportunity brokers deal in chattels, as stock of goods and store equipment (usually) are personal property. It is therefore important that they become acquainted with the laws governing the sale of chattels in general, and those governing the sale of particular chattels, such as liquor stocks.

**Z18**    Chattels may be pledged as security interests just as real estate may be mortgaged, with some exceptions. Even growing crops such as cabbage and melons may be used as security interests.

**Z19**    Those which cannot be used as security interests are: personal property not capable of manual delivery; personal wearing apparel, and stock in trade of a merchant (except in the case of a purchase money security interest). By manual delivery is meant handing from one person to another.

## TRANSFERRING OWNERSHIP OF CHATTELS

**Z20**    The **bill of sale** is to chattels what the deed is to real estate. It is the document used to transfer title of personal property. Sometimes a bill of sale is not used, and title merely passes by delivery to the possession of the vendee.

**Z21**    The seller who gives the bill of sale is called the **vendor**, and the buyer the **vendee**.

**Z22**    When a bill of sale is intended to transfer title to a group of items such as the furniture in a furnished house, it is important to take an accurate **inventory** and include it in the bill of sale.

**Z23**    **A Notice to Creditors of Bulk Transfer** must be published when selling the stock of a merchant. The law requiring this to be done for protection of creditors is called the **Bulk Sales Law**. See Z27.

## UNIFORM COMMERCIAL CODE - DIVISION 9

**Z24**    In an earlier chapter, we discussed how real property is pledged as security for a debt by use of a trust deed or other type of security instrument. The sole instrument used to create a security interest in personal property is the **security agreement**. A standard form called the **Financing Statement (UCC-1)**, is commonly used in **filing with the Secretary of State** to provide constructive notice of the existence of the security agreement. In case of a foreclosure sale, the priorities of various creditors is according to the order of their filings. The Financing Statement is merely a form used in connection with the filing, and is no substitute for the security agreement which provides for the actual grant of a security interest.

**Z25** Information and copies of Financing Statements pertaining to a particular debtor may be obtained from the Secretary of State by filing a **"Request for Information or Copies" form (UCC 3)**. The Secretary of State will provide a certificate giving the names and addresses of any secured creditors and the times of their filings of Financing Statements.

**Z26** Division 9 of the Uniform Commercial Code covers all forms of transactions which are intended to create a security interest in personal property. Local filing with the county recorder rather than with the Secretary of State is done for some types of security. Sophisticated lenders often record the Financing Statement both with the State and in the county where the property is located for added protection. We have mentioned only one aspect of Division 9 here. There is much more to it, and it should be thoroughly studied by the business opportunities broker.

## BULK SALES LAW

**Z27** **The Uniform Commercial Code - Division 6**, was primarily enacted to protect wholesalers and others who give credit to merchants from being defrauded by a secret sale of the business without first paying off all debts incurred in the purchase of goods. It is sometimes called the **California Bulk Sales Law**. It applies to materials, supplies, merchandise, equipment or other inventory.

**Z28** The law does not apply to the sale of goods of a merchant in the ordinary course of trade, but only when sold "in bulk." That is, when sold in their entirety, or when a substantial part is sold.

**Z29**   When a business is sold and its goods are to be transferred, the **transferee (purchaser)** is required by law to give public notice to the transferor's (seller's) creditors. This protects the transferee from any claims which are unknown to him against his merchandise once the stock has been purchased. This law also applies to businesses where there is no particular stock in trade, such as bakeries, restaurants, garages, machine shops, cleaners, etc.

**Z30**   The sale of any retail or wholesale business is conclusively presumed by law to be fraudulent unless the steps listed below are followed. **At least 12 business days** prior to the bulk transfer the transferee must:

1. Record a **Notice to Creditors of Bulk Transfer** with the county recorder of the county in which the business is located.

2. The notice must be published at least once in a newspaper of general circulation in a certain prescribed area.

3. The notice must be sent by registered or certified mail to the county tax collector in the county where the property is located.

**Z31**   The Notice to Creditors of Bulk Transfer must contain the following information:

1. That a bulk transfer is about to be made.

2. Names and business addresses of the transferor within the past three years so far as known to the transferee.

3. The name and address of the transferee.

4. The location and general description of the property to be transferred.

5. The place and the date where the bulk transfer is to take place.

**Z32** Failure to comply with this law makes the transfer void as far as the seller's creditors are concerned. That is, they can still claim the property as security for the unpaid accounts due them. The Statute of Limitations allows one year from date of transfer to initiate such claims.

**Z33** In addition to doing these things in connection with a sale, the law requires it to be done if the property is to be assigned, or is to be used as a security interest.

**Z34** If the business is to be sold at public auction, the same procedure must be followed. The Notice to Creditors of Bulk Transfer, which is recorded and published, shall also contain the name and address of the auctioneer and the time and place of the auction.

**Z35** If an auctioneer sells a business without the notice being recorded and published, he is personally liable for any losses to the merchant's creditors.

**Z36** An auctioneer who sells businesses must have a real estate license.

## FICTITIOUS BUSINESS NAMES

**Z37** Many operators of businesses use **fictitious names**. A business name which does not include the surname of the individual, or one that suggests the existence of additional owners, is said to be fictitious. A partnership must include the surname of each partner in its business name, and a corporation must include the corporate name stated in its articles, or they are considered to be fictitious names. A business must file a fictitious business name statement with the county clerk no later than 40 days from the start of business. Within 30 days after the statement has been filed, it must be published in a newspaper of general circulation once a week for four consecutive weeks in the county where the business is located. An affidavit confirming the publication must be recorded within 30 days after the completion of the publication. A fictitious business name statement expires at the end of 5 years. To discontinue using a fictitious name a statement of abandonment must be recorded. The statement must be executed, published and recorded in the same manner as a ficticious business name statement.

## FRANCHISING

**Z38** **Franchising** has become very popular. This simply involves a large business firm (the franchisor) giving the right of a dealership to a buyer (the franchisee). The franchisee may use the franchisor's trade name and trademark, products, services, etc. in his independent business. Examples are a Kentucky Fried Chicken restaurant, Century 21 Real Estate, and Travelodge.

**Z39** The **Franchise Investment Law** requires the franchisor to provide a prospective franchisee with detailed information regarding the franchise agreement. This information is contained in a prospectus which must be delivered to the prospective purchaser at least 10 business days prior to any binding franchise agreement, or a minimum of 10 business days before the receipt of any consideration, whichever occurs first.

**Z40** Persons authorized to sell franchises are:

1. A person identified on the franchisor registration application and who offers the franchise.

2. Licensed broker or salesperson.

3. Agents licensed by the Commissioner of Corporations.

**Z41** Take note that a broker may sell a franchise even though he is not identified in the franchisor registration application, and an individual who is identified in the registration application need not be a broker to sell the franchise.

## CALIFORNIA SALES AND USE TAX

**Z42** The State of California partly finances the cost of State government and public schools by means of taxing retail sales.

**Z43**   Most types of tangible personal property when sold at retail are subject to the tax. By tangible property is meant something with substance, such as a clock, brush or automobile. A mortgage is personal property, but not tangible as it does not have substance.

**Z44**   Certain tangible personal property is exempt from the tax. The list is rather lengthy, but the following exemptions are of interest to the agent: food for human consumption, including most items purchased in grocery stores and meat markets for home meals; gas, electric, and water services by public utilities; livestock, poultry, feed, fertilizer, seeds and annual plants. Hot food to go is taxed. Cold food to go is not.

**Z45**   The law imposes the tax upon the retailer for the privilege of selling goods, and the retailer in turn must collect the tax from the customer.

**Z46**   All persons or firms in the business of selling taxable personal property must secure a "**seller's permit**" from the **State Board of Equalization**. These permits are free. They are applied for on a form provided by the State Board of Equalization, the governmental agency charged with collecting sales and use taxes.

**Z47**   A permit must be secured for each separate place of business, and must be displayed at that place. They are good until revoked. Wholesalers as well as retailers must obtain permits.

**Z48**   As of July 15, 1991, the statewide sales and use tax ranged from 7.25% to 8.25% in different areas. On this date some additional items were taxed for the first time, including snack foods and candy, bottled water, newspapers, and periodicals.

**Z49**   Any holder of a permit is responsible for the taxes owed by anyone running a concession on the premises (concessionaire), unless that person has secured his own permit. Business proprietors should therefore determine that concessionaires secure these permits.

**Z50**  Sellers are required by law to keep records of all sales and purchases, and keep them available to the Board of Equalization for inspection.

**Z51**  Payment of the tax must be made to the Board of Equalization quarterly unless otherwise ordered. Failure to pay in the required time may result in a penalty of 10%.

**Z52**  Failure to comply with the law may result in the permit being revoked. The Board must give the accused merchant the privilege of presenting his defense at a hearing before taking any action.

**Z53**  If the person or firm responsible for the tax **fraudulently** fails to make returns, a penalty of 25% may be imposed in addition to the 10% previously mentioned.

**Z54**  Whenever a sale of goods is made to someone for the purpose of resale at retail, as in the case of a sale by a wholesaler, the tax need not be collected or paid by the wholesaler, but he is held responsible for the tax unless he proves that it was a wholesale transaction. Therefore, he secures from the retailer a certificate to the effect that the property was purchased for resale. This provides the means of establishing proof that the tax need not have been collected from the retailer.

**Z55**  Whenever a retail business is sold, the Board of Equalization should be notified so that their auditors may determine the amount of tax owed by the seller up to the time of sale and collect that amount. If this is done, a **clearance receipt** is issued. This protects the purchaser, who may otherwise be responsible for the unpaid taxes of his predecessor. Such responsibility is called **successor's liability**.

**Z56**  A sales tax must be paid on the fixtures and equipment of a business which has a sales tax permit when sold to a new proprietor, but not on "good will" or merchandise.

**Z57**  The **Use Tax** applies to certain retail purchases on which a retailer does not collect and remit a tax. It applies mostly to purchases made by residents of California from dealers in other states who ship goods into California direct to consumers. It also applies to vehicles purchased outside of the State. The purchaser is responsible for paying this tax.

## ALCOHOLIC BEVERAGE BUSINESS

**Z58**  Because of the numerous sales of business opportunities involving liquor stores, bars, wineries, etc., the Real Estate Commissioner requires applicants for licenses to have a general knowledge of the provisions of the California law controlling liquor sales.

**Z59**  The Constitution of the State reserves to the State the right to control the manufacture, sale, purchase and possession of alcoholic beverages. The State law controlling this right is known as the **Alcoholic Beverage Control Act**. It is administered by the **Department of Alcoholic Beverage Control**. The Department issues licenses and has the power to deny, suspend or revoke a license upon due cause. This is an exercise of the police power of the State. By **police power** is meant the right of the State to protect the safety, health, welfare, peace and morals of its citizens.

**Z60**  Any person who is responsible and of good moral character is eligible for an alcoholic beverage license. Even an alien may qualify. However, the Department may refuse to issue a license to any person who has previously violated the Alcoholic Beverage Control Act, or who has a disqualifying criminal record. A complete background disclosure and fingerprinting are required of each applicant. A broker should not encourage his client to make an investment in this category of business until it is determined that the client meets all requirements.

**Z61**  The Department may refuse to issue a license if the applied-for establishment is too near a school, church, public playground; if there is an over-concentration of alcoholic beverage licenses in the area, or if the location is in a high crime area. Delinquent tax payments by the owner of the business may also cause problems in qualifying for a license.

Z62   The number of general licenses issued in any one area is limited to prevent an over-concentration of licenses. General licenses mean that they are not limited to certain types of beverages, as opposed to a license to sell beer and wine only. An on-sale general license is one issued where consumption of liquor, beer or wine is served on the premises. An off-sale license is one issued to a store selling packaged goods which are not to be consumed there, but are to be removed from the business location.

Z63   Before an applicant files a license transfer application with the Department of Alcoholic Beverage Control, generally the following steps must be taken:

1.   The applicant must establish an escrow.

2.   A Notice to Creditors of Bulk Transfer must be filed with the County Recorder.

3.   The transferee must post on the premises a notice of application for ownership change or notice of application to sell alcoholic beverages.

4.   A notice of application must be published in a newspaper of general circulation if applying for an on-sale license.

5.   The filling out of the necessary application papers required by the Department includes a statement affirming that the purchase price has been deposited in escrow.

Z64   The processing of the application could take up to 50 days or more. By law, a license will not be issued prior to a minimum period of 30 days.

Z65   Anyone who wishes to protest the issuance of a license has up to 30 days from the date the notice was first posted. Issuance of a license will be withheld while a valid protest is pending or being appealed.

**Z66**   After a license is issued, the transferee has 30 days from date of issuance to put it into use, unless the building is under construction.

**Z67**   All licenses must be issued to specific persons at specific locations. Licenses may be sold separately from the stock and the business.

**Z68**   The maximum purchase price that a transferee may pay for an on-sale or off-sale general license originally issued after June 1, 1961 is $6,000. This applies for a period of 5 years. After the 5 year period, there is no limit as to the amount that may be paid. This is done to preclude speculation in these licenses. Further, there are limits as to amounts that may be paid for good will and personal property so that the $6,000 rule may not be circumvented. The Alcoholic Beverage Control Board should be contacted regarding any questions pertaining to the transfer of these licenses.

The following is from an article by the DRE Business Brokers Advisory Committee which was published in a Department of Real Estate Bulletin.

> "It is important to understand that even though you have the 'legal right' to represent buyers and sellers in business opportunity sales by being a real estate licensee, you need additional education and training in order to safely negotiate your way through a transaction. Courses in business appraisal, general accounting, small business management, taxation, business law, and business brokerage would be beneficial.
>
> It is interesting to note that business brokers often specialize in the sale of specific types of businesses. For example, one agent may only handle restaurant sales while another licensee works exclusively with the dry cleaning industry. These individuals realize that specific knowledge is often needed for each type of business transaction, and wisely work only within the parameters of their expertise. While any real estate agent may sell a business opportunity, there is much more to the transaction than merely filling out the proper forms."

# Business Opportunities

# CHECK QUESTIONS

1. Title to personal property is conveyed when:
   (A) A deed is recorded
   (B) Bill of sale is given to buyer
   (C) The chattel mortgage is signed
   (D) None of the above. ( ) Z20

2. Which of the following business opportunity transactions requires a real estate license:
   (A) Sale                    (B) Month to month rental
   (C) Exchange                (D) All of the above. ( ) Z3

3. When taking a listing, if the agent is unable to verify information about a business which was provided by the owner he should
   (A) Reject the listing
   (B) State on the listing, "not verified by agent."
   (C) Take the listing and sell the property subject to the buyer verifying all facts about the business
   (D) None of the above. ( ) Z8

4. If a party purchases a business and the real estate in which it is housed, it is best to:
   (A) Consolidate the two and have one escrow
   (B) Have separate escrows, but close the business escrow first
   (C) Have two separate escrows, but close the real estate escrow first
   (D) Have separate escrows and close them concurrently. ( ) Z4

5. In business opportunity transactions the agent is responsible to:
   (A) The party who is to pay his commission
   (B) The buyer
   (C) The seller                                    Z6
   (D) Vendor and vendee. ( ) Z10

6. The person who is responsible for transferring all licenses and permits in a business opportunity transaction is:
   (A) The seller              (B) The broker
   (C) The buyer               (D) The escrow officer. ( ) Z11

7.  Before giving a prospective buyer a list of businesses to see on his own, and have him sign a customer registration form, the broker must:
    (A) Check the financial records of the business
    (B) Check the zoning
    (C) Get written authorizations from the owners of the businesses
    (D) Review the buyer's financial statement.                    (  )  Z5

8.  The buyer of a business opportunity has some protection as to condition of the title of the assets he is acquiring through:
    (A) An ALTA title policy
    (B) A chattel title insurance policy
    (C) Filing a "Request for Information or Copies" (UCC 3) with the Secretary of State
    (D) A business opportunity lien search.                          (  )  Z25

9.  Chattels which may be pledged as security interests are:
    (A) Personal wearing apparel
    (B) Growing crops of vegetables
    (C) Grocery store stock in trade                                        Z18
    (D) All of the above.                                          (  )  Z19

10. The vendee is the:
    (A) Trustee in a chattel mortgage
    (B) The purchaser
    (C) The beneficiary
    (D) Sandwich lessee.                                           (  )  Z21

11. Under the Uniform Commercial Code - Division 9, which form is used in filing notice of a security agreement with the Secretary of State?
    (A) Notice of Security Agreement
    (B) Constructive Notice
    (C) Financing Statement
    (D) Notice of Lien.                                            (  )  Z24

12. If an auctioneer sells a business without a Notice to Creditors of Bulk Transfer being recorded and published, he is personally liable:
    (A) For up to $50,000 per creditor
    (B) For any losses to the merchant's creditors
    (C) Up to $10,000 per merchants creditor
    (D) None of the above.                                         (  )  Z35

13. According to the Bulk Sales Law, a notice of intended sale must be published in a newspaper how many days before the transfer:
    (A) 12 business days          (B) 18 business days
    (C) 4 days                    (D) 20 days.                     (  )  Z30

14. The Franchise Investment Law requires the franchisor to provide the prospective franchisee with detailed information regarding the franchise agreement at least how many business days prior to a binding franchise agreement or receipt of any consideration:
    (A) 3 days                      (B) 10 business days
    (C) 15 days                     (D) 30 business days.          (  )  Z39

15. Which of the following is subject to the California Sales tax:
    (A) Tools                       (B) Seeds
    (C) Grocery store food items    (D) Fertilizer.                (  )  Z44

16. The Department of Alcoholic Beverage Control may refuse to issue a license if:
    (A) The applicant is an alien
    (B) The applicant does not have a specific location for use of the license
    (C) The place of business is a private club
    (D) The location is one mile from a school.                         Z61
                                                                   (  )  Z67

17. By law, an alcoholic beverage license will not be issued prior to a minimum period of:
    (A) 60 days    (B) 90 days    (C) 45 days    (D) 30 days. (  )  Z64

18. The maximum amount that may be paid for an on-sale or off-sale alcoholic beverage license for a period of 5 years from date of issuance is:
    (A) $50,000    (B) $6,000    (C) $25,000    (D) $10,000. (  )  Z68

19. When brokering a business, to insure that the seller has paid all sales tax up to the time of sale, which of the following documents should be secured from the Board of Equalization for the protection of the buyer?
    (A) Sales tax payment guarantee  (B) Clearance receipt
    (C) Deposit receipt              (D) None of the above.         (  )  Z55

20. Firms selling taxable, tangible personal property must get a seller's permit from:
    (A) The Department of Real Estate
    (B) Board of Equalization
    (C) State Taxing Authority
    (D) Department of Corporations.                                (  )  Z46

21. An escrow is mandatory in business opportunity transactions when:
    (A) The business is a restaurant
    (B) Crops are involved
    (C) An alcoholic beverage license is to be transferred
    (D) The price is one million dollars or more.                  (  )  Z11

# ANSWERS TO CHAPTER CHECK QUESTIONS

## "A" Chapter - Real Estate License Law:
1. (A)  2. (D)  3. (D)  4. (C)  5. (B)  6. (A)  7. (C)
8. (D)  9. (B)  10. (B)  11. (D)  12. (A)  13. (D)  14. (D)
15. (C)  16. (C)  17. (A)  18. (A)  19. (B)  20. (D)  21. (D)
22. (B)  23. (B)  24. (D)  25. (D)  26. (C)  27. (B)  28. (A)
29. (C)

## "B" Chapter - Property:
1. (C)  2. (D)  3. (D)  4. (C)  5. (C)  6. (B)  7. (A)
8. (B)  9. (D)  10. (A)  11. (D)  12. (C)  13. (D)  14. (B)

## "C" Chapter - Various Ways Property is Owned and Acquired:
1. (B)  2. (B)  3. (A)  4. (D)  5. (D)  6. (A)  7. (A)
8. (D)  9. (B)  10. (B)  11. (A)  12. (C)  13. (D)  14. (C)
15. (B)  16. (A)  17. (C)

## "D" Chapter - Deeds:
1. (B)  2. (C)  3. (D)  4. (A)  5. (D)  6. (C)  7. (D)
8. (D)  9. (C)  10. (C)  11. (A)  12. (B)

## "E" Chapter - County Records:
1. (C)  2. (D)  3. (D)  4. (B)  5. (A)  6. (C)  7. (C)
8. (B)  9. (C)

## "F" Chapter - Titles/Title Insurance:
1. (D)  2. (B)  3. (C)  4. (C)  5. (B)  6. (D)  7. (D)
8. (D)  9. (C)  10. (A)  11. (B)

## "G" Chapter - Escrows:
1. (D)  2. (C)  3. (D)  4. (C)  5. (D)  6. (C)  7. (D)
8. (D)  9. (A)  10. (A)  11. (B)

## "H" Chapter - Subdivisions:
1. (D)  2. (D)  3. (B)  4. (C)  5. (C)  6. (D)  7. (C)
8. (A)  9. (C)  10. (C)  11. (D)  12. (C)  13. (C)  14. (B)
15. (B)  16. (C)  17. (C)  18. (D)  19. (C)  20. (D)  21. (A)

## "I" Chapter - Agency/Power of Attorney:

| 1. (B) | 2. (A) | 3. (D) | 4. (D) | 5. (A) | 6. (B) | 7. (A) |
| 8. (C) | 9. (C) | 10. (C) | 11. (D) | 12. (C) | | |

## "J" Chapter - Contracts:

| 1. (C) | 2. (A) | 3. (D) | 4. (C) | 5. (C) | 6. (B) | 7. (D) |
| 8. (D) | 9. (D) | 10. (B) | 11. (B) | 12. (D) | 13. (B) | 14. (D) |
| 15. (C) | 16. (B) | 17. (A) | 18. (D) | 19. (C) | 20. (D) | 21. (A) |
| 22. (D) | | | | | | |

## "K" Chapter - Listings, Deposit Receipts, Options and Probate Sales:

| 1. (B) | 2. (C) | 3. (B) | 4. (C) | 5. (D) | 6. (B) | 7. (C) |
| 8. (D) | 9. (C) | 10. (C) | 11. (C) | 12. (A) | 13. (B) | 14. (D) |

## "L" Chapter - Encumbrances:

| 1. (B) | 2. (B) | 3. (A) | 4. (B) | 5. (C) | 6. (B) | 7. (D) |
| 8. (C) | 9. (C) | 10. (C) | 11. (D) | 12. (B) | | |

## "M" Chapter - Mortgages, Deeds of Trust and Sales Contracts:

| 1. (D) | 2. (D) | 3. (A) | 4. (C) | 5. (A) | 6. (B) | 7. (C) |
| 8. (B) | 9. (D) | 10. (D) | 11. (A) | 12. (B) | 13. (A) | 14. (D) |
| 15. (A) | 16. (A) | 17. (C) | 18. (D) | 19. (D) | 20. (B) | 21. (C) |
| 22. (B) | 23. (C) | | | | | |

## "N" Chapter - Notes:

| 1. (B) | 2. (C) | 3. (A) | 4. (A) | 5. (C) | 6. (C) | 7. (A) |
| 8. (B) | 9. (C) | 10. (C) | 11. (D) | 12. (B) | 13. (C) | 14. (C) |

## "P" Chapter - State and Federal Loan Laws:

| 1. (B) | 2. (B) | 3. (B) | 4. (C) | 5. (B) | 6. (A) | 7. (D) |
| 8. (B) | 9. (A) | 10. (D) | 11. (B) | 12. (B) | 13. (D) | 14. (C) |
| 15. (C) | 16. (A) | 17. (A) | 18. (D) | | | |

## "Q" Chapter - Government Home Financing Agencies and Conventional Mortgage Lenders:

| 1. (B) | 2. (B) | 3. (C) | 4. (C) | 5. (D) | 6. (C) | 7. (C) |
| 8. (B) | 9. (D) | 10. (C) | 11. (D) | 12. (C) | 13. (B) | 14. (A) |

## "R" Chapter - Leases:

1. (A)   2. (D)   3. (B)   4. (C)   5. (B)   6. (B)   7. (D)
8. (A)   9. (D)   10. (C)   11. (C)   12. (D)   13. (A)   14. (C)

## "S" Chapter - Judgments:

1. (D)   2. (B)   3. (B)   4. (C)   5. (C)   6. (B)

## "T" Chapter - Homesteads and Fair Housing

1. (A)   2. (D)   3. (D)   4. (C)   5. (D)   6. (B)   7. (C)
8. (C)   9. (C)   10. (A)   11. (D)   12. (C)   13. (B)   14. (A)
15. (D)   16. (D)   17. (B)   18. (B)   19. (D)   20. (B)

## "U" Chapter - Government Land Use Planning and Controls:

1. (D)   2. (C)   3. (C)   4. (D)   5. (A)   6. (D)   7. (C)
8. (B)   9. (D)

## "V" Chapter - Home Construction/Termites:

1. (D)   2. (D)   3. (D)   4. (A)   5. (B)   6. (A)   7. (C)
8. (C)

## "W" Chapter - Appraising:

1. (D)   2. (C)   3. (D)   4. (C)   5. (C)   6. (B)   7. (A)
8. (B)   9. (D)   10. (C)   11. (A)   12. (D)   13. (C)   14. (D)
15. (B)   16. (C)   17. (A)   18. (C)   19. (A)   20. (B)   21. (C)
22. (B)   23. (C)   24. (D)   25. (B)

## "X" Chapter - Land Descriptions:

Answers are contained within the chapter.

## "Y" Chapter - Taxes:

1. (B)   2. (C)   3. (D)   4. (D)   5. (A)   6. (B)   7. (A)
8. (C)   9. (C)   10. (A)   11. (C)   12. (B)   13. (D)   14. (C)

## "Z" Chapter - Business Opportunities:

1. (B)   2. (D)   3. (B)   4. (D)   5. (D)   6. (A)   7. (C)
8. (C)   9. (B)   10. (B)   11. (C)   12. (B)   13. (A)   14. (B)
15. (A)   16. (B)   17. (D)   18. (B)   19. (B)   20. (B)   21. (C)

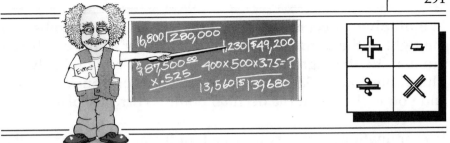

# REAL ESTATE ARITHMETIC

Inability to solve fairly simple arithmetic problems causes some license applicants to lose enough points so that they fail to pass license examinations. The Primer cannot undertake to give complete instruction in arithmetic, but will set forth a number of problems similar to those given in some examinations. It is now permissible to use a silent electronic calculator in taking the State exams. One of these can make the solving of these problems much easier and more accurate.

It is recommended that those who feel they are weak in this subject enlist the aid of a friend who can be helpful. It is especially desirable that one have knowledge of the use of the decimal system. Problems can often be worked by use of ordinary fractions, however the use of decimals with an electronic calculator is usually the much better way. The student should have the ability to convert fractions and percentages to decimals.

The decimal system is based on the use of multiples of ten. Our money system is based upon decimals. That is why it is easier for us to make change than for the English, whose system of money is not based upon multiples of ten.

The location of the decimal point (period) determines the value of the number. One is written 1. Ten is written 10. One tenth is .1 One hundredth is .01 All fractions may be changed to decimals. For instance, 5 1/2 may be written 5.5

In multiplying decimals, you end up with as many numbers to the right of the decimal point in your answer as the combined number to the right in the numbers you are multiplying. Illustration: 5.25 x 3.5 equals 18.375. Do this on your calculator and you will see that the decimal point is correctly placed.

In examinations you may be asked for instance, to compute the annual interest on a straight note of $6,750 at 5 1/4% interest. $6,750 x .0525 equals $354.375, or bringing it to whole cents, $354.38. You will note that the decimal point for 5% was moved two places to the left. This was because 5% means five parts in a hundred, or five hundredths. Therefore 5% is written .05, and 5 1/4% is .0525

## TYPICAL PROBLEMS

135 is 5% of what number? Simply divide 135 by .05. The answer is 2,700.

What is the quarterly interest on a mortgage loan of $5,500 at 12% annual interest? 5,500 x .12 equals 660.00 or $660 annual interest. To get quarterly interest divide by 4. Answer is $165.00.

A property earns $1,100 net after allowing for all expenses and the mortgage payment. A buyer wants 5% spendable cash return on his money. How much of his cash should be invested in the property? Divide the $1100 spendable cash by the rate of return wanted, or just divide the $1,100 by .05. Your answer is $22,000.

An owner insists upon receiving $82,500 net for his property and will pay the broker a 5% commission. What sale price must be asked to accomplish this? Subtract the commission from 100, leaving 95%. Simply divide .95 into the net price to get the sales price, or divide $82,500 by .95. The answer is $86,842.11.

A broker sells a home for $97,500 and collects a 6% commission. The salesperson who secured the listing gets 35% of the commission. What does the salesperson receive? $97,500 x .06 equals $5,850. $5,850 x .35 equals $2,047.50.

Sometimes an examination contains a teaser like this. Three lots sell for a total of $10,000. The second lot brings $1,200 more than the first. The third lot brings $1,600 more than the second. What did each lot sell for?

The problem is to find out what the first lot sold for, then the rest is simple. Let us call the sale price of the first lot, just "lot."

The lot plus (lot + 1,200) plus (lot + 2,800) equals $10,000. Therefore, 3 lots priced like number one plus $4,000 equals $10,000, or 3 lots like number one equal $6,000. One would therefore sell for $2,000. Then it is a simple matter to add the additional amounts brought by lots 2 and 3, and the problem is solved.

Try this one: Three lots sell together for $5,000. The second lot sells for $600 more than the first, and the third lot brings $800 more than the second. What did each lot sell for?

What is the amount of monthly interest on a straight note for $50,000 at 10% annual interest? $50,000 x .10 divided by 12 equals $416.67.

How long does it take to pay off a note for $20,000 at $200 per month plus interest at the rate of 13% per annum? Answer is 100 months. The rate of interest does not affect the length of time to pay off, as the payments are **plus** interest. Watch for this type of problem. If the payments **include** interest, that is another matter and you need an amortization table, or better yet a financial calculator to solve the problem.

You may be asked to figure the net income from a property, being given a list of the monthly rents, the vacancy factor and the itemized expenses. This is merely a matter of addition and subtraction and should present no difficulty. Remember however, that some items may not be expenses to be deducted in figuring a net income. These include mortgage interest, depreciation and capital improvements. Repairing an air conditioner system would be an expense. Installing an air conditioning system in a building that didn't have one would be a capital improvement and not an expense.

# REAL ESTATE PROBLEMS

"Math" plays such an important part today in State exams that we are going to give you a number of practice problems. In examinations, arithmetic problems will probably be of the "multiple choice" type, with three false answers and one correct one. Here are some examples of the general type of questions which you may be asked. Answers follow the questions.

1. A home sold for $225,000 and the commission was 5%. What amount did the broker receive?

2. The salesperson who made the sale receives 60% of the commission. What amount did he receive?

3. When the seller in question (1.) sold, he took back a straight note and trust deed in the amount of $15,500 as part of the purchase price, carrying interest @ 10 1/2%, payable quarterly. What is the quarterly interest payment on this loan?

4. Your town requires a minimum of 6,000 square feet of land to erect a residence. Your lot is 55 feet on the street and is 90 feet deep. Could you build on it?

5. If the lot (in question 4) has a set-back restriction of 20 ft. from the front line and 5 feet from each of the side lines, what is the net building area?

6. Your lot with 65 feet frontage and depth of 150 feet sold for $12,500. How much per front foot did you receive? Per square foot?

7. A broker sold a duplex for $280,000 and received $16,800 commission. What percentage of the sale price did he receive?

8. If you contracted to have a 1,600 square foot home built on your lot and it cost you $83,200, what was the cost per square foot?

9. You paid a bonus of $300 to get a $10,000 loan. How many "points" did you pay?

10. Smith bought a lot and sold it for $24,000, giving him a profit of 16% over what he paid for it. How much did he pay for it, and what amount of profit did he make?

11. A salesman sold a motel for $360,000. The listing provided for a 5% commission. The broker paid his salesmen 45% of the commission on sales made by them. How much did this person receive on this sale?

12. Assuming that in making the sale in question 11, the owner was required by the buyer to reduce his price to take care of the following expenses: painting amounting to $5000, installing new carpets and linoleum totaling $6000, removing trees at a cost of $800 and making termite repairs costing 2% of his original asking price, what was the total sale price? What would the salesperson's part of the commission be on this sum?

13. A lot with 157 feet frontage by 233 feet deep sold for $18,290.50. How much did the seller receive per front foot? Per square foot?

14. Your new home ended up having 1230 square feet of living area and the contractor's charge was $49,200. How much per square foot did it cost you?

15. A salesman earned $5,500 commission on the sale of a business lot. The broker charged the seller 10% commission and the salesman's share was 55% of the entire commission. What price was the lot sold for?

16. Jones owned two acres on a highway, with a depth of 217.80 feet. He sold the land for $120 per front foot. What was the total selling price?

17. An industrial lot is 400 x 500 feet in size. It sold for $3.75 per square foot. What was the price paid?

18. Jones bought a half section of school land in the Mojave desert for $500 per acre. How much did he pay?

19. Referring to the previous question, Jones' land was in Section 16 of the township. He later sold the SW 1/4 of Section 16 for $1,000 per acre. What profit did he make on this parcel?

20. Broker Green sold a warehouse for $327,500. His commission was $17,193.80. What percentage did he charge?

21. Here is a type of problem the examiners like to use, as many students use the wrong reasoning. Smith sold a vacant lot for $12,000, and made a profit of 10% over his cost. Disregarding any taxes paid or other expenses, what did the lot cost him?

22. Jones bought a lot and later sold it for $84,000, giving him a profit of 12% over and above what he paid for the lot. What price did he pay and how much did he make?

23. A bank appraised a commercial building at $420,000. This showed an increase of 18% over their former appraisal. What was their previous valuation?

24. Unfortunately there is sometimes a loss instead of a gain in selling property. Let's try a couple of these.

   Broker Green sold a home he bought "on speculation" for $103,500. It turned out to be a poor buy for him, and when it sold he took a loss of 15% based on his cost. How much did he pay for the place?

25. Here's another problem of the same type. Jones sold a duplex for $275,000 and suffered a loss of 18% from his cost. What had he paid for it?

NOTE: These arithmetic problems can be tricky and should be carefully analyzed before you start. Note whether the problem states that the profit or loss is based on the cost to the seller, or on the selling price. The percentages in the foregoing problems applied to the **cost** of the property. Here's one where the profit given is on the **selling** price.

26. Broker Green sold a home for $200,000. Green made a profit based on the **selling price**, of 20%. How much did the home originally cost him?

### COMMISSION PROBLEMS

27. Broker Green sold a home for $220,000 and the agreed rate of commission was 6%. What was the amount of his check from escrow?

28. Green sold an apartment house for $576,500 and received a commission of 5 1/4%. How much did he earn?

29. A salesman who worked under an arrangement with his broker whereby he received 52 1/2% of the total commissions earned by him, sold properties paying the broker $87,500 gross in commissions during the first six months of the year. What was the salesman's share?

30. The salesman in the previous question earned $52,500 for himself during the following six months. How much did he make for the office during that period?

31. Broker Green charged 5% commission on a sale and collected $13,250. What was the amount of the sale?

32. Broker Green's commission on the sale of a 120 acre farm was $31,200. On farm land he charged 8% commission. What was the sale price per acre? What was the total sale price?

33. Green collected $6,159.00 from escrow as commission on the sale of a property for $102,650. What percentage of the sale price was charged by him?

## MISCELLANEOUS PROBLEMS

34. The seller paid 3 1/2 points for securing a loan of $18,500. How much did the lender deduct from the amount of the loan?

35. Jones sold 10 acres for $80,000 and made 15% profit on his original purchase price (his cost). How much did he pay for the acreage?

36. The annual expenses in maintaining an office building amount to 25% of the gross annual receipts from rentals. The property has been appraised at $1,100,000, based on the capitalization of the net income, using 10% as the capitalization rate. What is the gross annual income of the property?

37. Jones invested in a lot and tried for several months to sell it. He told the broker to reduce the price 12% from the price specified in the listing. The broker did so, and sold the lot for $13,200. How much did Jones originally list it for?

38. An acre of land is 1089 feet deep and fronts on a highway. What is the frontage on the highway?

39. An apartment house containing eight units pays the owner $24,300 net per annum after making all proper allowances for maintenance, repairs, taxes, insurance, management, etc. A broker sells this property to a client on the basis that it will yield him 9% return on his investment. What sale price did he quote?

40. An acre sold for $130,680. What was the price per square foot?

41. Mr. Glenn paid $850 per acre for the S 1/2 of the SW 1/4 of the NE 1/4 of Section 6. What did he pay for the parcel? Where was the section located in the township?

42. Brown sold his parcel containing 32,670 square feet on the basis of $40,000 per acre. How much did he receive?

43. A farmer whose acreage fronted on a county road was offered $4,640 for two acres with a road frontage of 200 feet. How deep would the parcel be? How much per square foot was the offer?

44. Bill and Jack hiked due East on a road that ran along the north edge of various sections. They walked 2 1/2 miles. If they started at the NW corner of Section 6, where did they end up? How many feet had they walked?

## ESCROW PRORATIONS

Another area in which knowledge of arithmetic is required in license examinations is the prorating of taxes, insurance and interest. In every transaction certain credits are due to either the buyer or seller at the time title to the property passes.

The owner of improved property usually pays for his fire insurance one year in advance, and if he sells within that time he has a rebate coming from the buyer. On the other hand, if the property is subject to a mortgage, he usually owes some interest at the time of the closing of the sale. As the buyer will have to pay it when it comes due, he is given a credit when the escrow is closed.

The tax year is not the calendar year (January 1st through December 31st), but runs from July 1st through the following June 30th. If all sales were closed on June 30th there would be no problem, but of course that is seldom the case. So if the taxes have been paid promptly, the seller is credited with a part of the taxes he has paid if the escrow closes before June 30th. He is debited if the closing date is after July 1st. The first installment of the taxes, due November 1st, pays the taxes from July 1st to the following January 1st. So this date must be considered if the taxes are paid in two installments.

45. The seller had paid taxes for the full year promptly and the escrow closed on June 30th. What proration of taxes was made?

46. With 1991-1992 taxes paid for the first half, escrow closed December 31, 1991. What proration was made?

47. Taxes on a home that sold for $200,000 were $1,600 for the current tax year and fully paid. The escrow closed April 1st. What credit was given and to whom, buyer or seller?

48. Taxes on a building were $1,200 a year and the first installment was paid. The property closed escrow May 15th of the tax year. What credit or debit was given to the buyer or seller?

49. A home sold on March 1, 1992. A one-year fire insurance policy was written effective September 1, 1991, and was paid in advance. The premium was $300. What credit was given to whom?

50. A three year fire policy was written on March 20, 1991, and was paid in advance. The home sold and escrow closed April 10, 1992. Cost of the policy was $1080. The seller received what rebate?

51. The Blacks bought a home for $200,000 and paid all cash for it. What amount of transfer tax was required on the deed? If the broker handled the escrow, where would he pay the transfer tax? Who would be charged for it?

52. In the previous question, let's assume the Blacks had taken over a loan of $150,000 already on the house. What amount of transfer tax does the deed require?

As previously stated, interest on real estate loans is normally not paid until it is earned, that is, at the end of the interest period rather than at the outset. So the borrower pays at the end of the month, quarter year, six months period or annually. This means that when a sale is made, the seller owes some interest, and the buyer is given credit in escrow as he has to pay the interest when it next becomes due. This happens when an existing loan on the property is taken over by the buyer. If a new loan is arranged when in escrow, then there is nothing to prorate. Payment periods on loans are stated in the note.

The following problem involves simple interest on a straight loan which is pretty rare these days, especially on homes. Nearly all home loans are amortized loans. With these, a part of the principal is paid along with interest on the declining balance each month or quarter. This makes the computation more involved, and escrow officers resort to prepared tables or financial calculators.

53. Jones borrowed $8,000 on a trust deed straight note dated February 1, 1992. He sold the property and escrow closed on August 15, 1992. He paid his quarterly interest @ 10% promptly. Did he owe the buyer any interest?

## ANSWERS TO REAL ESTATE PROBLEMS

Rather than give you flat answers, we'll try to indicate how we arrived at our answers to these problems.

(1.) 5% of $225,000 is $11,250. Multiply $225,000 by .05.

(2.) 60% of $11,250 is $6,750 (.60 x $11,250).

(3.) $406.88. Multiply $15,500 by .105 (10 1/2%) which gives an annual interest of $1,627.50. Divide this by 4 for the quarterly interest.

(4.) No, you would have only 4,950 square feet.

(5.) 3,150 square feet - do not duplicate the corners! Make a sketch on these problems.

(6.) $192.31 per front foot. You have 9,750 square feet, so the sq. ft. price is approximately $1.28.

(7.) 6%. Divide $16,800 by $280,000 to get .06, or 6%

(8.) $52.00 per sq. ft. Simply divide $83,200 by 1,600.

(9.) Three points, or 3%.

(10.) Don't take 16% of the selling price and then deduct it from the selling price. You'll not get the right answer. The selling price is 116% of the cost to Smith. Divide 1.16 into the $24,000 selling price and you get approximately $20,690, the cost to Smith. His profit, of course, was the difference between $24,000 and $20,690, or $3,310.

(11.) The broker's total commission was $18,000 (360,000 x .05). Of this amount the salesperson received 18,000 x .45 or $8,100.

(12.) Extra expenses are $5000 plus $6000 plus $800 plus $7200 (.02 x 360,000) or $19,000, making $341,000 the final sales price. The broker's commission on this sum (.05 x 341,000) is $17,050. The salesperson's share at 45% is $7672.50 (.45 x $17,050).

(13.) Multiply the width by the depth to get square footage. 157 x 233 equals 36,581 square feet. Divide 157 front feet into $18,290.50 and you get about $116.50 per front foot. Divide 36,581 square feet into the selling price and the answer is $.50 per square foot.

(14.) Divide 1230 into the cost, $49,200 and it shows that you spent $40.00 per square foot.

(15.) If the salesperson received $5,500 as 55% of the commission, the total must have been $10,000. So this is 10% of a $100,000 sale price. Your exam problems will not always come out in such even figures.

(16.) Two acres (43,560 sq. ft. per acre) contain 87,120 square feet. Divide the depth into this, and 400 feet is the frontage. At $120 per front foot, this amounts to $48,000.

(17.) 200,000 square feet at $3.75 per square foot equals $750,000.

(18.) As a standard section contains 640 acres, Jones bought 320 acres. 320 x $500 equals $160,000.

(19.) Jones sold 160 acres at $1,000 per acre and received $160,000. He paid $80,000. Profit was $80,000.

(20.) Divide the sale price into the commission, or $17,193.80 301 ÷ $327,500 = 0.0525, or 5.25%.

(21.) If you take 10% of $12,000 and deduct it from the selling price, this does not give the right answer. The selling price of $12,000 is actually 110% of the cost of the lot to Smith. So divide 1.10 into $12,000 (selling price) and you get $10,909.09, the cost to Smith. You can prove this by adding 10% of this figure (1090.90) and the total is $12,000. Let's try another of this type. Be sure to take time to read the questions carefully!

(22.) Use the same formula. $84,000 is 112% of the cost. Divide 84,000 by 1.12 which gives you 100%, the cost to Jones. This is $75,000, showing a sale profit of $9,000. This amount is 12% of $75,000.

(23.) The previous appraisal figure would be 100% and the last one 118%. You know the latest figure, so divide this by 1.18 to get the 100%. This turns out to be $355,932. To prove, take 18% of 355,932 and then add it to 355,932 and you get $420,000.

(24.) His sale price was 15% less than his cost, so amounted to 85% of the cost. Divide his cost of $103,500 by .85 and you get $121,765, the amount he paid for it. Note that on this "loss" problem we deducted the percentage of loss from 100% instead of adding it before we divided. To prove this problem, take 15% of your answer (.15 x 121,765) which is $18,265. Subtract this from 121,765 and you get $103,500, the figure you started with.

Note that we sometimes round figures and disregard the off dollar or cents.

(25.) The cost of the duplex to Jones was 100% and the $275,000 price he received represented 82%. Divide the .82 into 275,000 and you get $335,366, the original cost to Jones.

(26.) Here we are dealing with the selling price instead of the owner's cost. 20% of the selling price (.20 x 200,000) is $40,000, the profit. The selling price less this profit (200,000 less 40,000) leaves $160,000, the cost to the seller.

(27.) This is about the simplest of commission problems. 6% is written .06 Multiply .06 times 220,000 and the answer is $13,200.

(28.) Green collected $30,266 (576,500 x .0525)

(29.) The salesperson received 87,500 x .525 or $45,938.

(30.) The salesman made $52,500 which was 52 1/2% of the total commissions earned by him. Divide 52,500 by .525 and the total earned by his efforts was $100,000. The office share was therefore $47,500.

(31.) $13,250 is 5% of $265,000. Divide 13,250 by .05.

(32.) $31,200 is 8% of 390,000. Divide 390,000 by 120, the acreage, and the price per acre is $3,250.

(33.) Divide the sale price into the amount collected and you arrive at 6%.

(34.) Lender deducted .035 times 18,500, or $647.50.

(35.) He paid approximately $69,565. As 15% profit was on his cost, divide 1.15 into 80,000 and get this amount. To prove, take 15% of 69,565 and add it to this amount, and it should total $80,000. Remember, this profit is based on the cost, not the sale price.

(36.) As the property has been capitalized at 10% of the net annual income, take 10% of the appraised value, giving you the net annual income of $110,000. As this represents 75% of the gross annual income, divide it by .75, giving you $146,666 as the gross income from which the expenses were deducted.

(37.) $13,200 was 88% (100 minus 12%) of the original listing price. Divide .88 into $13,200 and the answer is $15,000.

(38.) An acre contains 43,560 square feet. If the lot is 1089 feet deep, divide this into 43,560 and you find the frontage is 40 feet on the highway.

(39.) To capitalize the net income of $24,300 you divide by the rate of return desired, in this case 9%. He quoted $270,000.

(40.) With 43,560 square feet in the acre, divide this into $130,680 and the answer is $3.00 per square foot.

(41.) Refer to the land description chapter in the Primer if you are rusty on fractional section descriptions. This would contain 20 acres, so he paid $17,000 (20 x $850). It was located in the NW corner of the township.

(42.) Divide the number of square feet in an acre (43,560) into 32,670 and you'll find he sold 3/4 of an acre (.75). Therefore he received $30,000.

(43.) There are 87,120 square feet in two acres. Divided by 200 (the frontage) would give a depth of 435.6 feet. For price per square foot, divide $4640 by 87,120 and it gives you approximately 5.33 cents per square foot.

(44.) They walked to approximately the center of the north edge of Section 4. (See township plat in the "Land Descriptions" chapter.) As a section is one mile on edge (5,280 feet) they walked 13,200 feet, or 2 1/2 sections.

(45.) None. Taxes were paid exactly to date.

(46.) None. First half of the 1991-92 fiscal year taxes were paid exactly to the closing date.

(47.) Seller was credited $400, as he was paid to July 1st and only nine months of the tax year had elapsed.

(48.) Taxes were $100 per month and the first installment paid them to the previous January 1st. On May 15th, 4 1/2 months were unpaid while the seller held title. At $100 per month this amounted to $450 to be credited to the buyer, plus any fees and penalties.

(49.) The seller was credited with $150 as one-half of the policy term remained. Don't forget to consider all months as having 30 days for proration purposes.

(50.) The policy had been in effect for 12 months and 20 days (12 2/3 months). Cost per month was $30.00. For 12 months the cost was $360.00. For 2/3 month, $20.00. Total cost to escrow closing date, $380. $1080 - $380 = $700.

(51.) A tax totaling $220.00 is required as the tax is $.55 for each $500 or fraction thereof. Transfer taxes are paid to the Recorder. The seller by custom usually pays the tax.

(52.) The required tax would total $55.00 on the $50,000 they paid. The tax does not apply to the amount of trust deeds taken over by the buyer. The tax applies to cash paid and any new liens created by the sale.

(53.) Yes. He had paid interest to August 1st. Quarterly interest was $200 (10% of $8,000 divided by four). One-half month's interest (1/6 of a quarter) was unpaid on August 15th. This would be $33.33 credited to the buyer.

This page intentionally left blank.

# Sample Examination

The purpose of this "sample exam" is to give you an idea as to the extent of your knowledge of the material in the Primer, and also to help you continue the learning process. Although the correct answers are given following each section of this test, it is advised that when you are not sure of the answers, that you refer to the paragraph references. By doing this you will not only learn the specific answer, but will gain a better understanding of the subject matter so that you will be able to answer related questions.

This test begins with 200 multiple choice questions, the form of questions used in State examinations. Then there are additional questions of various types concerning exclusive authorization and right to sell listing and deposit receipt forms, a closing statement problem and a land problem.

## MULTIPLE CHOICE QUESTIONS

1. To verify means to:
   (1) Make void
   (2) To amplify
   (3) To vary the terms
   (4) To swear or affirm.          (  )   **E16**

2. If a flood should cause a stream to suddenly wash away land from along its banks, the process is called:
   (1) Avulsion
   (2) Alluvion
   (3) Accretion
   (4) Collusion.          (  )   **C27**

3. Prescription most nearly means gaining title:
   (1) By grant deed
   (2) By duress
   (3) By open and notorious possession for a long time
   (4) Through death of a relative.          (  )   **B16**

4. In appraising, the cost approach is more applicable to well designed new buildings than to older buildings because of:
   (1) Obsolete materials in old buildings
   (2) Depreciation in old buildings
   (3) Actual cost of new buildings is available
   (4) None of the above.          (  )   **W23**

5. What form of real estate ownership must have at least 100 investors?
   (1) Limited partnership
   (2) General partnership
   (3) Real estate investment trust
   (4) Group investment trust.           ( )   C24

6. An instrument which would enable you to legally act for another person in his stead is:
   (1) Notice of non-responsibility
   (2) Power of attorney
   (3) Subordination agreement
   (4) Unilateral contract.           ( )   I 25

7. Ownership of an undivided interest which passes to heirs upon death is called:
   (1) Ownership in severalty     (2) Joint tenancy
   (3) Tenancy in common     (4) Tenancy by inheritance. ( )   C3

8. When land is divided for sale or lease into five or more parcels, the Commissioner must issue a Final Subdivision Public Report:
   (1) Before any lot is sold or leased
   (2) Before the fourth lot is sold or leased
   (3) At once after fifth lot is sold or leased
   (4) Only if a map is recorded.           ( )   H8

9. Ownership in severalty means ownership:
   (1) As an undivided interest     (2) As joint tenants
   (3) By several people     (4) By an individual.     ( )   C2

10. An enforceable contract may not be entered into under the age of eighteen by:
    (1) An emancipated single man
    (2) An unemancipated minor
    (3) A married woman
    (4) A single woman on active duty in the U.S. armed forces.( )   D28

11. Joint tenancy ownership has the following unique feature:
    (1) Ownership by two or more persons
    (2) Right of survivorship
    (3) Ownership of specific portions
    (4) Ownership of undivided interests.           ( )   C5

12. One who inherits real estate by will is:
    (1) Administrator     (2) Devisee
    (3) Testator     (4) Trustor.           ( )   C26

13. In order to create an easement by prescription which of the following would not be required:
    (1) Payment of taxes on the easement
    (2) Continuous use for 5 years
    (3) Lack of permission from owner
    (4) Some claim of right.  ( )  **B16**

14. A declaration of homestead may be invalid if the declarant
    (1) Has a judgment against him
    (2) Intends to sell the property
    (3) Makes false statement in the declaration
    (4) Mortgages home after filing declaration.  ( )  **T7**

15. The income from a property if it were fully rented is called the:
    (1) Effective gross income  (2) Net income
    (3) Scheduled gross income  (4) Maximum income.  ( )  **W40**

16. When an agent receives two offers to buy his principal's property at the same time, he should:
    (1) Submit offer with largest cash deposit
    (2) Submit highest offer only
    (3) Submit both offers
    (4) Submit deal which will pay him most commission.  ( )  **I 2**

17. A broker who holds a bona fide option on property he offers for sale is not:
    (1) A principal  (2) An agent
    (3) An optionee  (4) A potential buyer.  ( )  **K31**

18. A grant deed is executed when it is:
    (1) Conveyed  (2) Signed by the grantor
    (3) Delivered to the grantee  (4) Transferred.  ( )  **D10**

19. Rent under a percentage lease usually is related to:
    (1) Net profit of tenant
    (2) Number of sales made by tenant
    (3) A pedestrian traffic court
    (4) Gross dollar sales made by tenant.  ( )  **R17**

20. To convey title is to:
    (1) Sell on conditional contract
    (2) Place in escrow
    (3) Alienate the property
    (4) Search the abstract.  ( )  **D13**

21. The type of listing which usually gives the broker the greatest assurance of obtaining a commission in property which is sold is:
    (1) Open listing from a friend
    (2) Exclusive right to sell contract in writing
    (3) Properly signed exclusive agency contract
    (4) An oral exclusive agency.                                     (  )    K9

22. The greatest right to the possession and enjoyment of real property is evidenced by:
    (1) Leasehold interest              (2) Prescriptive right
    (3) Equitable estate                (4) Fee simple estate title.   (  )    B7

23. The buyer of property is usually the:
    (1) Beneficiary                     (2) Grantee
    (3) Assignee                        (4) Grantor.                   (  )    D5

24. The deed usually given at private sale in California is the:
    (1) Warranty deed                   (2) Sheriff's deed
    (3) Quitclaim deed                  (4) Grant deed.                (  )    D5

25. The purchaser by means of a "land contract of sale" is:
    (1) An equitable owner              (2) Record owner
    (3) Owner in fee                    (4) Owner at sufferance.       (  )    M50

26. By recording a deed the owner, as to his interest, gives to the public:
    (1) Objective notice                (2) Constructive notice
    (3) Factual notice                  (4) Actual notice.             (  )    E2

27. The holder of an unrecorded deed who resides in the property, as to his interest gives:
    (1) Constructive notice             (2) Actual notice
    (3) Contingent notice               (4) Declarant notice.          (  )    E2

28. The agreement in a "junior" lien which permits a first lien to be refinanced without suffering loss of priority is called:
    (1) A release clause
    (2) A subordination clause
    (3) A lien waiver
    (4) An acknowledgment waiver.                                      (  )    M39

29. The terms loyalty and diligent and faithful service best refer to what kind of a relationship:
    (1) Mesne                           (2) Ethical
    (3) Fiduciary                       (4) Business.                  (  )    I 2

30. The instrument used by some sovereign powers to transfer the title of property to private owners was:
   (1) Patent      (2) Quitclaim deed
   (3) Royal deed      (4) Mesne.      ( )    **F1**

31. A standard policy of title insurance insures against which one of the following:
   (1) Liens not of record
   (2) Lack of capacity
   (3) Unrecorded easements
   (4) Rights of parties in physical possession.      ( )    **F7**

32. The trustor in connection with a trust deed is the party who:
   (1) Lends the money      (2) Signs the note
   (3) Holds property in trust      (4) Receives a note.      ( )    **M22**

33. An unpaid lumber bill may result in:
   (1) A notice of non-responsibility
   (2) Notice of completion
   (3) Notice of default
   (4) Mechanic's lien.      ( )    **L9**

34. An action by the State Legislature in time of emergency to stop foreclosures of liens would be termed:
   (1) A stop order      (2) An amortization
   (3) Declaratory relief      (4) A moratorium.      ( )    **S17**

35. Information of things affecting the title of a property prior to the use of computers was recorded by title companies in what were known as:
   (1) Title record books      (2) Lot books
   (3) Title history books      (4) Property books.      ( )    **F3**

36. A chronological detailed account of all actions and events affecting the title to a property is known as:
   (1) Chronological title records
   (2) Report of title condition
   (3) Chain of title
   (4) Title history.      ( )    **F14**

37. Deeds which contain use restrictions usually contain:
   (1) A subordination clause      (2) A forfeiture clause
   (3) A zoning ordinance      (4) A time limit for resale.      ( )    **D30**

38. Restricting the right to alienate means:
   (1) Dictating conditions of resale
   (2) Prohibiting sale or lease to foreigners
   (3) Restricting against occupancy by aliens
   (4) Imposing area restrictions.      ( )    **D13**

39. The agency under HUD/FHA which sells securities backed by Title II
F.H.A. loans is called:
(1) Bureau of Veterans Affairs
(2) Ginny Mae (GNMA)
(3) Reconstruction Finance Corporation
(4) Home Owners Loan Corporation.                    (  )   Q22

40. An organization which accepts and distributes exclusive right to sell
listing contracts among its members under a co-operative selling plan,
is said to conduct:
(1) A realty interchange        (2) A warranted listing service
(3) A multiple listing service  (4) A realty clearing house.  (  )   K10

41. Money in connection with an F.H.A. loan is usually advanced by:
(1) A state finance agency
(2) An approved private lending institution
(3) Wealthy individuals
(4) A federal agency.                                (  )   Q5

42. When a deduction is made in an income tax return for gradual decrease
in value of an apartment house, the deduction is for:
(1) Amortization        (2) Depletion
(3) Depreciation        (4) Degradation.             (  )   W24

43. When the value of an income property is computed by using as factors
the net income and an overall capitalization rate, the appraisal process
is termed:
(1) The accrual method
(2) The income approach
(3) Comparative method
(4) Reproduction cost method.                        (  )   W32

44. The net income of a property is arrived at by deducting all chargeable
operating costs from:
(1) The intrinsic value
(2) Fair market price
(3) Warranted value
(4) Effective gross annual income.                   (  )   W36

45. A chattel is:
(1) Farm property
(3) An encumbrance
(2) A document
(4) Item of personal property.                       (  )   Z15

46. An acre contains the following number of square feet:
(1) 43,650      (2) 32,520      (3) 43,560      (4) 5,280.   (  )   X23

47. The NW1/4 of the SW1/4 of the NE1/4 of the SE1/4 of any standard section contains:
    (1) 10 acres       (2) 11/4 acres
    (3) 5/8 acre       (4) 21/2 acres.
    (Make a simple sketch - read the description backwards).   ( )    X8

48. The SE1/4 of the SE1/4 of the SW1/4 of the NE1/4, and the NE1/4 of the SE1/4 of a standard section contain a total of:
    (1) 160 acres       (2) 320 acres
    (3) 42.5 acres       (4) 240 acres.      ( )    X8

49. A straight line drawn from the SW corner of a standard section to the exact center of the section, thence due south to the south line of the section, thence due west to point of beginning, would enclose land containing:
    (1) 320 acres       (2) 160 acres
    (3) 80 acres       (4) 40 acres.      ( )    X21

50. A description of an irregular piece of land based on permanently located land marks, distances, and angles is a description termed:
    (1) Metes and bounds       (2) Fractional section
    (3) Recorded map       (4) Township and range.   ( )    X4

51. The delinquent date for the first installment of real estate taxes is:
    (1) October 15       (2) November 1
    (3) December 5       (4) December 11.      ( )    Y18

52. When a veteran acquires a home under the California Farm and Home Loan Purchase Plan, title is held by:
    (1) The veteran
    (2) An approved lending institution
    (3) Federal Mortgage Discount Agency
    (4) The State.      ( )    Q34

53. The most common and simplest way to place restrictions on all lots in a large new subdivision is to:
    (1) Insert them in all deeds to lots
    (2) Enter into a contract with each purchaser
    (3) Publish them in a legal newspaper
    (4) Record a declaration of restrictions.      ( )    D30

54. The systematic paying of a loan in full by regular equal payments including principal and interest is usually called:
    (1) Liquidation       (2) Amortization
    (3) Acceleration       (4) Underwriting.      ( )    N7

55. Before a broker could find the seller to get acceptance of an offer, the buyer told broker the "deal is off" and demanded return of his $500 deposit. The broker should:
(1) Hold deposit until he learned if seller would accept
(2) Refund to buyer forthwith
(3) Keep half for his work and return balance
(4) Put the deposit in escrow and "sit tight."  (  )  **K25**

56. Ms. Poindexter purchased an older apartment house, and shortly after taking possession of the building she learned for the first time that the air conditioning unit was in such bad condition that it had to be replaced. The seller was aware of this but informed neither the agent nor the buyer. He felt that he was on safe ground since there was an "as is" clause in the sales contract. The seller was:
(1) Correct in not revealing this information as the basic rule is "caveat emptor", let the buyer beware
(2) On safe ground as the disclosure was the responsibility of the agent
(3) Completely protected by the "as is" clause
(4) Possibly liable for damages as the seller has the duty to disclose building deficiencies which are not within the reach of the buyer after diligent attention and observation.  (  )  **I 24**

57. A corporation cannot:
(1) Buy vacant land  (2) Mortgage its property
(3) Own undivided interests  (4) Be a joint tenant.  (  )  **C21**

58. After issuance by the DRE of a Final Subdivision Public Report, the Commissioner would have to be notified if which one of the changes was made regarding the subdivision?
(1) Prices of the lots were raised
(2) Change in mortgage interest rates
(3) Public sewers were eliminated and buyers of lots would have to use septic tank systems instead
(4) A purchaser was restricted to buying a maximum of three lots.  (  )  **H22**

59. Failure to use an easement may result in loss of rights if it was secured by:
(1) Prescription  (2) Quitclaim deed
(3) Grant deed  (4) Reservation in deed.  (  )  **B16**

60. If you are the beneficiary of a second trust deed and are concerned that the trustor may default in payments to the beneficiary of the first trust deed without your knowledge, your practical remedy is to:
(1) Phone the beneficiary of the first lien frequently
(2) Keep in touch with the trustee of the first lien
(3) Record a request for a notice of default
(4) Check often with the trustor.  (  )  **M35**

61. Potable water is provided to various properties by:
   (1) Wells  (2) Irrigation districts  H29
   (3) Municipal utility districts  (4) All of the above.  (  )  H37

62. According to law, the usual urban land lease cannot exceed:
   (1) 99 years  (2) 12 years  (3) 30 years  (4) 51 years. (  )  R16

63. After a notice of completion is recorded, a subcontractor may file an effective mechanics' lien within:
   (1) 120 days  (2) 90 days  (3) 60 days  (4) 30 days. (  )  L12

64. A deposit made by a lessee with a lessor to guarantee against default is:
   (1) Prepaid rent
   (2) Available for cost of maintenance
   (3) A trust fund
   (4) Available to pay taxes.  (  )  R32

65. Two of the underlying factors of value are:
   (1) Size and demand  (2) Utility and scarcity
   (3) Supply and attractiveness  (4) Price and terms.  (  )  W5

66. It is unlawful to use as a security interest:
   (1) Merchant's stock in trade
   (2) Commercial vehicles
   (3) Store fixtures
   (4) Manufacturing machinery.  (  )  Z19

67. "Out of state" subdividers and applicants for real estate licenses must file an irrevocable consent, so that a valid service may be filed against them by delivering a process to the Secretary of State if personal service cannot be made. With whom must the irrevocable consent be filed?
   (1) Secretary of State
   (2) Corporations Commissioner
   (3) County recorder
   (4) Real Estate Commissioner.  (  )  A41

68. You enter into a contract to purchase a lot in a Land Project, but later decide that you want to back out of the deal. From the date of the contract, for how many days does the Real Estate Law permit rescission of the contract by the buyer without cause of any kind?
   (1) 14  (2) 5  (3) 10  (4) 30.  (  )  H34

69. You inherited 10 acres of vacant M zoned land which you want to sell. A buyer would most likely want to acquire it for a:
   (1) Museum  (2) Apartment house
   (3) Factory  (4) Motel.  (  )  U5

70. According to law, the Assessor must assess property at:
    (1) Full cash value (market value)
    (2) Lease value
    (3) Conservative loan value          **Y5**
    (4) Book value.         ( )   **Y6**

71. A county's General Plan must include:
    (1) Land use and circulation    (2) Housing and open space
    (3) Conservation and safety    (4) All of the above.     ( )   **U2**

72. Cost to property owners for improvements under the Street Improvement Act of 1911 are assessed based on:
    (1) Benefits to individual properties
    (2) City-wide benefits
    (3) County-wide benefits
    (4) District benefits.        ( )   **Y38**

73. The townships in the extreme northwest corner of California are located by reference to:
    (1) N.M.P.M.           (2) H.B.& M.
    (3) M.D.B.& M.        (4) S.B.B.& M.     ( )   **X6**

74. You own a vacant lot in a residential neighborhood which would be ideal for development with a nursery school. However, the zoning does not permit this use and the planning commission denies your request for a conditional use permit. You would appeal their decision to:
    (1) The city council
    (2) The zoning appeals board
    (3) The Board of Equalization        **U12**
    (4) The city's planning department.    ( )   **U15**

75. If you have paid a judgment against you and wish to release the cloud on your title you would:
    (1) Secure a quitclaim deed from the judgment creditor
    (2) File a quiet title suit
    (3) Secure a writ of enforcement
    (4) Record a satisfaction of judgment.    ( )   **S7**

76. You bring suit against a building contractor who plans to make a quick sale of his property to prevent you from collecting on a contract. To protect your position, you would secure:
    (1) A pax vobiscus        (2) Nolo contendere
    (3) Res judicata          (4) An attachment.     ( )   **S8**

77. Complying with the law entitled "Disclosure Upon Transfer of Residential Property" is primarily the responsibility of:
    (1) The agent           (2) The pest control operator
    (3) The lender          (4) The seller.       ( )   **I 16**

78. One of the following is wrong. An "advance fee" broker is required to:
    (1) Submit a quarterly report to the Commissioner
    (2) Submit his contract forms to the commissioner for approval
    (3) Possess a real estate license
    (4) Place all advance fees received in a trust account until five days
        after the final accounting is made.                    **A60**
                                                        (  )   **A61**

79. Broker Jones listed a home at a price of $178,500. He found a buyer who
    would not offer more than $170,000, but offered Jones $2,000 on the side
    if he could put the deal over. Jones submitted the entire proposal to the
    seller, including the offer of the bonus. Jones acted:
    (1) Unlawfully            (2) Unethically
    (3) Inconsiderately       (4) Properly.             (  )   **I 2**

80. In the standard floor construction of a dwelling, the foundation rests on
    the concrete or masonry:
    (1) Sill       (2) Footing      (3) Sole       (4) Lintel.   (  )   **V5**

81. Which of the following does not pertain to the Subdivided Lands Law?
    (1) Final Public Report      (2) Notice of Intention         **H6**
    (3) Eminent domain           (4) Standard subdivision.       **H7**
                                                        (  )   **H8**

82. FNMA (Fannie Mae) activities are concerned with:
    (1) The secondary mortgage market
    (2) Secondary financing
    (3) Conventional financing
    (4) Cal-Vet financing.                             (  )   **Q23**

83. One of the following statements is in error. A negotiable note must be:
    (1) Payable within one year
    (2) Made to a bearer or his order
    (3) Made for a definite sum of money
    (4) Payable at a stated time.                       (  )   **N12**

84. The board along the peak of a frame roof to which rafters are nailed is
    called a:
    (1) Ridge board           (2) Header
    (3) Joist                 (4) Batten.               (  )   **V6**

85. Straight line method relates to:
    (1) Metes and bounds descriptions
    (2) Depreciation
    (3) Highway surveys
    (4) Base lines and meridians.                       (  )   **W30**

86. A piece of lumber is one foot wide two inches thick and ten feet long. How many board feet does it contain?

    (1) 10       (2) 20       (3) 30       (4) 40.     ( )    **V6**

    **Page    205**

87. A water pipe broke in a furnished apartment and was causing damage. Tenant shut off water and phoned owner. Owner would not fix the pipe, so the tenant called in a plumber and paid him $100 to fix it. Tenant's best course of action was:

    (1) Forget it

    (2) Deduct it when paying next monthly rental

    (3) Sue in small claims court

    (4) File a mechanic's lien.          ( )    **R26**

88. One of the following is not correct regarding a prepaid rental service:

    (1) Brokers must have a special license to engage in this type of business

    (2) All of the advance fee over $25 must be refunded if the client obtains a rental other than through the services of the licensee

    (3) The prospective tenant must make demand for the refund within 10 days of expiration of the contract        **A46**

    (4) None of the above.          ( )    **A47**

89. A broker must have a Real Property Securities endorsement to his license in connection with the real estate securities he is selling when he:

    (1) Guarantees the purchaser against loss

    (2) Guarantees payment of principal and interest

    (3) Personally assumes payment to protect the note       **A51**

    (4) All of the above.          ( )    **A52**

90. The agency responsible for enforcement of the Business Opportunity brokerage regulations is:

    (1) Insurance Commissioner

    (2) Attorney General

    (3) Board of Equalization

    (4) Department of Real Estate.          ( )    **Z1**

91. A month to month tenancy under a lease is termed:

    (1) Estate at sufferance

    (2) Estate from period to period

    (3) Leased fee estate

    (4) Estate for months.          ( )    **R9**

92. Persons authorized to sell franchises are:

    (1) Licensed brokers

    (2) Agents licensed by the Commissioner of Corporations

    (3) Persons identified on the franchisor registration application

    (4) All of the above.          ( )    **Z40**

93. A ficticious business name statement must be filed with the county clerk within how many days from start of business:
(1) 30 days    (2) 35 days    (3) 40 days    (4) 5 days.  ( )  **Z37**

94. The Statute of Frauds requires which one of the following to be in writing to be enforced by law?
(1) Month to month rental agreement
(2) A one year lease
(3) An eight month lease
(4) A 13 month lease.           ( )  **R11**

95. Structural pest control certification reports are required by:
(1) State law           (2) Some lenders
(3) Some buyers      (4) Both numbers 2 and 3.  ( )  **V12**

96. When a Real Property Securities Dealer fills out a disclosure statement it is signed by the dealer. Who, of the following, would also be required to sign?
(1) Owner of the real property
(2) Borrower
(3) Lender
(4) Investor.                ( )  **A54**

97. A lessee holds a "sandwich lease" when he:
(1) Sublets           (2) Assigns the lease
(3) Renews the lease    (4) Has an estate for years.  ( )  **R23**

98. The buyer of a 15 year old wood frame home purchased the property subject to a pest control certification report by a licensed pest control operator, and repair of any termite, dry rot, and fungus damage in accessible areas. The transferor or the agent in the transaction is required to effect delivery of the inspection report, certification, and the notice of work completed:
(1) Within 5 days of availability from the pest control operator
(2) Before close of escrow
(3) As soon as practical before transfer of title
(4) Within 3 days after close of escrow.     ( )  **V12**

99. Under federal law a taxpayer may sell his home and pay no income tax on the first $125,000 of profit from the sale beginning at what age?
(1) 62        (2) 50        (3) 65        (4) 55.  ( )  **Y43**

100. When a sum is required for overdue repairs it refers to a form of depreciation called:
(1) Economic obsolescence    (2) Functional obsolescence
(3) Deferred maintenance      (4) Residual.  ( )  **W26**

101. Which of the following conditions lowers a property's value:
    (1) Excessive demand
    (2) High degree of utility
    (3) Functional obsolescence
    (4) Neighborhood conformity. ( ) W27

102. In appraising an old single family dwelling, which of the following factors would be given the greatest weight?
    (1) Calculations based on value of Federal Stamps affixed to the deed
    (2) Current costs of the dwelling, assuming the value of the land can be closely estimated
    (3) Capitalization of typical rental values in neighborhood
    (4) Current prices paid for similar homes in the neighborhood. ( ) W37

103. Under the Cal-Vet loan program the eligible veteran must normally make application within how many years from the date of release from active duty:
    (1) 30        (2) 15        (3) 10        (4) 8. ( ) Q36

104. Broker secured a verbal listing. He sold the property and the owner refused to pay him a commission. The broker:
    (1) Could recover his share in court
    (2) Could not recover his share on a verbal agreement
    (3) Should ask the Commissioner to arbitrate
    (4) Should go to the Labor Commissioner. ( ) J5

105. George Riddell did not pay the real estate taxes on his dwelling and the property was finally sold to the State. During the 5 year redemption period Riddell:
    (1) Remained in possession and held title
    (2) Remained in title but had to vacate the premises
    (3) Neither held title nor remained in possession
    (4) None of the above. ( ) Y22

106. A sales contract is a security device. Which is true:
    (1) Seller uses it to convey title without a trustee
    (2) Similar to a lease. Buyer has possession but no part of the title or future rights in it
    (3) The buyer has absolute assurance of receiving the title under a real property sales contract.
    (4) Seller keeps the title and buyer is merely equitable owner. ( ) M50

107. Brother and sister own in joint tenancy. Sister marries and deeds half of her interest to husband. Title holding is:
    (1) Each party 1/3 joint tenant.
    (2) Each party 1/3 tenant in common
    (3) Brother joint tenant-husband and wife community property
    (4) Each party a tenant in common. ( ) C9

108. Mechanics' lien law recognizes alternatives as being the same as completion of the work. Which of the following is not completion:
    (1) A legal notice of completion is recorded
    (2) All labor on the project stops for a period of 30 days
    (3) The property is occupied by the owner and all work on the project has stopped.
    (4) A cessation of labor for a period of 30 days and the      **L11**
    owner files a notice of cessation.      ( ) **L13**

109. A seller contacted his non-purchase money trust deed beneficiary who agreed to an assumption by the buyer. In this circumstance:
    (1) The seller still has secondary liability
    (2) The buyer will have secondary liability
    (3) The seller will have no liability whatsoever
    (4) The buyer will have no liability whatsoever.      ( ) **M43**

110. Which of the following is not usual to a trust deed foreclosure:
    (1) Posted Notice of Sale
    (2) Notice of Default      **M28**
    (3) Advertised Notice of Sale      **M30**
    (4) Deed of Reconveyance.      ( ) **M31**

111. Statewide assessment of which one of the following types of real property is performed by the State Board of Equalization:
    (1) Banks      (2) Colleges
    (3) Public utilities      (4) Charitable trusts.      ( ) **Y39**

112. A man received a property free and clear of all encumbrances, reservations and tenancies. Under this "bundle of rights" he can:
    (1) Sell part of it      (2) Lease it
    (3) Occupy it      (4) All of the above.      ( ) **W4**

113. Mortgages differ in certain respects from trust deeds. The widest degree of time difference occurs in the area of:
    (1) Possession      (2) Title      **M16**
    (3) Period of redemption      (4) Recording.      ( ) **M31**

114. Which one of the following would be required to hold a California real estate license:
    (1) Person acting under order of the court
    (2) A trustee selling under a deed of trust
    (3) A person negotiating a 6 month, month to month rental      **A5**
    (4) A resident manager of an apartment building.      ( ) **A10**

115. A foreclosure sale of the first T.D. brought $7,000. First T.D. is $8,000, second T.D. is $2,000. How much will second T.D. get:
    (1) 2/7ths of the proceeds      (2) $2,000 less costs
    (3) $1,000      (4) Nothing.      ( ) **M32**

116. You submit an offer of $100,000 and receive a counter offer of $110,000. Seller signs all four copies of the counter offer. Which of the following is incorrect:
(1) Take all four copies to buyer for approval
(2) Give one copy to seller
(3) Get signature of buyer
(4) Inform seller when buyer signs counter offer. ( ) A79 #8

117. Which following violation statement is incomplete:
(1) Making any substantial misrepresentation
(2) Making any false promises of a character likely to influence, persuade or induce
(3) A continued course of misrepresentation or making false promises through real estate agents or salespersons
(4) Representing more than one party in a transaction. ( ) A79 #4

118. A contract signed under menace is:
(1) Permissible (2) Voidable
(3) Legal (4) Enforceable. ( ) J7

119. Real property security dealers are licensed by:
(1) Real Estate Commissioner
(2) Corporations Commissioner
(3) Secretary of State
(4) F.D.I.C. ( ) A51

120. Mr. Palumbo owned a lot with an appurtenant easement giving him the right to run sewer lines over Mr. Martin's property. If Mr. Palumbo sells his lot to Mr. Savino, but does not mention the easement in his deed, the easement:
(1) Remains with Palumbo (2) Transfers to Mr. Savino
(3) Reverts to Mr. Martin (4) Is lost by escheat. ( ) B14

121. A principal is considered to be "in the business": and must have a real estate license if he sells a minimum of what number of trust deed notes to the public? A6
(1) 4 (2) 8 (3) 12 (4) 15. ( ) A7

122. Broker Green secured seller's signature to a listing and gave seller copy. He then secured buyer's signature to a sales agreement and deposit receipt, and gave him a copy. Seller signed deposit receipt form but made changes which he initialed. Green gave him copy of amended form. Buyer then signed amended form but Green had no more copies, so buyer didn't get one. Green communicated buyer's acceptance of the amended contract to the seller. The Real Estate Law would:

(1) Permit buyer to withdraw
(2) Permit Green's license to be suspended
(3) Permit seller to withdraw
(4) Prohibit Green from collecting his commission.      ( )  A79
                                                              #8

123. To be valid, a grant deed must:
   (1) Be delivered by grantor to grantee personally
   (2) Recite every warranty it carries
   (3) State the money consideration                           D7
   (4) Be delivered personally or by agent of grantor and      D11
       be accepted by the grantee.                   ( )  D12

124. The "highest and best use" to which a lot could be put is determined by:
   (1) What use would presently produce the largest gross income
   (2) What use would cause the property to have its highest value
   (3) How tall a building the neighborhood would warrant
   (4) What similar vacant lots are being leased for.   ( )  W13

125. Two brothers, John and Bill, owned valuable property left to them by
   their father, as joint tenants. Both married later, and then Bill died
   intestate. His widow would acquire:
   (1) No interest in the property
   (2) Half interest as joint tenant with John
   (3) Half interest as tenant-in-common
   (4) One quarter interest in the property.          ( )  C5

126. Deposit receipt form with offer signed by prospective buyer gave broker
   10 days in which to get seller's acceptance. Buyer gives broker a cash
   deposit. Seller has not accepted offer. The offer is:
   (1) Unenforceable if offer is withdrawn by the buyer prior to seller's
       acceptance
   (2) Unenforceable if buyer forfeits deposit
   (3) Enforceable as broker has contract with buyer
   (4) Enforceable by the seller only.                ( )  K25

127. Sale by use of the usual land contract of sale usually gives the buyer:
   (1) Possession              (2) Title in the fee
   (3) A homestead interest    (4) An estate for years.   ( )  M50

128. A commission for the probate sale of real estate is not collectible if it
   exceeds:
   (1) The real estate board schedule
   (2) The amount determined by heirs
   (3) The amount approved by the court
   (4) Limits set by the Commissioner.                ( )  K40

129. Which would be your most likely source for a first trust deed loan on your home?
    (1) Through Fannie Mae
    (2) From an insurance company
    (3) Savings and loan association
    (4) A Private individual.                                    (  )  Q51

130. In arranging a VA loan for a buyer, Broker Green would never:
    (1) Go to a Federal Savings and Loan Association
    (2) Inquire into the applicant's present obligations
    (3) Ask for a loan commitment
    (4) Apply for a $35,000 loan direct from the VA.            (  )  Q29

131. If your petition to the City Planning Commission for a variance is rejected, you may appeal to:
    (1) The City Engineer
    (2) The City Council
    (3) The City Assessor
    (4) No one.  The decision may not be appealed.             (  )  U15

132. All counties are required by law to adopt:
    (1) An ordinance requiring 60 ft. streets
    (2) A general plan
    (3) A special use plan
    (4) An all inclusive plan.                                  (  )  U2

133. Jones owns acreage through which runs a natural drainage ditch, but it is too small to handle the flow during excessively heavy rains. So, he dug a by-pass ditch which diverted part of the water onto adjacent land which was currently unused for any purpose. Jones was:
    (1) Within his right, as it is "any man for himself" as far as natural flood waters are concerned
    (2) Guilty of an illegal act as he did not get permission from the County Engineer
    (3) Within his rights as adjoining land was unused and there was no danger created to life, limb and property
    (4) In violation of law as one cannot divert natural flow onto the property of another.                                         (  )  B12

134. Unless he complies with certain provisions of the law, such as posting a bond, etc., one who subdivides land into five or more parcels for the purpose of sale or lease cannot sell lots or parcels unless any trust deed on the property contains a:
    (1) Date of definite termination
    (2) Provision for releasing individual lots from the lien
    (3) Provision for releasing the lien from five or more parcels at a time
    (4) Clause permitting it to be subordinated.                (  )  H25

135. A binding real estate contract can be entered into by a married man as soon as he has reached the age of:
(1) Any age
(2) Twenty
(3) Eighteen
(4) Twenty-one.
( ) D28

136. A lease document should contain which one of the following:
(1) A description of the premises
(2) The mortgage loan balance on the property
(3) The zoning
(4) The assessed value.
( ) R15

137. A 70 year-old single man without dependents filed a valid declaration of homestead on a dwelling. Property was valued at $115,000 and was encumbered with a deed of trust, balance of $16,000. The owner was found negligent in an automobile accident, and judgment of $5,000 was obtained against him. The injured person upon obtaining execution stood a chance to:
(1) Force a sale and collect as judgment has priority over the trust deed
(2) Collect nothing as an equity over the exemption and trust deed was lacking
(3) Collect $2,000 as this is amount of equity over value exempt from execution
(4) Collect $5,000 as a single man cannot make valid declaration of homestead on so large a house.
( ) T9

138. A farmer owned 20 acres and sold the front 10 acres facing on the road, reserving a 10 ft. easement in the deed so he could have access to the rear half. He then moved away for 12 years, and when he returned the buyer had blocked the 10 ft. strip with a fence, claiming the easement had lapsed for non-use.
(1) The buyer was right as the easement had not been used for 10 years
(2) Buyer was right as easement had not been used for 5 years
(3) Buyer was right but should have notified seller before fencing property
(4) Buyer was wrong because it is not necessary to use the easemen retained in a deed to keep it valid.
( ) B16

139. The beneficiary under a deed of trust who forecloses on property which does not bring enough at a foreclosure sale to pay the note and expenses may secure a deficiency judgment if:
(1) The trust deed note was part of the purchase price of the property
(2) The foreclosure was completed in 110 days
(3) The loan was made to refinance the property and foreclosure brought by court action
(4) The foreclosure was made under the trustee's power to sell. M37
( ) M38

140. Which of the following is incorrect regarding tenancy in common. The owners:
   (1) All have equal rights of possession
   (2) All must own equal interests
   (3) All owners have undivided interests
   (4) Several persons may be in ownership under tenancy in common.

   ( )   C3

141. A lot owner started building a home and ran out of money. To complete it he borrowed $20,000 from a friend, giving him a first trust deed which was at once recorded. Later he got into a dispute with the contractor who paved the driveway, and the latter filed a mechanic's lien, which:
   (1) Had priority over the trust deed note as work on the house had started when trust deed note was given and recorded.
   (2) Lacked priority over the trust deed as it was subsequently recorded
   (3) Had priority as this is always true of a mechanic's lien
   (4) Lacked priority because paving was not a part of the house.

   ( )   L15

142. Joint tenancy ownership to be effective must always have:
   (1) Ownership of community interest
   (2) Unity of severalty, possession, occupancy and estate
   (3) Mutual interest as tenants in common
   (4) Unities of interest, possession, time and title.        ( )   C10

143. A subdivider recorded a declaration of restrictions for the benefit of all lot owners in the tract and made special reference to the recording in each deed delivered. They provided that no two-story dwellings could be built as they would block the ocean view. It was specified that restrictions would run 50 years. Twenty-one years later a two-story house was started. Other lot owners in the tract brought suit to prohibit the construction, claiming the restrictions were still valid.
   (1) They were wrong as such restrictions cannot run over 20 years
   (2) They were wrong, because the subdivider had died in the meantime
   (3) They were right as the restrictions are good for the term specified in the declaration
   (4) They were wrong as you cannot prohibit building of two-story houses.        ( )   D30

144. Broker Green was happy when he got buyer and seller to execute a sales agreement and then sign escrow instructions. He also had in his pocket a $5,000 cash deposit by buyer paid outside escrow. Then buyer and seller mutually agreed to rescind the transaction and seller instructed Green to return deposit in his possession to the buyer. The proper action by Green was to:

(1) Tell seller he had earned his commission and was retaining the $5,000 as part payment

(2) Agree to refund any part in excess of his commission in accordance with the forfeiture clause in the standard sales agreement

(3) Put the $5,000 in his trust account and let the parties sue if they wanted to

(4) Return the $5,000 to buyer as per instructions and make demand upon seller for his full commission.      ( )    **J15 K4**

145. What would you say is the real basis for value of the average property, i.e., the economic characteristics of value:
(1) Opportunity for a profit if purchased
(2) Its relative scarcity and the demand for it
(3) How it is zoned
(4) Replacement cost.      ( )    **W5**

146. The validity of a grant deed does not require:
(1) Identification of grantor and grantee
(2) A description of the property to be conveyed    **D6**
(3) A statement of the actual monetary consideration    **D7**
(4) Proper delivery.      ( )    **D11**

147. In foreclosing a property under a trust deed the first step the trustee should take is:
(1) Publish the notice of sale
(2) Notify the trustor that he is in default
(3) Bring a suit in court
(4) Record a notice of default.      ( )    **M30**

148. In order to secure an enforceable option to buy, the optionee should:
(1) Actually pay a valuable consideration which is agreed to by the optionor
(2) Always pay optionor at least $1,000 in cash
(3) Never give jewelry or other valuables as a consideration
(4) Never give a note as the consideration.      ( )    **K37**

149. A trustor whose property is being foreclosed upon, until 5 business days before the trustee's sale has:
(1) Redemption interest      (2) Equity of redemption
(3) A security interest      (4) The right of reinstatement. ( )    **M34**

150. Broker Green's listing on a business lot was an exclusive right to sell for 90 days, and provided that he himself could buy it within the listing period for the $200,000 listed price, less 5%. Green found a buyer who would pay $250,000, so he bought the lot for $190,000, double escrowed, and made an earning of $60,000 instead of a mere $10,000. The seller was angry when he later heard about Green's profit:

(1) Green was a smart operator and deserved to make the profit

(2) Green should have told his principal he was making a profit, whether principal liked it or not.

(3) Green placed his license in jeopardy by not getting principal's written consent after disclosing amount of profit involved.

(4) The seller got the price he agreed to take and should be a "good sport" about it.                                    (   )   A79
                                                                                          #10

151. An escrow is mandatory in business opportunity transactions when:
(1) The business is a restaurant
(2) Crops are involved
(3) An alcoholic beverage license is to be transferred
(4) All of the above.                                              (   )   Z11

152. The commission rate which may be charged to the seller of residential property is:
(1) Never more than 10%
(2) Whatever the seller agrees to
(3) The 5% allowed by law
(4) The rate published by the Commissioner.                        (   )   K28

153. The fair market value of the average single family home is:
(1) Not usually greater than the lot value plus what it would cost to reproduce the house plus a developer's profit
(2) Nearly always determined by the summation process
(3) Usually arrived at by capitalizing the average monthly rental value
(4) Determined by computing the present worth of possible future earnings.                                                 W17
                                                                   (   )   W19

154. In order for a grant deed to convey good title, it must have:
(1) A verified signature of the grantor
(2) An acknowledged signature of the grantee
(3) Grantor's signature acknowledged by two witnesses
(4) A description sufficient to identify the land.                 (   )   D6

155. An alienation clause in a mortgage is also referred to as:
(1) Amortization clause          (2) Reconveyance clause
(3) Due-on-sale clause           (4) Default clause.               (   )   M48

156. Smith gave Brown a thirty day option to buy a business lot. Brown said he would not have enough cash to pay for the lot, but if he exercised the option he would pay part cash and give Smith his personal note for the balance of the purchase price. Smith agreed, and this arrangement was provided for in the option agreement. Later Brown assigned the option to Robinson for a consideration of $5,000. Robinson then tendered Smith, the optionor, the amount of cash provided by the option and his personal note for the balance. Smith refused to deliver. Robinson could:

**(1)** Not force sale as the assignment of the option was without the consent of Smith, who had agreed to take Brown's note as part of the purchase price

**(2)** Not force the sale as options in general are not assignable

**(3)** Not force the sale as any option providing for purchase price to be paid wholly or partially by a note is not enforceable

**(4)** Force the sale as optionor had agreed to take a note as part of the purchase price.                                    ( )  **K38**

157. In arriving at the net income you would capitalize to arrive at value of an income property, you would not deduct from the potential gross income which one of the following:

**(1)** Janitor services

**(2)** Loss of rent due to vacancies

**(3)** Manager's salary

**(4)** Interest on encumbrances.                              ( )  **W36**

158. An experienced income property investor usually arrives at a fair price by:

**(1)** Taking seller's price and deducting about 10%

**(2)** Computing present worth of future earnings

**(3)** Capitalizing the present gross income

**(4)** Computing reproduction cost less an amount for          **W31**
physical deterioration.                                  ( )  **W33**

159. Mr. and Mrs. Smith had nothing of value when they married, but after marriage invested in real estate, taking title as tenants in common. Mr. Smith died leaving a will in which he named his brother as sole beneficiary. The brother would receive:

**(1)** Half of the real estate as Mrs. Smith is entitled to one-half of the property if husband wills his interest to another

**(2)** All of the property as it was not held in joint tenancy

**(3)** None of the property, as it was accumulated by the joint efforts of Mr. and Mrs. Smith

**(4)** One-fourth of the property, as Mrs. Smith by law would get her one-half plus half of her husband's share.              ( )  **C3**

160. Loss of value to an income property known as external obsolescence may be caused by:

**(1)** A rapidly deteriorating neighborhood

**(2)** Plumbing fixtures becoming obsolete

**(3)** Building becoming old-fashioned

**(4)** Failure to paint building regularly.                     ( )  **W28**

161. A partial release clause in a trust deed is often used in connection with:

**(1)** Apartment houses

**(2)** Subdivisions

**(3)** Properties subject to condemnation

**(4)** Properties with multiple leases.                        ( )  **M41**

162. California law requires that a real estate licensee must disclose to a prospective purchaser of 1 to 4 residential units all facts materially affecting the value or desirability of a property an investigation would reveal. This law includes which of the following:
    (1) A reasonably competent and diligent visual inspection of the property by the agent
    (2) A two year statute of limitations
    (3) Buyer must exercise reasonable care to protect himself
    (4) All of the above.                ( )    I14

163. Home was owned clear of liens by Smith. He sold to Jones taking a first trust deed as part of selling price. Later Jones sold to White who assumed and agreed to pay the trust deed note. White defaulted and Smith foreclosed, but at the sale the successful bidder bought the home for $2,000 less than the balance owed on the trust deed. Smith sued both Jones and White to secure deficiency judgment. He could secure judgment against:
    (1) Jones, as he was the original buyer
    (2) White, as he assumed and agreed to pay the note
    (3) Both Jones and White, due to joint responsibility
    (4) Neither Jones nor White, as the trust deed was a purchase money trust deed.           ( )   M37

164. The California Department of Veterans Affairs will not purchase a farm or home and sell to the veteran on contract if:
    (1) The veteran was born in California but drafted in another state
    (2) The veteran was born and entered military service in another state, but has since resided in California for over 5 years
    (3) He was born in another state but volunteered for service in California
    (4) He was born in Alaska but drafted when living in California.          ( )   Q35

165. You list an old home on a corner in an older residential area. The home has an addition on the front which has been used as a small neighborhood grocery store, but which has been vacant for some time. Your prospect wants to re-establish the grocery business, and wants to know if there is anything to prohibit it.
    (1) You can assure him it is permitted as it has been used as a grocery store
    (2) It is permissible as there is a similar store two blocks away
    (3) You should check with the zoning authorities as the business may have been a holdover when area was re-zoned
    (4) You can assure buyer it is o.k. as the seller would know if a business could not be started.          ( )    U7

166. One morning at breakfast the family saw a telephone pole being placed on the rear of their yard. Upon calling the telephone company, they were informed that the original subdivider had recorded an easement for their benefit along the rear of all lots. On checking the deed, father found no reference to the telephone company, but it recited "Subject to easements and rights of way of record." The easement was:
    (1) Ineffective as it was over 10 years old
    (2) Valid because the area needed telephones
    (3) Invalid because the deed did not specifically mention it
    (4) Valid because an easement of record is sufficient notice to purchasers.                                  E2
                                                              (  )  B14

167. Broker sold property for client who signed purchase and sale contract. He then learned that client had previously been declared incompetent by the Courts. The sales agreement was:
    (1) Enforceable because broker and buyer were not informed
    (2) Voidable because broker did not inquire as to seller's mental health
    (3) Enforceable because sales price was adequate
    (4) Void because incompetents cannot contract.         (  )  D29

168. An ALTA title insurance policy does not insure against:
    (1) Mechanics' liens not of record
    (2) Unrecorded easements
    (3) Errors in survey                                        F7
    (4) Default by a trustor.                               (  )  F9

169. The second installment of county taxes becomes due and payable on February 1 of each year. A penalty attaches if not paid:
    (1) By noon on April 5
    (2) By 5 PM on April 10
    (3) By midnight of April 5
    (4) By 5 PM on first Monday in March.                  (  )  Y18

170. With respect to an official planning commission, the State law requires one to be appointed by:
    (1) Every incorporated city only
    (2) Each county only
    (3) Only those counties with population over 200,000
    (4) Each city and county.                              (  )  U15

171. One of the following statements is in error. A subdivider who sells on a conditional land contract is required by law to:
    (1) Give a policy of title insurance
    (2) Disclose all existing liens
    (3) Give a good legal description in the contract
    (4) Apply buyer's payments to any delinquent payments       M56
        on existing liens.                                 (  )  M57

172. After selling on conditional sales contract, a builder discovered that buyer was having the home painted another color. In order to protect himself against possible liens, the builder could:
(1) Warn the painters he would not be responsible
(2) File a lis pendens
(3) File notice of completion
(4) Post notice of non-responsibility and record it.                ( )   L21

173. The loan regulations in the Real Estate Law do not regulate the amount of the broker's commission if a first loan is negotiated which
(1) Exceeds $30,000            (2) Is less than $8,000
(3) Exceeds $5,00             (4) Is less than $5,000.        ( )   P8

174. The amount of the transfer tax to be entered on a grant deed, at the rate of 55 cents for each $500 or fraction thereof, is always determined by:
(1) The total selling price
(2) The cash payment made by the buyer
(3) The value of the seller's equity conveyed
(4) The cash payment and amount of any new financing secured by the property.                ( )   Y33

175. One of the following is not controlled by zoning regulations:
(1) Type of building          (2) Deed covenants
(3) Property use              (4) Height limits.           ( )   U6

176. When property is acquired by right of eminent domain, a political subdivision must pay the owner just compensation which is the same as:
(1) Book value
(2) Fair market value
(3) Assessed value
(4) Last sale price as shown by revenue stamps on the deed. ( )   C28

177. One of the following encumbrances affects the physical use of property:
(1) An easement              (2) A trust deed
(3) A money judgment         (4) Delinquent taxes.        ( )   B15

178. There are implied warranties by the grantor in a grant deed. One of the following is not among them:
(1) Property has not been encumbered by grantor except as disclosed
(2) The interest being conveyed has not previously been conveyed to others
(3) That the price paid is fair market value
(4) None of the above.                ( )   D12

179. The term used when the termination of a contract provides for putting the parties in their original position is:
(1) Cancellation             (2) Rescission
(3) Abrogation               (4) Surrender.              ( )   J13

180. When a trust deed foreclosure is started, the trustor may make up the back delinquent payments with penalties and costs, up to a certain point when the advertising starts. After that he must pay off the entire loan to save his property. The time given to him to make up payments after start of foreclosure proceedings is:
    (1) 10 days
    (2) 30 days
    (3) 90 days
    (4) Up to 5 business days before the sale.  (  )  M34

181. When a broker estimates the value of an apartment house to be eight times the scheduled annual income, before deducting any expenses, he is using what is called in the business a:
    (1) Gross rent multiplier     (2) Net factor
    (3) Coordinate factor         (4) Adjusted divisor.  (  )  W40

182. Authority of a corporation to enter into real estate agreements lies with the:
    (1) Board of directors
    (2) Corporation attorney
    (3) President and secretary
    (4) Duly appointed general manager.  (  )  C22

183. Which one of the following is true for both joint tenancy and community property interests:
    (1) Ownership interests are always equal
    (2) Title may be held in one name only, the husband or wife
    (3) The interest may be willed to others
    (4) None of the above (There can be a large variety of questions on holding title - carefully review the paragraphs covering this subject. Understand the characteristics of the different ways of holding title.)
    (  )  C5
    through  C17

184. Mr. and Mrs. Jones bought some land with savings which they had accumulated during their married life. As Mr. Jones was older and in poor health, they decided to put title in her name alone, and the deed was prepared accordingly. In such a case the presumption at law would be that the property was:
    (1) Her separate property
    (2) Community property
    (3) Joint tenancy property
    (4) Property held as tenants in common.  (  )  C11

185. A licensed real estate broker negotiated a second trust deed loan of $4,500 for a loan period of two years and 9 months, and charged the maximum commission allowed by the Loan Broker Law. His commission was:
    (1) $900     (2) $675     (3) $225     (4) $450.  (  )  P13

186. A "security device" is a means of making property available to assure the payment of a debt. Therefore, one of the following is not such an instrument:
(1) Conditional sales contract  (2) Deed given to protect a loan    **D30**
(3) A second deed of trust      (4) A deed covenant.         (  )  **M47**

187. Owner sold a vacant lot on land contract, $5,000 down and balance on monthly terms including interest until paid. Needing more money, he sold the contract itself. The law required him to:
(1) Record the contract
(2) Convey title to the lot to the contract buyer
(3) Give a policy of title insurance
(4) Pay off all existing assessments.            (  )  **M58**

188. You buy a home which is financed by an FHA first loan. The impound account to take care of insurance premiums and taxes as they become due amounts to $250. Any balance in this account at the close of escrow should be credited to:
(1) The lender            (2) Apply it on reduction of the loan
(3) The buyer             (4) The seller.             (  )  **G15**

189. The holder of an easement in gross is most likely to be:
(1) A homeowner
(2) An electric utility company
(3) A farmer
(4) A lumber company.                     (  )  **B18**

190. The servient tenement is:
(1) Land benefitted by an easement
(2) A type of apartment building
(3) Land subject to an easement
(4) None of the above.                     (  )  **B17**

191. A declaration of homestead always terminates when declarant:
(1) Moves from the premises  (2) Leaves his wife
(3) Rents the place          (4) Sells the place.        (  )  **T14**

192. An option is seldom enforceable if:
(1) No value consideration is given for it
(2) A note is given as the consideration
(3) If it is assigned to another
(4) If given to an alien.                   (  )  **K37**

193. To commingle a client's money or property means to:
(1) Impound it
(2) Confuse it with that of others
(3) Guarantee its safety
(4) Repay in installments.                  (  )  **A87**

194. Under no circumstances can a person make a valid declaration of homestead if:
(1) The declared homestead is not the person's principal dwelling place
(2) Is unmarried
(3) Has it mortgaged
(4) Has no wife or children.　　　　　　　　　( )　T4

195. A fiduciary relationship usually exists between:
(1) Buyer and seller　　　　　(2) Lessor and lessee
(3) Agent and principal　　　　(4) Optionor and optionee.　( )　I 2

196. The instrument which must be verified instead of acknowledged for recordation is:
(1) A mechanic's lien　　　　(2) A general lien
(3) A quitclaim deed　　　　　(4) A long term lease.　　( )　E17

197. When a trust deed is satisfied (paid) the trustee prepares a:
(1) Satisfaction of mortgage
(2) Conditional release form
(3) Reconveyance deed
(4) Quitclaim deed.　　　　　　　　　　( )　M28

198. The type of "value" expressed in dollars which most nearly indicates the highest price an owner may expect to receive if he offers the property for sale is:
(1) Loan value　　　　　　　(2) Insurance value
(3) Market value　　　　　　　(4) Book value.　　　　( )　W7

199. Green, a real estate broker, sells trust deed notes. He agrees to buy back said trust deeds from investors in case of default. Which of the following is correct:
(1) Green must be endorsed as a Real Property Securities Dealer
(2) Green must have a Security Licence from the Corporations Commissioner
(3) Green must have a Loan Broker endorsement on his license to negotiate loans　　　　　　　　　　　　A51
(4) None of the above.　　　　　　　　　　( )　A52

200. Under the Uniform Commercial Code - Division 9, which form is used in filing notice of a security agreement with the Secretary of State:
(1) Notice of Security Agreement
(2) Constructive Notice
(3) Financing Statement
(4) Notice of Lien.　　　　　　　　　　( )　Z24

# MULTIPLE CHOICE ANSWERS

| | | | | |
|---|---|---|---|---|
| 1. (4) | 41. (2) | 81. (3) | 121. (2) | 161. (2) |
| 2. (1) | 42. (3) | 82. (1) | 122. (2) | 162. (4) |
| 3. (3) | 43. (2) | 83. (1) | 123. (4) | 163. (4) |
| 4. (2) | 44. (4) | 84. (1) | 124. (2) | 164. (2) |
| 5. (3) | 45. (4) | 85. (2) | 125. (1) | 165. (3) |
| 6. (2) | 46. (3) | 86. (2) | 126. (1) | 166. (4) |
| 7. (3) | 47. (4) | 87. (2) | 127. (1) | 167. (4) |
| 8. (1) | 48. (3) | 88. (1) | 128. (3) | 168. (4) |
| 9. (4) | 49. (3) | 89. (4) | 129. (3) | 169. (2) |
| 10. (2) | 50. (1) | 90. (4) | 130. (4) | 170. (4) |
| 11. (2) | 51. (4) | 91. (2) | 131. (2) | 171. (1) |
| 12. (2) | 52. (4) | 92. (4) | 132. (2) | 172. (4) |
| 13. (1) | 53. (4) | 93. (3) | 133. (4) | 173. (1) |
| 14. (3) | 54. (2) | 94. (4) | 134. (2) | 174. (4) |
| 15. (3) | 55. (2) | 95. (4) | 135. (1) | 175. (2) |
| 16. (3) | 56. (4) | 96. (4) | 136. (1) | 176. (2) |
| 17. (2) | 57. (4) | 97. (1) | 137. (2) | 177. (1) |
| 18. (2) | 58. (3) | 98. (3) | 138. (4) | 178. (3) |
| 19. (4) | 59. (1) | 99. (4) | 139. (3) | 179. (2) |
| 20. (3) | 60. (3) | 100. (3) | 140. (2) | 180. (4) |
| 21. (2) | 61. (4) | 101. (3) | 141. (1) | 181. (1) |
| 22. (4) | 62. (1) | 102. (4) | 142. (4) | 182. (1) |
| 23. (2) | 63. (4) | 103. (1) | 143. (3) | 183. (1) |
| 24. (4) | 64. (3) | 104. (2) | 144. (4) | 184. (2) |
| 25. (1) | 65. (2) | 105. (1) | 145. (2) | 185. (4) |
| 26. (2) | 66. (1) | 106. (4) | 146. (3) | 186. (4) |
| 27. (2) | 67. (4) | 107. (4) | 147. (2) | 187. (2) |
| 28. (2) | 68. (1) | 108. (2) | 148. (1) | 188. (4) |
| 29. (3) | 69. (3) | 109. (1) | 149. (4) | 189. (2) |
| 30. (1) | 70. (1) | 110. (4) | 150. (3) | 190. (3) |
| 31. (2) | 71. (4) | 111. (3) | 151. (3) | 191. (4) |
| 32. (2) | 72. (1) | 112. (4) | 152. (2) | 192. (1) |
| 33. (4) | 73. (2) | 113. (3) | 153. (1) | 193. (2) |
| 34. (4) | 74. (1) | 114. (3) | 154. (4) | 194. (1) |
| 35. (2) | 75. (4) | 115. (4) | 155. (3) | 195. (3) |
| 36. (3) | 76. (4) | 116. (1) | 156. (1) | 196. (1) |
| 37. (2) | 77. (4) | 117. (4) | 157. (4) | 197. (3) |
| 38. (1) | 78. (1) | 118. (2) | 158. (2) | 198. (3) |
| 39. (2) | 79. (4) | 119. (1) | 159. (1) | 199. (1) |
| 40. (3) | 80. (2) | 120. (2) | 160. (1) | 200. (3) |

# Notes

# SAMPLE EXAM - LISTING PROBLEM

## EXCLUSIVE AGENCY AUTHORIZATION AND RIGHT TO SELL
### THIS IS INTENDED TO BE A LEGALLY BINDING AGREEMENT— READ IT CAREFULLY.
### CALIFORNIA ASSOCIATION OF REALTORS® STANDARD FORM

1. **RIGHT TO SELL.** I hereby employ and grant __John M. Green__ hereinafter called "Agent," the exclusive and irrevocable Agency right commencing on __November 17__, 19 86 , and expiring at midnight on __February 15__, 19 87 , to sell or exchange the real property situated in __the City of Walnut__ . County of __Pacific__ , California described as follows: __3202 Maple Street, being Lots 19, 20 & 21, Block A, Rancho Annex Tract as per Map recorded in Book 616 of Maps of official records of Pacific County.__

2. **TERMS OF SALE.** The purchase price shall be $ __105,000__ , to be paid on the following terms: __All cash to seller.__

    (a) The following items of personal property are to be included in the above-stated price: __Washer and dryer.__

    (b) Agent is hereby authorized to accept and hold on my behalf a deposit upon the purchase price.

    (c) Evidence of title to the property shall be in the form of a California Land Title Association Standard Coverage Policy of Title Insurance in the amount of the selling price to be paid for by __Seller__ .

    (d) I warrant that I am the owner of the property or have the authority to execute this agreement. I hereby authorize a FOR SALE sign to be placed on my property by Agent. I authorize the Agent named herein to cooperate with sub-agents.

3. **Notice: The amount or rate of real estate commissions is not fixed by law. They are set by each broker individually and may be negotiable between the seller and broker.**

COMPENSATION TO AGENT. I hereby agree to compensate Agent as follows:

    (a) $ __6,300__ or __6__ % of the selling price if the property is sold during the term hereof, or any extension thereof, by Agent, on the terms herein set forth or any other price and terms I may accept, or through any other agent. $ __6,300__ or __6__ % of the price shown in 2, if said property is withdrawn from sale, without the consent of Agent, or made unmarketable by my voluntary act during the term hereof or any extension thereof.

    (b) The compensation provided for in subparagraph (a) above if property is sold, conveyed or otherwise transferred within _____ days after the termination of this authority or any extension thereof to anyone with whom Agent has had negotiations prior to final termination, provided I have received notice in writing, including the names of the prospective purchasers, before or upon termination of this agreement or any extension thereof. However, I shall not be obligated to pay the compensation provided for in subparagraph (a) if a valid listing agreement is entered into during the term of said protection period with another licensed real estate broker and a sale, lease or exchange of the property is made during the term of said valid listing agreement.

    (c) It is expressly understood that this is an Exclusive Agency listing and except as to a sale to any prospective purchaser who has initially been introduced to or shown the property and been informed of the price by Agent, during the above term or any extension hereof, I reserve the right to sell the property to any purchaser without any obligation for commission to Agent except as above provided.

    (d) I agree to notify Agent in writing within 24 hours of my acceptance of any offer of sale, lease or exchange including identity of parties, price and terms.

4. I agree not to offer the property for sale or exchange at a lower price than stated above.

5. In any action or proceeding to enforce this agreement, the prevailing party shall receive reasonable attorney's fee and costs.

6. In the event of an exchange, permission is hereby given Agent to represent all parties and collect compensation or commissions from them, provided there is full disclosure to all principals of such agency. Agent is authorized to divide with other agents such compensation or commissions in any manner acceptable to them.

7. I agree to save and hold agent harmless from all claims, disputes, litigation, and/or judgments arising from any incorrect information supplied by me or from any material fact known to me concerning the property which I fail to disclose.

8. This property is offered in compliance with state and federal anti-discrimination laws.

9. Other provisions: _____

10. I acknowledge that I have read and understand this Agreement, and that I have received a copy hereof.

Dated __November 17__, 19 86      __Walnut__ , California

Owner __Richard M. Brown__      Owner __Mary L. Brown__

Address __212 Fir Street__      City-State-Phone __Nectarine, California 687-2655__

11. In consideration of the above, Agent agrees to use diligence in procuring a purchaser.

Agent __John M. Green__      Address-City __1000 Main Street, Walnut, CA__

By __John M. Green__      Phone __555-6250__ Date __11/17/86__

NO REPRESENTATION IS MADE AS TO THE LEGAL VALIDITY OF ANY PROVISION OR THE ADEQUACY OF ANY PROVISION IN ANY SPECIFIC TRANSACTION. IF YOU DESIRE LEGAL ADVICE, CONSULT YOUR ATTORNEY

To order, contact—California Association of Realtors®
525 S. Virgil Ave., Los Angeles, California 90020
Copyright © 1983, California Association of Realtors®     FORM EA-11

Reprinted by permission, California Association of Realtors®. Endorsement not implied.

## SAMPLE EXAM - LISTING FORM QUESTIONS

1. If on February 17, 1987, Broker Green presents the Browns with an offer on a deposit receipt form signed by the buyers, the offer being in accordance with the terms of the listing, has he earned a commission?

2. If, in consideration of the listing terms, the Browns (sellers) decide to take a trip around the world for six months, and notify Broker Green that they do not wish to sell until they return, is Green entitled to a commission?

3. A listing may merely authorize the agent to find a buyer who will meet the terms of the listing. Can Broker Green accept a deposit from a prospective buyer in working under the listing contract he has used for the Brown property?

4. If this listing on community property had been signed by Mr. Brown only, was it a good authorization to sell?

5. What could happen to Broker Green if he had taken this listing for a term "until sold"?

6. If Broker Green had forgotten to give Mr. Brown a copy of the exclusive listing when he signed it, what was Green's position?

## ANSWERS TO LISTING FORM QUESTIONS

1. No. The listing had expired. The seller may sign the offer form, however, if he is still interested in selling.

2. Yes. See No. 3 of listing form.

3. Yes. See K3 and No. 2(b) of listing form.

4. No. See C16.

5. His license could be suspended or revoked. See A79, #6.

6. His license could be suspended or revoked. See A79, #8.

# SAMPLE EXAM - DEPOSIT RECEIPT PROBLEM

**REAL ESTATE PURCHASE CONTRACT AND RECEIPT FOR DEPOSIT**
THIS IS MORE THAN A RECEIPT FOR MONEY. IT IS INTENDED TO BE A LEGALLY BINDING CONTRACT. READ IT CAREFULLY.
CALIFORNIA ASSOCIATION OF REALTORS® STANDARD FORM

___Brawley___, California. ___October 1___, 19 86

Received from ___George M. and Alice B. Roberts___
herein called Buyer, the sum of ___One Thousand Dollars & no/100___ Dollars $ 1,000
evidenced by cash ☐, cashier's check ☐, or _____☐, personal check ☒ payable to ___William Archer Company___, to be held uncashed until acceptance of this offer, as deposit on account of purchase price of
___One Hundred Thousand Dollars and no/100___ Dollars $ 100,000
for the purchase of property, situated in ___City of Brawley___, County of ___Imperial___, California
described as follows: ___1820 Melon Ct., Brawley, California___

1. Buyer will deposit in escrow with ___Bank of Atlas___ the balance of purchase price as follows:

A. Buyer to deposit an additional Ten Thousand Dollars ($10,000) cash in escrow within fifteen days of acceptance hereof. Buyer to take property subject to existing First Trust Deed and Note of approximately Thirty Thousand Five Hundred Dollars ($30,500) payable $149.93 per month including 9% interest, balance all due and payable March 1, 1998. Buyer to execute Second Trust Deed and Note for the balance of the purchase price, payable $500.00 per month plus 12% interest running until paid.

B. Legal Description: Lot 12, Block B, Burns Tract, as per map recorded February 6, 1938 in Book 61, Page 48, Official Map records of Imperial County.

Set forth above any terms and conditions of a factual nature applicable to this sale, such as financing, prior sale of other property, the matter of structural pest control inspection, repairs and personal property to be included in the sale.

2. Deposit will ☒ will not ☐ be increased by $ 10,000 to $ 11,000 within ___15___ days of acceptance of this offer.

3. Buyer does ☒ does not ☐ intend to occupy subject property as his residence.

4. The following supplements are incorporated as part of this agreement:

Other

☒ Structural Pest Control Certification Agreement    ☐ Occupancy Agreement    ☐ _____
☐ Special Studies Zone Disclosure    ☐ VA Amendment    ☐ _____
☐ Flood Insurance Disclosure    ☐ FHA Amendment    ☐ _____

5. Buyer and Seller shall deliver signed instructions to the escrow holder within ___5___ days from Seller's acceptance which shall provide for closing within ___30___ days from Seller's acceptance. Escrow fees to be paid as follows:

Buyer and seller agree to split escrow fee 50/50

6. Buyer and Seller acknowledge receipt of a copy of this page, which constitutes Page 1 of ___ Pages.

Buyer (signed) George M. Roberts    Seller (signed) John Seller

Buyer (signed) Alice B. Roberts    Seller (signed) Jane Seller

A REAL ESTATE BROKER IS THE PERSON QUALIFIED TO ADVISE ON REAL ESTATE. IF YOU DESIRE LEGAL ADVICE CONSULT YOUR ATTORNEY.

THIS STANDARDIZED DOCUMENT FOR USE IN SIMPLE TRANSACTIONS HAS BEEN APPROVED BY THE CALIFORNIA ASSOCIATION OF REALTORS® IN FORM ONLY. NO REPRESENTATION IS MADE AS TO THE APPROVAL OF THE FORM OF SUPPLEMENTS, THE LEGAL VALIDITY OF ANY PROVISION, OR THE ADEQUACY OF ANY PROVISION IN ANY SPECIFIC TRANSACTION. IT SHOULD NOT BE USED IN COMPLEX TRANSACTIONS OR WITH EXTENSIVE RIDERS OR ADDITIONS.

To order, contact—California Association of Realtors®
525 S. Virgil Ave., Los Angeles, California 90020
Copyright © California Association of Realtors® (Revised 1978), 1984)    FORM D-11-1

BROKER'S COPY

(Reverse side of form on next page.)

# DEPOSIT RECEIPT CONTINUED

**REAL ESTATE PURCHASE CONTRACT AND RECEIPT FOR DEPOSIT**

The following terms and conditions are hereby incorporated in and made a part of Buyers Offer

7.    Title is to be free of liens, encumbrances, easements, restrictions, rights and conditions of record or known to Seller, other than the following: (1) Current property taxes, (2) covenants, conditions, restrictions, and public utility easements of record, if any, provided the same do not adversely affect the continued use of the property for the purposes for which it is presently being used, unless reasonably disapproved by Buyer in writing within _____5_____ days of receipt of a current preliminary title report furnished at _sellers'_ expense, and

(3) _____ .

Seller shall furnish Buyer at ___sellers'___ expense a standard California Land Title Association policy issued by Ticor Title Ins. Company, showing title vested in Buyer subject only to the above. If Seller (1) is unwilling or unable to eliminate any title matter disapproved by Buyer as above, Seller may terminate this agreement, or (2) fails to deliver title as above, Buyer may terminate this agreement; in either case, the deposit shall be returned to Buyer.

8.    Property taxes, premiums on insurance acceptable to Buyer, rents, interest, and _____

shall be pro-rated as of (a) the date of recordation of deed; or (b)_____. Any bond or assessment which is a lien shall be __paid__ by _seller.    Seller_ shall pay cost of transfer taxes, if any.

9.    Possession shall be delivered to Buyer (a) on close of escrow, or (b) not later than_____days after close of escrow or (c)_____.

10.    Unless otherwise designated in the escrow instructions of Buyer, title shall vest as follows: _George M. and Alice B. Roberts,husband & wife,as community property_

(The manner of taking title may have significant legal and tax consequences. Therefore, give this matter serious consideration.)

11.    If Broker is a participant of a Board multiple listing service ("MLS"), the Broker is authorized to report the sale, its price, terms, and financing for the information, publication, dissemination, and use of the authorized Board members.

12.    **If Buyer fails to complete said purchase as herein provided by reason of any default of Buyer, Seller shall be released from his obligation to sell the property to Buyer and may proceed against Buyer upon any claim or remedy which he may have in law or equity; provided, however, that by placing their initials here Buyer:** _GMR AR_ **Seller: (** _JS J.S._ **) agree that Seller shall retain the deposit as his liquidated damages. If the described property is a dwelling with no more than four units, one of which the Buyer intends to occupy as his residence, Seller shall retain as liquidated damages the deposit actually paid, or an amount therefrom, not more than 3% of the purchase price and promptly return any excess to Buyer.**

13.    If the only controversy or claim between the parties arises out of or relates to the disposition of the Buyer's deposit, such controversy or claim shall at the election of the parties be decided by arbitration. Such arbitration shall be determined in accordance with the Rules of the American Arbitration Association, and judgment upon the award rendered by the Arbitrator(s) may be entered in any court having jurisdiction thereof. The provisions of Code of Civil Procedure Section 1283.05 shall be applicable to such arbitration.

14.    In any action or proceeding arising out of this agreement, the prevailing party shall be entitled to reasonable attorney's fees and costs.

15.    Time is of the essence. All modification or extensions shall be in writing signed by the parties.

16.    This constitutes an offer to purchase the described property. Unless acceptance is signed by Seller and the signed copy delivered to Buyer, in person or by mail to the address below, within ___3___ days, this offer shall be deemed revoked and the deposit shall be returned. Buyer acknowledges receipt of a copy hereof.

Real Estate Broker _William Archer Co._    Buyer _(signed) George M. Roberts_

By _(signed)  William Archer_    Buyer _(signed) Alice B. Roberts_

Address _100 Main St.,Brawley,CA_    Address _107 Manhat St.,Los Angeles_

Telephone _(619) 627-9862_    Telephone _(213) 682-1276_

**ACCEPTANCE**

The undersigned Seller accepts and agrees to sell the property on the above terms and conditions. Seller has employed _William Archer Company_

as Broker(s) and agrees to pay for services the sum of _Six Thousand_ Dollars

($ _6,000.00_ ), payable as follows: (a) On recordation of the deed or other evidence of title, or (b) if completion of sale is prevented by default of Seller, upon Seller's default or (c) if completion of sale is prevented by default of Buyer, only if and when Seller collects damages from Buyer, by suit or otherwise and then in an amount not less than one-half of the damages recovered, but not to exceed the above fee, after first deducting title and escrow expenses and the expenses of collection, if any. In any action between Broker and Seller arising out of this agreement, the prevailing party shall be entitled to reasonable attorney's fees and costs. The undersigned acknowledges receipt of a copy and authorizes Broker(s) to deliver a signed copy to Buyer.

Dated _10/1/86_ Telephone _627-9552_ Seller _(signed) John Seller_

Address _1820 Melon Street,Brawley_ Seller _(signed) Jane Seller_

Broker(s) agree to the foregoing. Broker _William Archer Co._ Broker _____

Dated _10/1/86_ By _William Archer_ Dated _____ By _____

To order, contact—California Association of Realtors®
525 S. Virgil Ave., Los Angeles, California 90020
Copyright © California Association of Realtors® (Revised 1984)    FORM D-11-2

Page _2_ of _2_ Pages

**BROKER'S COPY**

Reprinted by permission, California Association of Realtors ®
Endorsement not implied.

## SAMPLE EXAM - DEPOSIT RECEIPT QUESTIONS

Answer the following questions based on the completed and signed Deposit Receipt just preceding. Write YES or NO in the answer space or give the figure called for. Do not refer to the answers which follow until you test your knowledge.

1.  Do you find anything in the Deposit Receipt that might cause the broker to be disciplined by the Commissioner? _____

2.  If it developed that the first trust deed balance was only $20,000 instead of $30,500, would buyer have good grounds in a suit to rescind the contract and recover his deposit? _____

3.  On November 1, 1986, the seller demanded the deposit be forfeited, as the specified 30 days were up and the Roberts had not complied. However, the broker extended the time for one month. Was the broker acting within his rights? _____

4.  Broker Archer put the $1,000 cash deposit in his safe. After three weeks it was robbed and he was unable to produce it when it was called for to complete the escrow. The Commissioner revoked his license. Did he have good grounds? _____

5.  What was the amount of the note signed by the buyers which was secured by the second trust deed? _____

6.  Let's assume buyer and seller mutually agreed to drop the deal (rescind it), and that sellers ordered the broker to return the $1,000 deposit to the buyers. The broker kept half the deposit which he considered forfeited and paid buyers the balance. Did he act properly? _____

7.  If the holders of the 2nd trust deed had to foreclose and failed to recover the unpaid amount of the note, do you believe they could secure a deficiency judgment against the Roberts? _____

8.  The Roberts insisted upon a subordination clause in the 2nd trust deed. Do you think they acted wisely? _____

9.  Would the 2nd trust deed note pay off before the final payment is due on the 1st trust deed? _____

10. If Alice Roberts were to take title in her name alone, would the property be presumed to be separate property. _____

11. If George and Alice Roberts had been brother and sister instead of husband and wife, would that fact prohibit them from taking title as joint tenants? _____

12. Taxes on the property were $530 for the year 1986 - 1987, and were unpaid. How much do the sellers owe the Roberts if the deed is delivered on November 1, 1986. _____

13. A fire insurance premium of $720 was paid for a three year policy on the property by the sellers on November 1, 1984, the date the policy became effective. What part of this must the Roberts pay the sellers if their deed is delivered November 1, 1986? _____

14. Two months after close of escrow, the sellers learned for the first time that the buyers were the mother and step-father of Archer, and that an escrow for resale of the property at a price of $110,000 had been opened before their escrow was closed. If they complained to the Commissioner, is it likely that Archer might lose his license? _____

15. Let's assume that before Archer had secured the signature of the sellers to this deposit receipt, the Roberts had served him with a notice of withdrawing the offer, and demanding return of their deposit. Could Archer properly insist on holding their deposit until he could contact the sellers and get their acceptance? _____

16. If Mr. and Mrs. Roberts were to join with some relatives in taking title, would that be known as ownership in severalty? _____

## ANSWERS TO DEPOSIT RECEIPT QUESTIONS

1. No. On its face the form seems to be in good order. No doubt other provisions could be inserted to avoid future misunderstandings.

2. Yes. This would be a change in terms and conditions and might be unfavorable to the buyers. In this case it would mean a larger 2nd trust deed note, probably with less desirable terms.

3. No. The contract does not provide for the broker to extend the time to take care of such a condition. See No. 16 of the Deposit Receipt.

4. Yes. One of the Commissioner's rules requires a broker to immediately place deposit money in a trust account or in a neutral escrow.     **A87**

5. $58,500.

6. No. Deposit money usually belongs to either buyer or seller during the course of the transaction. Broker should comply with the order and then demand commission of the seller if he thinks he has earned it. If seller refuses to pay, then broker may consult his attorney for advice on bringing action to recover.

7. No. No deficiency judgment can be secured when purchase money trust deed is foreclosed.     **M37**

8. Yes. If they should desire to refinance the first trust deed later on, this would simplify it.     **M39 & M40**

9. Yes. Any unpaid balance on the 1st trust deed must be paid in full on March 1, 1998. The second trust deed would normally be paid off about August 1, 1996. 117 monthly payments must be made at $500 per month on the principal. This assumes that the note would call for first payment to be made December 1, 1986.

10. No. Read paragraphs **C11 & C12**.

11. No. See paragraph **C5 & C6**.

12. $176.67. The tax year started July 1, 1986. Sellers owned the property for 4 months or one third of the tax year, therefore should pay one third of the $530.     **Y12**

13. $240.00. One third of the term is still unexpired, therefore buyers should pay one third of the premium.

14. Yes. Archer owed his principals (the sellers) full disclosure, and should reveal if any employee or relative is the buyer. In this case, it looks as if Archer connived to make a secret profit by using relatives as "dummies."

15. No. An offer may be withdrawn any time before it is accepted, and the buyer is legally notified of the acceptance.     **K25**

16. No. Severalty means ownership by an individual.     **C2**

# SAMPLE EXAM - CLOSING STATEMENT PROBLEM

Here are the figures on a typical transaction. With this information, answer the five questions below.

**Date of Sale:** July 1, 1986. Use this date for prorations.

**Price:** $100,000. Cash $40,000, balance by loan assumed by buyer.

**Financing:** $60,000 first trust deed straight note loan. Interest payable annually at 10% paid to April 1, 1986.

**Commission:** Seller to pay 6% of sales price.

**Insurance:** Value of house is $80,000. Insured for 80% of value. Three-year fire insurance rate is 62 cents per $100 valuation. Policy is dated July 1, 1984. Premium is paid in full.

**Taxes:** Tax rate is 1.10%. Assessed value was $100,000 for the seller and remained the same for the buyer. 1985-86 tax had been paid by seller.

**Other expense to seller:** $800 paid through escrow, including transfer tax, title insurance, etc.

## SAMPLE EXAM - CLOSING STATEMENT QUESTIONS

(Check either buyer or seller as indicated, and insert answer in dollars)

1. What amount of interest was due on date of sale?
   Charged to:   Buyer ( )   Seller ( )         $

2. Credit on proration of taxes.
   Charged to:   Buyer ( )   Seller ( )         $

3. What credit is due on insurance proration?
   Charged to:   Buyer ( )   Seller ( )         $

4. What net amount of cash did seller get from escrow?
   (Refer to G15)                              $

5. What amount of transfer tax was required on deed? Remember trust deed was assumed. Transfer tax is 55 cents for each $500 or fraction thereof, applied on seller's equity. (See Y33)         $

## ANSWERS TO CLOSING STATEMENT QUESTIONS

1.  Three months interest, or $1,500 was accrued on July 1, 1986. It was the responsibility of the seller, so was charged to him.

2.  Taxes had been paid to July 1, 1986 by the seller. No proration required.

3.  The insurance was paid one year in advance of the date of the date of sale. The seller was to be credited $132.27.

4.  The seller gets the buyer's $40,000 cash plus $132.27 he paid in advance on the insurance, minus the $6,000 commission, $1,500 interest due and $800 other expense. He nets $31,832.27.

5.  $44.00 (See Y33)

# SAMPLE EXAM - LAND PROBLEM

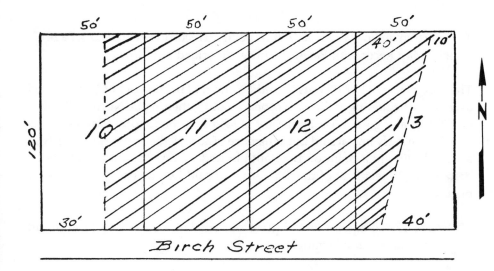

Plat of Lots 10, 11, 12, and 13, in Block B, Tract 3750, as per Map recorded in Book 173, Page 67, Official Map Records of Pacific County.

All lots in the plat are rectangular, with lot lines running due north and south, and due east and west. Sufficient dimensions are given.

## SAMPLE EXAM - LAND PROBLEM QUESTIONS

1.  Write a legal description of the shaded parcel which has been sold. Use separate sheet of paper for description.

2.  Give area of shaded parcel in square feet _____.

3.  Based on frontage of parcel on Birch Street, shaded parcel brought $500 per front foot. The sales price less 10% commission was _____?

## ANSWERS TO LAND PROBLEM QUESTIONS

1. It is the odd shaded portion of Lot 13 that causes the trouble. It requires a running description, starting at a given corner and then tracing the boundary. We started at the SW corner and traced clockwise. Other starting points on any of four corners would do. The following is a good description.

That portion of Block B, Tract 3750, as per map recorded in Book 173, Page 67, Official Map Records of Pacific County, described as follows:

The East 20 feet of Lot 10; Lots 11 and 12; and that portion of Lot 13 described as follows: beginning at the SW corner of Lot 13, thence due North a distance of 120 feet along the West boundary of said Lot, thence due East along the North boundary line of said Lot a distance of 40 feet, thence Southwesterly in a straight line to a point on the South boundary line of said Lot located a distance of 10 feet East of the SW corner of said Lot, thence to the point of beginning.

2. Area 17,400 square feet. Square out shaded area in Lot 13 and add remaining shaded triangle.

3. 130 feet on Birch Street @ $500 per front foot = $65,000 less 10% commission = $58,500.

# COMBINATION INDEX
### &
# LIST OF BRIEF DEFINITIONS
## OF REAL ESTATE TERMS AND PHRASES
### WITH PARAGRAPH REFERENCES BY KEY NUMBER

Following is a list of the more common words and phrases used in the real estate business. The definitions which follow them are very much abbreviated, so *Primer* paragraph key numbers are added for reference when available. Check the references for more detailed information.

### WORDS AND PHRASES

**Abandonment**
To release claim or forfeit rights - as in the case of a homestead.     **T14**

**Abeyance**
Pending or temporarily suspended. Such as an action held in abeyance.

**Abstract of title**
A digest or summary of documents or records affecting title to property.
**F13**

**Acceleration clause**
Provision sometimes inserted in a mortgage or trust deed note causing it to become payable at once under certain conditions - such as in event property is sold, leased, etc.     **M48**

**Acceptance**
Giving consent to an offer - as when seller signs an offer to purchase.

**Accession**
Acquiring title to unauthorized improvements to your land.     **C31**

**Accretion**
Addition to your land as by deposits from a stream or lake.     **C27**

**Acknowledgment**
A formal declaration before a notary public (or other qualified officer) in signing a document, that it is your voluntary act.     **E11**

**Acquisition**
The process by which property is procured - through purchase, inheritance, gift, foreclosure, etc.

**Acre**
An area of land containing 43,560 square feet.     **X23**

**Action to quiet title**
A lawsuit to determine status of a title. Often to remove a "cloud" on the title.

**Actual Notice**
Notice given by open possession and occupancy of property.     **E2**

**Administrator**

One appointed by a court to handle details of an estate of a deceased person. **C26**

**Adult**

A person who has reached an age established by law to attain certain privileges, such as to vote, contract, etc. Those of lessor age are minors. (See minors.)

**Ad valorem**

Based upon the value - property taxes for example. **Y4**

**Adverse possession**

Openly holding possession of land under some claim of right which is opposed to the claim of another. **C32**

**Affiant**

One who makes a sworn statement, such as an affidavit.

**Affidavit**

A sworn statement in writing before an officer authorized to administer oaths. **E18**

**Agency**

Act of representing a principal in the capacity of an agent. **I 1**

**Agent**

One who is authorized to represent another person, as in a real estate transaction. **I 1**

**Agreement of sale**

A written contract whereby buyer and seller agree on terms of the sale. A "Deposit Receipt" form in common use provides for such an agreement.

**Alcohol Beverage Control (Department of)**

Licenses the manufacture, distribution and sale in California. **Z59**

**Alias**

An assumed name.

**Alien**

A resident who is a citizen of a foreign country.

**Alienate**

Act of transferring title to property. **D13**

**Alienation clause**

Provision in a mortgage or trust deed providing for full payment if the property is sold. **M48**

**Alluvion (alluvium)**

Deposit of soil on or adjoining property, as by flow of a river or stream, or by tides. **C27**

**ALTA Policy of Title Insurance**

A lender's broad type policy. **F9**

**Amortize**

Pay off debt in equal periodic installments of principal and interest; or gradual recovery of an investment. **N7**

**Annexation**

Adding land to another jurisdiction. Such as bringing a tract within the limits of a city from a county.

**Annual percentage rate**

The relative cost of credit as determined in accordance with Regulation Z of the Board of Governors of the Federal Reserve System for implementing the Federal Truth in Lending Act. **P35**

**Annuity**

Money paid annually or in other agreed periods.

**Appraisal**

An opinion as to value based upon facts and experience, by one skilled in such work. **W2**

**Appurtenance**

A thing or right which attaches or becomes incident to the land, so as to become a part of the realty. A house, fence, etc. which, when the land is conveyed, goes with it without special mention in the deed. **B14**

**Assessed value**

Value placed on property by the assessor as basis for the levy of taxes. **Y3**

**Assessments (special)**

Levies against particular properties for cost of improvements which particularly benefit them. (Sewers, sidewalks, drains, etc.) **Y35**

**Assessor**

An official, usually county or city, who determines the value of property for tax purposes. **Y3**

**Assign**

To endorse over to another, such as a promissory note, or lease. **R21**

**Assignee**

One to whom a property or a right is transferred.

**Assignor**

One who assigns a property right to another.

**Assumption of mortgage (or trust deed)**

Taking title to property and assuming personal liability for payment of existing notes for which the property is security. **M 43**

**Attachment**

Seizure of property by court order in connection with a lawsuit. **S 8**

**Attorney-in-fact**

A person to whom a power of attorney is given authorizing him to do all or specific acts for another. **I 26**

**Authorization to sell**

Commonly called a "listing." **K 1-21**

**Avulsion**

Sudden removal of land by flowing water. **C 27**

**Balloon payment**

Usually an extra large payment on an installment note at the time it is payable in full. **P 23 & P 27**

**Base and meridian**
Principal survey lines in an area from which townships are numbered. **X5**
**Bench mark**
Permanent marker placed by surveyors at an important point, upon which local surveys are based.
**Beneficiary**
One who is recipient of benefits from a trust; such as a lender of money secured by a trust deed. **M22**
**Bequeath**
To leave personal property by will. **C26**
**Bequest**
When personal property is bequeathed by will - an inheritance.
**Bilateral contract**
A contract by which both parties agree to perform certain acts. **J20**
**Bill of sale**
Signed document which transfers ownership of personal property. **Z20**
**Blanket mortgage (trust deed)**
A single lien covering two or more lots or parcels of land. **M41**
**Blighted area**
A district affected by detrimental influences of such extent or quantity that real property values have seriously declined as a result of adverse land use and/or destructive economic forces; characterized by rapidly depreciating buildings, retrogression and no recognizable prospects for improvement. However, renewal programs and changes in use may lead to resurgence of such areas.
**Blockbusting**
The practice on the part of unscrupulous speculators or real estate agents of inducing panic selling of homes at prices below market value, especially by exploiting the prejudices of property owners in neighborhoods in which the racial make-up is changing. **T30**
**Board of Equalization**
A State agency which, among other things, collects sales taxes and assesses public utility properties. **Z46**
**Bona fide**
In good faith - honest.
**Bond (Surety)**
A pledge to pay a sum of money in case of failure to fulfill obligations, inflicting damage, or mishandling funds. Usually written by a company for a fee.
**Book Value**
The value of a property as carried on the owner's accounts. **W24**
**Breach**
Failure to fulfill an obligation or perform a duty.
**Broker loan statement**
A statement of charges to be made in connection with a loan, for information of borrower. **P9**

**Building restrictions**

Laws or ordinances requiring sound construction for protection of health and safety.

**Bulk sales law**

State law requiring that the sale of a business be advertised beforehand, for protection of creditors. **Z27**

**Bundle of rights**

All of the legal rights incident to ownership of property including rights of use, possession, encumbering and disposition. **W4**

**Business opportunity**

A going business, including physical assets, good will and perhaps a property lease. **Z3**

**Cal-Vet loans**

This is the California Farm and Home Loan Purchase Plan. A plan to assist California veterans to finance a home or farm. **Q34-44**

**Capital gain**

Profit from increase in value of an investment.

**Capitalization**

In appraising, using a rate of return required of investors and the net income of a property as a basis of computing value. **W32-36**

**Caveat emptor (Latin)**

Means "let the buyer beware." Dealing "at arms' length."

**Certificate of reasonable value (CRV)**

The Federal Department of Veterans Affairs appraisal commitment of property value. **Q33**

**Chain of title**

Detailed account of all actions and events affecting a title to property as far back as the original government patent, if possible.

**Chattel**

Personal property; movable property.

**Chattel real**

An interest related to real estate, although not real estate; such as a mortgage note, a lease, etc.

**Clearance receipt**

Receipt issued by the Board of Equalization showing that seller of a business has accounted for sales taxes. **Z55**

**Client**

In real estate, one who employs you - your principal.

**Closing statement**

An accounting of funds made to the buyer and seller separately. Required by law to be made at the completion of every real estate transaction. **G15**

**Cloud on the title**

Anything affecting clear title to property. Term usually used in connection with minor nuisance items. Must be eliminated by quitclaim deed or court action. **L23**

**Collateral security**

Additional sums or things of value posted to guarantee fulfillment of a contract.

**Collusion**

A secret arrangement between two or more persons to defraud someone.

**Color of title**

A title which appears to be good on the surface, but actually is not good.

**Commercial acre**

What remains of an acre after allowing for deduction for streets, alley, etc. Something less than an acre. A loose term.

**Commercial paper**

Notes assigned in the course of trade, bills of exchange, etc.

**Commingling**

Situation where an agent has confused his own funds or property with that of his client - bad business.                                               **A87**

**Commission**

An agent's earnings in negotiating a real estate transaction; usually a percentage of the selling price, lease rental, etc.                         **K28**

**Community property**

That property acquired by husband and wife working as a partnership.
                                                                              **C11**

**Compaction**

Tamping of filled ground to make it more suitable for building. Done extensively in subdividing of hilly ground where there is much cutting and filling.

**Comparable sales**

Sales which have similar characteristics as the subject property and are used for indications of value in the appraisal process. Commonly called "comparables", they are recent selling prices of similar properties situated in a similar market.                                              **W37**

**Comparative analysis**

Appraising a property by comparing it with others of similar qualities with known recent sales prices. Known as sales comparison approach to value.                                                                    **W37**

**Competent parties**

Persons mentally fit; legally capable of contracting.

**Compound interest**

Earnings on the original investment and the accumulated interest therefrom.

**Condemnation**

Ruling by a public agency that property is not fit for use. Also refers to taking of private property for public use by right of eminent domain. **C28**

**Conditional sale contract (Real property sales contract)**

The purchase of property on contract, usually on the installment basis. Buyer does not receive a deed until he has made all payments called for by the contract.                                                           **M50-62**

**Conditions**

Limitations imposed in a deed. (See "covenants".)  D30

**Condominiums**

Apartments or other types of property in which the owner has fee title to the air space occupied, with an undivided interest in areas used by all occupants.  H16

**Consideration**

Something (usually of value) to induce a person to enter into a contract.

**Constructive notice**

Notice given by the public records, as opposed to actual notice.  E2

**Contiguous**

Adjoining, touching. As two contiguous parcels of land.

**Contract.** Agreement to do certain things, or not to do them.  J2

**Conventional loan**

A loan not guaranteed or insured by a governmental agency.  Q45

**Conveyance**

Transfer of title from one person to another; the instrument which accomplishes this (deed).  D3

**Cooperative (or community) apartment house**

Each owner receives a deed to an undivided interest in the entire property with the right to occupy a particular apartment.  H15

**Corner influence**

In appraising, the additional value given to a corner lot due to its advantages, especially in business property.

**Corporation**

An "artificial being" created by law with many rights of an individual in doing business.  C21

**Cost**

What a buyer pays for property. Not necessarily the value.  W47

**County records**

A recording system for documents maintained by each county as provided by State law.  E1

**Covenant**

Agreement in a deed to control the use and acts of future owners. Used also in other instruments such as leases and conditional sale contracts.  D30

**Customer**

The person you deal with as agent for your principal or client. Your prospective buyer, lessee, etc.

**Damages**

Compensation the court may award to a person who has been injured physically or financially by another.

**Declaration of abandonment**

Documents recorded to terminate a homestead.  T14

**Declaration of homestead**

Document recorded to declare a homestead under State law. **T3**

**Declaration of covenants, conditions and restrictions (CC & R's)**

A list of restrictions to a tract imposed by a subdivider and recorded. Deeds to lots make reference to this document and it saves reciting the contents in each separate deed. **D30**

**Decree**

A decision by a court or others authorized to make decisions.

**Dedication**

Acceptance of land from an owner by a political subdivision (city, county, etc.) for particular use by the public. May be voluntary or statutory (required). **C29**

**Deed**

A written instrument which conveys title to real estate. **D2**

**Deed essentials**

Those things necessary to create a valid deed. **D6**

**Deed in lieu of foreclosure**

A deed to real property accepted by a lender from a defaulting borrower to avoid the necessity of foreclosure proceedings by the lender.

**Deed of reconveyance**

Deed given by trustee under deed of trust when loan is paid. **M28**

**Default**

Failure to perform a duty or keep a promise, such as to make payments on a note.

**Deferred maintenance**

Existing but unfulfilled requirements for repairs and rehabilitation. Postponed or delayed maintenance causing decline in a building's physical condition. **W26**

**Deficiency judgment**

A judgment awarded by a court against a person when, after foreclosure of the security for the loan, insufficient money is realized at a sale to pay the balance of the loan. **M13**

**Delivery**

Formal transfer of a deed to the new owner, without the right to recall it. Essential to a valid transfer. **D11**

**Deposit receipt**

A term used by the real estate industry to describe the written offer to purchase real property upon stated terms and conditions accompanied by a deposit toward the purchase price, which becomes the contract for the sale of the property upon acceptance by the owner. **K22**

**Depreciation**

Loss of value to real estate improvements from any cause. **W25-30**

**Desist and refrain order**

A directive by the Commissioner to stop activities when it appears that the law is being violated, until a hearing can be held. **H23**

**Devise**

Gift of real estate by will. **C26**

**Directional growth**

Appraisal term. Direction in which main development in a city is growing.

**Documentary transfer tax**

A State enabling act allows a county to adopt a documentary transfer tax to apply on all transfers of real property located in the county. Notice of payment is entered on face of the deed or on a separate paper filed with the deed. **Y32 & 33**

**Duress**

Unlawfully causing someone to do an act against his will by use of force. **J7**

**Earnest money**

A sum of money given to bind an agreement or an offer. Receipted for in a "Deposit Receipt" form. A deposit.

**Easement**

The limited right or interest of one person in another's property; example: right to cross it, maintain a road, right of way to install and maintain public utility services, etc. **B15**

**Economic life**

Life of a building during which it earns enough to justify maintaining it and not razing it.

**Egress**

A means of leaving property without trespassing.

**Eminent domain**

The right of government to take private property for public use, provided it serves a necessary public use and just compensation is paid to the owner. **C28**

**Encroachment**

Building in whole or in part on another's property. **B19 & B20**

**Encumbrance**

Anything which affects the title of real estate. **L1**

**Endorsement**

The signing on the back of a check or note for the purpose of transfer.

**Endorsement in blank**

Signing to transfer rights to a check or note without qualification, making endorser equally responsible for payment. **N17**

**Endorsement without recourse**

Signing to transfer a check or note in this manner makes no guarantee to future holders. **N18**

**Equitable owner**

One who has hypothecated his property. He has conveyed title in trust perhaps, but retains the right to use and enjoy the property. Also, the buyer under a real property sales contract. **N20**

**Equity (owner's)**

Value of owner's interest in property in excess of the liens against it. **N20**

**Equity of redemption**

Owner's right to redeem property after foreclosure of a mortgage for a period provided by law. **M17**

**Escalator clause**

Provision in a lease whereby the rents increase under certain conditions. **R17-19**

**Escheat**

Process by which property reverts to the State for lack of private ownership. **C25**

**Escrow**

The depositing of papers and funds with a third neutral party along with instructions to carry out an agreement. Such as the transfer of title to a home. **G1 & G2**

**Escrow holder (escrow officer)**

One who undertakes to carry out escrow instructions. **G1**

**Estate**

The interest of a person in property; as to real property, the degree, quantity and extent of his interest.

**Estate for life**

Use of property only during the life of the person given the interest; after which it reverts to the original estate or others designated. **B9**

**Estate tax**

A California State tax on estates of deceased persons. **Y31**

**Estate at will**

A lease which may be terminated at will by either party.

**Estate for years**

A lease which has a definite term. **R8**

**Estoppel**

A legal theory under which a person is barred from asserting or denying a fact because of the person's previous acts or words.

**Ethics**

A standard of moral practice and fair play.

**Eviction**

Dispossession by process of law. The act of depriving a person of the possession of lands in pursuance of the judgment of a court.

**Exchange agreement**

A contract for the exchange of properties.

**Exclusive agency listing**

A listing agreement employing a broker as the sole agent for the seller of real property under the terms of which the broker is entitled to a commission if the property is sold through any other broker, but not if a sale is negotiated by the owner without the services of an agent. **K8**

**Exclusive right to sell listing**

A listing agreement employing a broker to act as agent for the seller of real property under the terms of which the broker is entitled to a commission if the property is sold during the duration of the listing through another broker or by the owner without the services of an agent.          **K9**

**Execute**

To sign and consent to carry out an agreement to completion.

**Executor**

Man named in a will to dispose of an estate.          **C26**

**Executrix**

Woman named in a will to dispose of an estate.          **C26**

**Federal Housing Administration (FHA)**

Federal government agency which insures loans.          **Q5**

**Fee simple estate**

Highest and best estate possible.          **B7**

**Felony**

A serious crime which may result in sentence to state prison.

**Fictitious name**

A business name which does not state the surname of the owner.

**A42 & Z 37**

**Fiduciary relationship**

A position of trust and confidence requiring loyalty.          **I 2**

**Financing real estate**

Arranging for a loan, giving property as security. Most property is bought partially with borrowed money, so this is an important phase of the real estate business.

**Fixtures**

Things which are attached to property which cannot be removed as ordinary personal property, as they become a part of the realty. Particular arrangements should be made in a lease to remove these items, such as shelves, showcases, etc.          **R15 (#11)**

**Foreclosure**

The sale of pledged property to cover a defaulted debt.          **M10**

**Forfeiture**

Loss of a deposit or earnest money for failure to perform.

**Fraud**

Causing loss of property due to use of deceit, cheating, false promises, etc.          **J7**

**Freeholder**

Owner of land in fee.

**Front foot**

The measure of land along the street frontage. Sometimes used as a unit in pricing business property.

**General lien**

One which may attach to all property of a person, such as under a judgment.          **L7**

**General plan**

    A plan for the future development of a city or county. Required by State law. **U2**

**Gift deed**

    A deed for which the consideration is love and affection, rather than money. **D19**

**Goodwill**

    An intangible but saleable asset of a business derived from the expectation of continued public patronage. **Z3**

**Grant**

    A conveyance of property by deed.

**Grant deed**

    Most usual instrument used to convey title to property in California. Carries implied warranties. **D5**

**Grantee**

    One who acquires title to property by deed. **D5**

**Granting clause**

    Clause in deed stating "I grant" or "I convey." Essential to a valid deed. **D6 & D9**

**Grantor**

    One who conveys title to property by deed. **D5**

**Gross income**

    Total income from a property before deducting vacancy and expenses. **W36**

**Gross rent multiplier**

    A number which, times the gross income of a property, produces an indication of value of the property. **W40**

**Ground lease**

    An agreement for the use of the land only, sometimes secured by improvements placed on the land by the user.

**H.B.& M**

    Humboldt base and meridian. Principal government survey lines in the northwest corner of California. **X6**

**Heirs**

    Those who by law obtain property upon death of another, either by will or operation of law.

**Highest and best use**

    In appraising, a determination as to how real estate can be used to produce its highest value. **W13**

**Holder in due course**

    One who in good faith takes a note for value and without knowledge of any defects, in the course of business. **N13**

**Homestead**

    A home upon which a declaration of homestead has been recorded. Gives certain protection against judgments. **T1-17**

**Hundred percent location**

The most valuable business property location in a community.

**Hypothecate**

To pledge property as security for a debt, but retaining its use. (As in connection with a trust deed loan.) **M3**

**Implied warranty**

A warranty assumed by law to exist in an instrument although not specifically stated. As in a grant deed. **D12**

**Improvements**

Things built on land which become a part of it. Examples: buildings, fences, paving, drains.

**Improvement acts**

State laws providing for the installation of improvements in certain districts, such as street widening and paving, installation of sewer lines and storm drains, etc. The cost is assessed against the properties directly benefited. **Y35-39**

**Incompetent**

One who is unable to manage his affairs because of feeblemindedness, senility, insanity, etc.

**Indemnity**

Guarantee against loss - as by an insurance policy.

**Inherit**

To obtain property as an heir.

**Ingress**

A means of entering a property without trespass.

**Injunction**

An order of a court to restrain against unjust acts in connection with a pending lawsuit or one adjudicated.

**Insolvent**

Inability of a person to pay all his debts. Where liabilities exceed assets.

**Installment note**

A note which provides for payment of a certain part of the principal and interest at stated intervals. **N6**

**Instrument**

A document in writing creating certain rights to its parties or transferring them. Examples: a deed, sales agreement, listing, lease, etc.

**Intestate**

Death without leaving a will. **C25**

**Intrinsic value**

Having value within itself, such as a gold coin.

**Involuntary lien**

A lien placed against property without necessity of the owner's consent. Taxes and assessments are examples. **L6**

**Irrevocable**

That which cannot be recalled or revoked (such as the delivery of a valid deed).

**Irrigation district**
> A district created by law to furnish water. It is a "quasi-political" district (having governing features similar to counties and cities). **H40**

**Joint note**
> A note signed by more than one person. All have equal responsibility for payment and must be sued together. **N15-16**

**Joint and several note**
> Same as joint note, but makers may be sued either jointly or individually in event of default. **N15-16**

**Joint tenancy**
> Equal ownership by two or more persons under four "essential unities." Featured by "right of survivorship." **C5 & C10**

**Joint tenancy deed**
> A deed which names grantees as joint tenants.

**Judgment**
> A court's final decree. Often involves awarding a payment of money.
> **L8 & S1**

**Judgment lien**
> A legal claim on all of the property of a judgment debtor which enables the judgment creditor to have the property sold for payment of the amount of the judgment. **S4**

**Junior lien**
> A lien which is subordinate to another lien which has prior claim on the security. Example: a second trust deed. The prior lien holders can collect before the junior lien is satisfied. **M32, M35 & M36**

**Jurisdiction**
> The right given by law by which courts, commissions, etc. enter into and decide cases.

**Key lot**
> One which is at right angle to another facing another street.

**Laches**
> "Sleeping on your rights." Failure to secure legal relief through too long delay.

**Land contract (same as real property sales contract)**
> An agreement whereby land is sold, usually on an installment basis, and buyer does not receive a deed until the contract is paid out. **M50-62**

**Land descriptions**
> Necessary to definitely determine the boundaries of land. Certain methods are recognized by law. **X1**

**Lease**
> An agreement by which real estate is rented for a certain period under certain specified conditions. **R3**

**Lease essentials**
> Things necessary to make a lease binding.

**Leasehold**
> Means simply the interest of one who leases property. **R5**

**Legal description**
　　A description of land recognized by law. **X1**

**Lessee**
　　A renter under a lease contract. **R4**

**Lessor**
　　An owner who has leased his property. **R4**

**Liable**
　　Responsible under the law.

**Life estate**
　　Rights to use property for a lifetime only. **B9**

**Lien**
　　An encumbrance against property making it liable for a money debt; taxes, trust deeds, special assessments, etc. **L3**

**Limited partnership**
　　A partnership consisting of a general partner or partners and limited partners in which the general partners manage and control the business affairs of the partnership. Limited partners are essentially investors taking no part in the management of the partnership and having no liability for the debts of the partnership in excess of their invested capital.
**C23**

**Liquid assets**
　　Those readily convertible to cash.

**Liquidate**
　　To sell off property at best available price to secure cash.

**Liquidated damages**
　　Extent of damages agreed upon in a contract in event of default. **J10**

**Lis pendens**
　　A recorded notice to advise persons interested in property that a lawsuit is pending which may affect it. **S13**

**Listing**
　　A contract authorizing a real estate broker to give service in connection with the property; buy, sell, lease, etc. **K1**

**Loan broker law**
　　A law enforced by the Real Estate Commissioner to prevent unfair practices in the real estate loan business. **P7-16**

**Map Act**
　　The Subdivision Map Act is a State law permitting cities and counties to exercise certain control over the subdivision of land within their boundaries. **H4-5**

**Marketable title**
　　Title to property which is free from any reasonable objections from the average purchaser.

**Market value**
　　The highest price a property would bring in dollars if freely exposed to the market for a reasonable period of time, etc. Refer to full definition. **W7**

**Material fact**

A fact, which if known to the broker's principal or customer, might seriously affect his decisions in a transaction.

**M.D.B.& M. (Mount Diablo Base and Meridian)**

A principal base line and meridian established by government survey from which land is located in central and northern California.     **X6**

**Mechanic's lien**

A lien right provided by law whereby persons who have furnished labor or materials may make legal claim against the property for unpaid services.                                                                      **L9-18**

**Menace**

Use of threats to induce one to enter into a contract.               **J7**

**Mesne profits**

Mesne means intermediate. Profits from a property during a period when a rightful owner is wrongfully deprived of the earnings.

**Metes and bounds**

A method of legally describing a property by describing its boundaries.
**X4**

**Mineral, Oil and Gas license**

Special license to deal in such lands.                                **A63**

**Minors**

Youths who have not reached a legal age to vote, contract, etc. Usually persons under 18, with certain exceptions.                          **D28**

**Misdemeanor**

A lesser crime. Sentences are usually to county jail, a fine, or both.

**Misplacement**

Making the wrong building improvement for the location. Causes depreciation and resulting loss of value.

**Month to month tenancy**

When rent is paid by the month - the usual arrangement for renting houses.                                                              **R9**

**Moratorium**

A law or governmental decree suspending liability for paying a debt or undertaking certain duties in an emergency.                          **S17**

**Mortgage**

An instrument which makes property security for the payment of a loan. Borrower has a period to redeem after foreclosure, and need not surrender property during that period.                           **M2-18**

**Mortgagee**

One who lends money secured by a mortgage or trust deed.       **M4**

**Mortgagee's statement**

A statement from holder of mortgage note as to present status of payments, balance owed, etc.                                        **M45**

**Mortgagor**

An owner who borrows money on a note secured by a mortgage or trust deed.                                                               **M4**

**Multiple listing**

A cooperative listing taken by one of an organization of brokers (usually a real estate association), which permits other members to find a buyer. Usually an "exclusive right to sell" listing.　　**K10**

**Mutual consent**

An essential to a good contract.　　**J6**

**Mutual water company**

A non-profit company of water users who own stock in the company and control its affairs.　　**H38**

**Negotiable instrument**

Those which are commonly transferred by endorsement in the course of trade - such as notes, checks and drafts.　　**N10**

**Net income**

Remaining income from property after vacancy and expenses are deducted.　　**W36**

**Net listing**

One which provides that agent gets his commission over and above a net sum to the seller.　　**K15**

**Notary public**

Person authorized by law to take acknowledgments and oaths and sign certificate and affix official seal.

**Notice of Abandonment**

Notice filed when work is discontinued on an unfinished building job.

**Notice of Completion**

Document filed to give public notice that a building job is completed. **L11**

**Notice of Default**

Notice filed by owner of a trust deed with the county recorder that borrower has defaulted and foreclosure proceedings may be started. **M29-36**

**Notice of Non-responsibility**

A notice provided by law, which when recorded, is designed to relieve an owner from liability for work or materials used on his property by lessee or purchaser under sales contract without his authorization.　　**L21**

**Notice to Quit**

A three day notice to a delinquent tenant to pay up or surrender possession of the premises.　　**R27**

**Obsolescence**

A form of depreciation to improvements due to obsolete design or unfavorable surroundings. Two forms are recognized, "functional" and "external."　　**W27 & W28**

**Off-sale license**

State liquor license issued to sellers of "packaged goods" to be taken from the premises.　　**Z58-68**

**On-sale license**

License to sell alcoholic beverages for consumption on the premises, such as cocktail bar, beer hall, etc.　　**Z58-68**

**Offset statement**

Statement of an owner or lien holder as to present status of a lien - the remaining principal balance on the note, interest due, etc.  **M45**

**Open housing law**

The Fair Housing Amendments Act of 1988 and other laws prohibit discrimination in the sale of real estate because of race, color, or religion of buyers.  **T18-T38**

**Open listing**

A non-exclusive listing given to one or more agents; may be oral or written, and first agent to get owner's acceptance to an offer earns the commission.  **K7**

**Option**

A written instrument which, for a consideration, gives one the right to buy (or lease) a property within a stated time limit on the terms set forth.  **K30-39**

**Optionee**

One who secures an option right.  **K32**

**Optionor**

An owner who gives an option.  **K32**

**Oral**

Verbal or spoken; not in writing. Examples: oral contract, oral lease.

**Original contractor (General contractor)**

The contractor who contracts with the owner to do the over-all building job for an agreed price.

**Outlawed claim**

A claim is outlawed when the claimant delays bringing suit beyond the time limit allowed by law. See Statute of Limitations.  **S12**

**Owner's equity**

What a property is worth over and above the liens against it.

**Partial release clause**

Clause in a mortgage or trust deed which provides for removal of certain property from the effect of the lien upon payment of an agreed sum. Subdividers must have these if their tract is subject to a "blanket lien."  **M41**

**Partnership**

A contract between two or more persons to unite their property, labor or skill, or some of them, in prosecution of some joint or lawful business, and to share profits in certain proportions.

**Party wall**

One built on the dividing line of properties for use of both owners.

**Patent**

An original conveyance of lands by the federal government.

**Payor and payee**

The payor pays the sum due on a note, and the payee receives the money.  **N4**

**Percentage lease**

A lease providing for rental based on the dollar volume of business done. Usually based on gross sales with an agreed minimum rental. **R17**

**Personal property**

Movable property; that which is not real property. **B3-6**

**Plaintiff**

One who brings a civil law suit.

**Planning commission**

A body appointed to study and recommend steps for orderly physical growth of a community. **U15**

**Pledge**

A deposit of personal property to secure a debt. A pawn.

**Plottage**

The increase in value to a parcel of land by increasing its utility by joining it with an adjoining parcel or parcels.

**Points**

In the language of the loan business, a point is one percent of the amount of the loan. Bonuses and commissions are often expressed in "points." **N24**

**Police power**

The power vested in the State to enact and enforce laws for the order, safety, health, morals and general welfare of the public. **U4**

**Power of attorney**

Authority given in writing by one person for another to act for him. **I 25**

**Power of sale**

A right given to a trustee to sell property under deed of trust if the borrower defaults. Power of sale provision may also be included in a mortgage, but is rarely done. **M26**

**Prescription**

A means of obtaining title to property through long open possession under some claim, in defiance of owner's rights. **B16**

**Presumption**

A fact assumed by law which must be proved to the contrary.

**Price**

The amount of money the owner asks for a property, or the amount paid for a property, not necessarily its value. **W46**

**Prima facie**

On its face; presumptive.

**Primary mortgage market**

Making original loans.

**Principal**

This term is used to mean the employer of an agent; or the amount of money borrowed, or the amount of the loan. Also, one of the main parties in a real estate transaction, such as a buyer, borrower, seller, lessor. **I 1**

**Priority**

Being ahead of in rank, time or place. In real estate, established largely by the order in which instruments affecting property are recorded. **E3**

**Probate sale**

Sale to liquidate the estate of a deceased person. **K40**

**Procuring cause**

When the efforts of a broker make a deal possible but the details are completed by others, he is said to be the procuring cause and may be entitled to a commission. **K19**

**Promissory note**

Written promise to pay a certain sum at a definite future time. **N3**

**Property**

In general, anything capable of ownership. **B2 & B3**

**Property management**

A branch of the real estate business.

**Proration (taxes, interest, etc.)**

To divide proportionately among the parties, as in closing an escrow. **G15**

**Public report (subdivision)**

A report on the conditions attendant to a new subdivision, prepared by the Real Estate Commissioner. **H11**

**Public Utility**

A private company giving public service, such as a water service. **H39**

**Purchase money mortgage (or trust deed)**

Given as part (or all) of the purchase price of property. Often referred to as a "purchase price" mortgage or trust deed. **M14**

**Quiet title**

A lawsuit to determine status of title; to remove a cloud on the title.

**Quitclaim deed**

Deed by which the grantor releases any claim or interest in a property he may possess. **D18**

**Range**

A strip of land running north and south and 6 miles wide, established by government survey. **X5**

**Real estate association**

An organization of real estate brokers and salespersons, and others interested in the real estate field.

**Real property**

In the strict legal sense, land, appurtenances, that which is affixed to the land, and that which by law is immovable. It usually refers to the "bundle of rights" inherent in ownership. **B2**

**Real Estate Settlement Procedures Act (RESPA)**

A federal law requiring the disclosure to borrowers of settlement (closing) procedures and costs by means of a pamphlet and forms prescribed by the United States Department of Housing and Urban Development. **P39**

**Real property securities broker statement**

A detailed statement on the real estate which secures the investment in a trust deed, land contract, etc., which must be given to a purchaser of the security. **A54**

**Real property sales contract**

An agreement whereby land is sold, usually on an installment basis, and buyer does not receive a deed until the contract is paid out.     **M50-62**

**Realtor**

A title restricted to use by a real estate broker who holds active membership in a real estate association affiliated with the National Association of Realtors.     **A84**

**Reconveyance**

Transfer of title to a former owner, as when a trustee under a deed of trust reconveys title when the note is paid in full.     **M28**

**Rescission of contract**

To set aside or annul a contract, either by mutual consent or by court order.     **J13 & J15**

**Recovery Account**

Part of the Real Estate Fund from which the Commissioner may compensate injured investors.     **A98**

**Redemption**

Re-acquiring property lost through foreclosure within the prescribed time limit.     **M16**

**Release clause**

Provision in a trust deed or mortgage to release portions of the property from the lien upon payment of an agreed amount of money. Subdividers are required to have these.     **M41**

**Request for notice of default**

Acknowledged request filed with the county recorder by holder of a junior lien so he may be notified of actions of prior lien holders.     **M35**

**Reservation**

A right withheld by a grantor when conveying property.

**Restriction**

A limitation on the use of property, usually imposed by a previous grantor.     **D30**

**Reversionary interest**

The right to an estate or its residue after present possession (as with a life estate or a lease) is terminated.     **B9 & R6**

**Right of survivorship**

The right of a joint tenant to the interest of a deceased joint tenant.   **C5**

**Right of way**

An easement to pass over, or maintain services, on property or a particular part thereof.

**Riparian right**

Rights of a landowner to use the water on, under or adjacent to his land, providing such use does not illegally injure other riparian owners.   **B11**

**Sale and leaseback**

A transaction in which at the time of sale the seller retains occupancy by concurrently agreeing to lease the property from the purchaser. The seller receives cash while the buyer is assured a tenant for his property.

**Sales and use tax**

A State and county levy on retail sales, collected from the vendor by the State Board of Equalization.                    **Z42-57**

**Sandwich lease**

A sublease which is subject to an original lease, the sublessee having further sublet the property. He holds an "in between" lease.       **R23**

**Satisfaction**

An instrument executed by a lien holder declaring that the debt has been paid. When recorded, it discharges the lien from the records.       **S7**

**S.B.B.& M.**

San Bernardino base and meridian. Principal government survey lines in Southern California.                    **X6**

**Schedule of commissions**

A list of fair charges for real estate services suggested by real estate associations and now outlawed.

**Secondary mortgage market**

The dealing in trust deeds and mortgages already in existence.

**Section of land**

A standard land measurement containing 640 acres, or one square mile.                    **X15 & X16**

**Security device**

An instrument or contract which results in real estate being made security for money owed, such as a trust deed, real property sales contract, etc.

**Security deposit**

Funds deposited by lessee to protect lessor if a default occurs. These are trust funds.                    **R32**

**Separate property**

That property which is owned and controlled separately by either husband or wife, as distinguished from community property.       **C12**

**Set-back ordinance**

Local laws requiring owners, when building, to keep improvements a certain distance from lot boundaries.

**Severalty ownership**

Sole ownership - as by a single person.                    **C2**

**Sheriff's deed**

One given by the sheriff upon court order when property is sold to satisfy a debt.

**Signing by mark**

Making a mark (witnessed) by a person unable to sign his name.       **D27**

**Sinking fund**

A fund invested, which with the accumulated compound interest, will in time amount to a certain sum - such as to replace an obsolete building.

**Solvent**

Able to pay all debts.

**Special assessment**

A legal charge against property for improvements which particularly benefit it. **Y35-39**

**Specific lien**

A lien affecting one particular property. **L7**

**Specific performance**

Court order requiring a person to do what he has agreed to do in a contract. **J11**

**Spouse**

Either one of a married couple.

**State Housing Act**

State law setting minimum construction requirements for certain types of structures. **V7**

**Statement of Identity**

A questionnaire by which title companies are helped in identifying a person; assists when the records show several persons with the same name, etc.

**Statute**

A law enacted by a legislative body.

**Statute of Frauds**

A State law requiring certain agreements to be in writing to be enforceable at law. **J5**

**Statute of Limitations**

A State law limiting the time in which certain court actions may be brought. (Such as for failing to pay a debt.) **S12**

**Statutory dedication.** Surrendering land for public use when required by law (as for streets in a subdivision). **C29-30**

**Straight line depreciation**

A method of depreciation under which improvements are depreciated at a constant rate throughout the estimated useful life of the improvement. **W30**

**Straight note**

One payable in a lump sum - not in installments. **N5**

**Subdivision Map Act**

State law enabling cities and counties to control and approve subdivision tracts. **H4**

**Subdivision maps**

When approved by the governing body and recorded they are the basis for good legal descriptions. **X3**

**"Subject to" a mortgage (or trust deed)**

Language used when buyer does not assume personal liability for payment of a mortgage or trust deed note against a property he buys. **M43**

**Sublease**

A lease given when the original lessee in turn sublets. **R21**

**Subordination clause**

Clause in a junior mortgage or trust deed enabling the first lien to keep its priority in case of renewal or refinancing. **M39**

**Successor's liability**

Liability of the new owner of a business for the unpaid sales taxes of the former owner, if he hasn't secured a clearance receipt from the Board of Equalization.                                                                                                **Z55**

**Surety**

A guarantee.

**Tangible property**

Personal property which has substance and can be manually delivered from one person to another.

**Tax deed**

One given when land is finally sold for non-payment of taxes.

**Taxes (real estate)**

A levy on property by political subdivisions, (county, city, school districts, or other special districts) to support administration and services.                                                                                                        **Y1-24**

**Tenancy at sufferance**

Occurs when a lease expires and owner permits tenant to continue in possession on a temporary basis.                                                                        **R10**

**Tenancy in common**

Ownership of equal or unequal undivided interests in property by two or more persons, without right of survivorship.                                                            **C3**

**Tenant in partnership**

Interest in property held as a partner.                                                        **C4**

**Termites**

Wood devouring insects - enemies of property owners.                                **V7-13**

**Testator and testatrix**

One who makes a will. Testator is a man, testatrix a woman.                        **C26**

**"Time is of the essence"**

Necessary provision in contracts. Contemplates prompt performance by the parties within the time limits set forth.

**Time-share estate**

A right of occupancy in a time-share project (subdivision) which is coupled with an estate in the real property.                                                            **H20**

**Time-share project**

A form of subdivision of real property into rights to the recurrent, exclusive use or occupancy of a lot, parcel, unit, or segment of real property, on an annual or some other periodic basis, for a specified period of time.                                                                                                                **H20**

**Time-share use**

A license or contractual or membership right of occupancy in a time-share project which is not coupled with an estate in the real property. **H20**

**Title**

Evidence of ownership and lawful possession.

**Title insurance**

Protection to a property owner against loss because of defective title. Policies are written by title companies.                                                                **F7**

**Topography**

The character of the land's surface - level, hilly, etc.

**Torrens title**

A system of land registration operated by a state. No longer used in California.

**Township**

A unit of land six miles square, or 36 square miles. Established by government survey. **X5**

**Trust deed (deed of trust)**

A conveyance of title to a trustee to be held until a loan secured by a property is paid, at which time title is reconveyed. **M20-38**

**Trustee**

A person or corporation which holds title in trust pending repayment of an obligation or the rendering of a service. In connection with trust deed, holds title until a note is paid. **M21**

**Trustee's deed**

One given by the trustee when foreclosed property is sold.

**Trustor**

Borrower on a trust deed note. **M22**

**Truth in lending**

The name given to the federal statutes and regulations (Regulation Z) which are designed primarily to insure that certain prospective borrowers and purchasers on credit receive credit cost information before entering into a transaction. **P33**

**Undivided interest**

A partial interest in a whole property, merged with the interest of others.

**Undue influence**

Taking advantage of a person because of his weakness or distress. **J7**

**Uniform Commercial Code - Division 9**

A law permitting filings with the Secretary of State of security devices making personal property loans secured liens. **Z24**

**Unilateral contract**

One which imposes an obligation on one party only; exchange of a promise for an act. **J20**

**Unities**

Essentials such as to a joint tenancy, the unities being time, title, interest, and possession. **C10**

**Unlawful detainer**

Failure of a tenant to vacate after being notified that he is in default. **R28**

**Urban property**

City property.

**Urban renewal and redevelopment**

Plan to improve substandard areas in populated communities.

**Usury**

Charging a high and illegal interest rate. Law sets maximum of 10% per annum or 5% above the Federal Reserve discount rate, whichever is higher, on non-exempt loans in California. **P32**

**VA loans**
    See Department of Veterans Affairs.                     **Q24-33**

**Valuation**
    Appraising. Estimating the worth of property in money.     **W1-3**

**Vendee**
    The buyer.

**Vendor**
    The seller.

**Verification**
    Confirmation of the truth of a document by sworn statement before a
    duly qualified officer.     **E16**

**Vest**
    To bestow upon - such as title of property.

**Veteran's tax exemption**
    A property tax exemption given to certain qualified veterans (or widows)
    in California.     **Y15**

**Void**
    Having no binding effect at law.

**Voidable**
    That which may be declared void, but which is not void until so adjudged
    by a court.

**Voluntary lien**
    A lien placed on property through the voluntary act of the owner, such
    as when he makes a mortgage loan.     **L6**

**Waive**
    To relinquish; to surrender the right to require anything.

**Warranty deed**
    A deed which recites certain warranties. Not used in California to any
    extent as grant deed coupled with title insurance has replaced it.

**Waste**
    Abuse of property by a tenant or someone holding a temporary interest
    (such as a life estate) which results in a loss of value.

**Water table**
    Depth of natural underground water from the surface.     **H41**

**Wrap-around mortgage**
    A financing device whereby a lender assumes payments on existing trust
    deeds of a borrower and takes from the borrower a junior trust deed with
    a face value in an amount equal to the amount outstanding on the old
    trust deeds and the additional amount of money borrowed.

**Writ**
    A written document issued by a court commanding a person to do
    certain acts, or sometimes to refrain from doing them.

**Writ of execution**
    A court order that property be sold to pay a judgment.     **S6**

**Zoning**
    Control of the use of land by county or city authorities; power to limit
    property to specific use.     **U4**

# COURSE PREREQUISITES

## TO TAKING BROKER & SALESPERSON LICENSE EXAMINATIONS

SECTION 1. Section 10153.2 of the Business and Professions Code is repealed.

SECTION 2. Section 10153.2 is added to the Business and Professions Code, to read:

10153.2 (a) An applicant to take the examination for an original real estate broker license shall also submit evidence, satisfactory to the Commissioner, of successful completion, at an accredited institution, of:

(1) A three-semester unit course, or the quarter equivalent thereof, in each of the following:

(A) Real estate practice.

(B) Legal aspects of real estate.

(C) Real estate appraisal.

(D) Real estate financing.

(E) Real estate economics or accounting.

(2) A three-semester unit course, or the quarter equivalent thereof, in any of the following:

(A) Advanced legal aspects of real estate.

(B) Advanced real estate finance.

(C) Advanced real estate appraisal.

(D) Business law.

(E) Escrows.

(F) Real estate principles.

(G) Property management.

(H) Real estate office administration.

(3) On and after January 1, 1986, an applicant shall submit evidence of successful completion of each of the courses listed in paragraph (1) and any three of the courses listed in paragraph (2).

(b) The Commissioner shall waive the requirements of this section for an applicant who is a member of the State Bar of California and shall waive the requirements for which an applicant has successfully completed an equivalent course of study as determined under Section 10153.5

(c) The Commissioner shall extend credit under this section for any course completed to satisfy requirements of Section 10153.3 or 10153.4.

SECTION 3. Section 10153.3 is added to the Business and Professions Code, to read:

10153.3. In order to take an examination for a real estate salesperson license after January 1, 1986, an applicant shall submit evidence, satisfactory to the commissioner, of successful completion, at an accredited institution, of a three-semester unit course, or the quarter equivalent thereof, in real estate principles.

The Commissioner shall waive the requirements of this section for an applicant who is a member of the State Bar of California or who has completed an equivalent course of study, as determined under Section 10153.5.

SECTION 4. Section 10153.4 of the Business and Professions Code is repealed.

SECTION 5. Section 101053.4 is added to the Business and Professions Code, to read:

10153.4 (a) Every person who is required to comply with Section 10153.3 to obtain an original real estate salesperson license shall, prior to the issuance of the license, or within 18 months after issuance, submit evidence, satisfactory to the Commissioner, of successful completion, at an accredited institution, of two of the courses listed in Section 10153.2, other than real estate principles, advanced legal aspects of real estate, advanced real estate finance, or advanced real estate appraisal.

(b) A salesperson who qualifies for a license pursuant to this section, shall not be required, for the first license renewal thereafter, to complete the continuing education pursuant to Article 2.5 (commencing with Section 10170), except for the course in ethics, professional conduct, and legal aspects of real estate pursuant to subdivision (a) of Section 10170.5.

(c) The salesperson license issued to an applicant who has satisfied only the requirements of Section 10153.3 at the time of issuance shall be automatically suspended effective 18 months after issuance if the licensee has failed to satisfy the provisions of subdivision (a). The suspension shall not be lifted until the suspended licensee has submitted the required evidence of course completion and the commissioner has given written notice to the licensee of the lifting of the suspension.

(d) The original license issued to a salesperson shall clearly set forth the conditions of the license and shall be accompanied by a notice of the provisions of this section and of any regulations adopted by the Commissioner to implement this section.

(e) The Commissioner shall waive the requirements of this section for any person who presents evidence of admission to the State Bar of California, and the Commissioner shall waive the requirement for any course for which an applicant has completed an equivalent course of study as determined under Section 10153.5.

SECTION 6. Section 10153.5 of the Business and Professions Code is repealed.

SECTION 7. Section 10153.5 is added to the Business and Professions Code, to read:

10153.5 As used in Sections 10153.2, 10153.3, and 10153.4, "an equivalent course of study" includes courses at a private vocational school or a supervised course of study, either of which has been found by the Commissioner, upon consideration of an application for approval, to be equivalent in quality to the real estate courses offered by the colleges and universities accredited by the Western Association of Schools and Colleges.

# THE CALIFORNIA REAL ESTATE COMMISSIONER'S

*Revised Code of Ethics for Real Estate Licensees*

A revised Code of Ethics has been adopted which became effective June 10, 1990. The text of the Code is set forth below. In addition to the Code of Ethics, there follows a section titled Suggestions for Professional Conduct.

## Code of Ethics and Professional Conduct

2785. **Professional Conduct.** In order to enhance the professionalism of the California real estate industry, and maximize protection for members of the public dealing with real estate licensees, whatever their area of practice, the following standards of professional conduct and business practices are adopted.

(a) **Unlawful Conduct in Sale, Lease and Exchange Transactions.** Licensees when performing acts within the meaning of Section 10131 (a) of the Business and Professions Code shall not engage in conduct which would subject the licensee to adverse action, penalty or discipline under Sections 10176 and 10177 of the Business and Professions Code including, but not limited to, the following acts and omissions:

(1) Knowingly making a substantial misrepresentation of the likely value of real property to:

(A) Its owner either for the purpose of securing a listing or for the purpose of acquiring an interest in the property for the licensee's own account.

(B) A prospective buyer for the purpose of inducing the buyer to make an offer to purchase the real property.

(2) Representing to an owner of real property when seeking a listing that the licensee has obtained a bona fide written offer to purchase the property, unless at the time of the representation the licensee has possession of a bona fide written offer to purchase.

(3) Stating or implying to an owner of real property during listing negotiations that the licensee is precluded by law, by regulation, or by the rules of any organization, other than the broker firm seeking the listing, from charging less than the commission or fee quoted to the owner by the licensee.

(4) Knowingly making substantial misrepresentations regarding the licensee's relationship with an individual broker, corporate broker, or franchised brokerage company or that entity's/person's responsibility for the licensee's activities.

(5) Knowingly underestimating the probable closing costs in a communication to the prospective buyer or seller of real property in order to induce that person to make or to accept an offer to purchase the property.

(6) Knowingly making a false or misleading representation to the seller of real property as to the form, amount and/or treatment of a deposit toward the purchase of the property made by an offerer.

(7) Knowingly making a false or misleading representation to a seller of real property, who has agreed to finance all or part of a purchase price by carrying back a loan, about a buyer's ability to repay the loan in accordance with its terms and conditions.

(8) Making an addition to or modification of the terms of an instrument previously signed or initialed by a party to a transaction without the knowledge and consent of the party.

(9) A representation made as a principal or agent to a prospective purchaser of a promissory note secured by real property about the market value of the securing property without a reasonable basis for believing the truth and accuracy of the representation.

(10) Knowingly making a false or misleading representation or representing, without a reasonable basis for believing its truth, the nature and/or condition of the interior or exterior features of a property when soliciting an offer.

(11) Knowingly making a false or misleading representation or representing, without reasonable basis for believing its truth, the size of a parcel, square footage of improvements or the location of the boundary lines of real property being offered for sale, lease or exchange.

(12) Knowingly making a false or misleading representation or representing to a prospective buyer or lessee of real property, without reasonable basis to believe its truth, that the property can be used for certain purposes with the intent of inducing the prospective buyer or lessee to acquire an interest in the real property.

(13) When acting in the capacity of an agent in a transaction for the sale, lease or exchange of real property, failing to disclose to a prospective purchaser or lessee facts known to the licensee materially affecting the value or desirability of the property, when the licensee has reason to believe that such facts are not known to nor readily observable by a prospective purchaser or lessee.

(14) Willfully failing, when acting as a listing agent, to present or cause to be presented to the owner of the property any written offer to purchase received prior to the closing of a sale, unless expressly instructed by the owner not to present such an offer, or unless the offer is patently frivolous.

(15) When acting as the listing agent, presenting competing written offers to purchase real property to the owner in such a manner as to induce the owner to accept the offer which will provide the greatest compensation to the listing broker without regard to the benefits, advantages and/or disadvantages to the owner.

(16) Failing to explain to the parties or prospective parties to a real estate transaction for whom the licensee is acting as an agent the meaning and probable significance of a contingency in an offer or contract that the licensee knows or reasonably believes may affect the closing date of the transaction, or the timing of the vacating of the property by the seller or its occupancy by the buyer.

(17) Failing to disclose to the seller of real property in a transaction in which the licensee is an agent for the seller the nature and extent of any direct or indirect interest that the licensee expects to acquire as a result of the sale. The prospective purchase of the property by a person related to the licensee by blood or marriage, purchase by an entity in which the licensee has an ownership interest, or purchase by any other person with whom the licensee occupies a special relationship where there is a reasonable probability that the licensee could be indirectly acquiring an interest in the property shall be disclosed to the seller.

(18) Failing to disclose to the buyer of real property in a transaction in which the licensee is an agent for the buyer the nature and extent of a licensee's direct or indirect ownership interest in such real property. The direct or indirect ownership interest in the property by a person related to the licensee by blood or marriage, by an entity in which the licensee has an ownership interest, or by any other person with whom the licensee occupies a special relationship shall be disclosed to the buyer.

(19) Failing to disclose to a principal for whom the licensee is acting as an agent any significant interest the licensee has in a particular entity when the licensee recommends the use of services or products of such entity.

(20) The refunding by a licensee, when acting as an agent for the seller, all or part of an offerer's purchase money deposit in a real estate transaction after the seller has accepted the offer to purchase, unless the licensee has the express permission of the seller to make a refund.

**(b) Unlawful Conduct When Soliciting, Negotiating, or Arranging a Loan Secured by Real Property or the Sale of a Promissory Note Secured by Real Property.** Licensees when performing acts within the meaning of subdivision (d) or (e) of Section 10131 of the Business and Professions Code shall not violate any of the applicable provisions of subdivision (a), or act in a manner which would subject the licensee to adverse action, penalty or discipline under Sections 10176 and 10177 of the Business and Professions Code including, but not limited to, the following acts or omissions:

(1)  Knowingly misrepresenting to a prospective borrower of a loan to be secured by real property or to an assignor/endorser of a promissory note secured by real property that there is an existing lender willing to make the loan or that there is a purchaser for the note, for the purpose of inducing the borrower or assignor/endorser to utilize the services of the licensee.

(2) (a) Knowingly making a false or misleading representation to a prospective lender or purchaser of a loan secured directly or collaterally by real property about a borrower's ability to repay the loan in accordance with its terms and conditions;

(b)  Failing to disclose to a prospective lender or note purchaser information about the prospective borrower's identity, occupation, employment, income and credit data as represented to the broker by the prospective borrower;

(c)  Failing to disclose information known to the broker relative to the ability of the borrower to meet his or her potential or existing contractual obligations under the note or contract including information known about the borrower's payment history on an existing note, whether the note is in default or the borrower in bankruptcy.

(3)  Knowingly underestimating the probable closing costs in a communication to a prospective borrower or lender of a loan to be secured by a lien on real property for the purpose of inducing the borrower or lender to enter into the loan transaction.

(4)  When soliciting a prospective lender to make a loan to be secured by real property, falsely representing or representing without reasonable basis to believe its truth, the priority of the security, as a lien against the real property securing the loan, i.e., a first, second or third deed of trust.

(5)  Knowingly misrepresenting in any transaction that a specific service is free when the licensee knows or has a reasonable basis to know that it is covered by a fee to be charged as part of the transaction.

(6) Knowingly making a false or misleading representation to a lender or assignee/endorsee of a lender of a loan secured directly or collaterally by a lien on real property about the amount and treatment of loan payments, including loan payoffs, and the failure to account to the lender or assignee/endorsee of a lender as to the disposition of such payments.

(7) When acting as a licensee in a transaction for the purpose of obtaining a loan, and in receipt of an "advance fee" from the borrower for this purpose, the failure to account to the borrower for the disposition of the "advance fee".

(8) Knowingly making false or misleading representation about the terms and conditions of a loan to be secured by a lien on real property when soliciting a borrower or negotiating the loan.

(9) Knowingly making a false or misleading representation or representing, without reasonable basis for believing its truth, when soliciting a lender or negotiating a loan to be secured by a lien on real property about the market value of the securing real property, the nature and/or condition of the interior or exterior features of the securing real property, its size or the square footage of any improvements on the securing real property.

# THE CALIFORNIA REAL ESTATE COMMISSIONER'S
## *Suggestions for Professional Conduct*

As part of the effort to promote ethical business practices of real estate licensees, the Real Estate Commissioner has issued the following Suggestions for Professional Conduct as a companion to the Code of Professional Conduct (Section 2785, Title 10, California Code of Regulations):

(a) **Suggestions for Professional Conduct in Sale, Lease and Exchange Transactions.** In order to maintain a high level of ethics and professionalism in their business practices, real estate licensees are encouraged to adhere to the following suggestions in conducting their business activities:

(1) Aspire to give a high level of competent, ethical and quality service to buyers and sellers in real estate transactions.

(2) Stay in close communication with clients or customers to ensure that questions are promptly answered and all significant events or problems in a transaction are conveyed in a timely manner.

(3) Cooperate with the California Department of Real Estate's enforcement of, and report to that department evident violations of, the Real Estate Law.

(4) Use care in the preparation of any advertisement to present an accurate picture or message to the reader, viewer or listener.

(5) Submit all written offers in a prompt and timely manner.

(6) Keep oneself informed and current on factors affecting the real estate market in which the licensee operates as an agent.

(7) Make a full, open and sincere effort to cooperate with other licensees, unless the principal has instructed the licensee to the contrary.

(8) Attempt to settle disputes with other licensees through mediation or arbitration.

(9) Advertise or claim to be an expert in an area of specialization in real estate brokerage activity, e.g., appraisal, property management, industrial siting, mortgage loan, etc., only if the licensee has had special training, preparation or experience in such area.

(10) Strive to provide equal opportunity for quality housing and a high level of service to all persons regardless of race, color, sex, religion, ancestry, physical handicap, marital status or national origin.

(11) Base opinions of value, whether for the purpose of advertising or promoting real real estate brokerage business, upon documented objective data.

(12) Make every attempt to comply with these Guidelines for Professional Conduct and the Code of Ethics of any organized real estate industry group of which the licensee is a member.

(b) **Suggestions for Professional Conduct When Negotiating or Arranging Loans Secured by Real Property or Sale of a Promissory Note Secured by Real Property.** In order to maintain a high level of ethics and professionalism in their business practices when performing acts within the meaning of subdivisions (d) and (e) of Section 10131 and Sections 10131.1 and 10131.2 of the Business and Professions Code, real estate licensees are encouraged to adhere to the following suggestions, in addition to any applicable provisions of subdivision (a), in conducting their business activities:

(1)  Aspire to give a high level of competent, ethical and quality service to borrowers and lenders in loan transactions secured by real estate.

(2)  Stay in close communication with borrowers and lenders to ensure that reasonable questions are promptly answered and all significant events or problems in a loan transaction are conveyed in a timely manner.

(3)  Keep oneself informed and current on factors affecting the real estate loan market in which the licensee acts as an agent.

(4)  Advertise or claim to be an expert in an area of real estate loan transactions only if the licensee has had special training, preparation or experience in such area.

(5)  Strive to provide equal opportunity for quality mortgage loan services and a high level of service to all borrowers or lenders regardless of race, color, sex, religion, ancestry, physical handicap, marital status or national origin.

(6)  Base opinions of value in a loan transaction, whether for the purpose of advertising or promoting real estate mortgage loan brokerage business, on documented objective data.

(7)  Respond to reasonable inquiries of a principal as to the status or extent of efforts to negotiate the sale of an existing loan.

(8)  Respond to reasonable inquiries of a borrower regarding the net proceeds available from a loan arranged by the licensee.

(9)  Make every attempt to comply with the standards of professional conduct and the code of ethics of any organized mortgage loan industry group of which the licensee is a member.

The conduct suggestions set forth in sub-sections (a) and (b) are not intended as statements of duties imposed by law nor as grounds for disciplinary action by the Department of Real Estate, but as guidelines for elevating the professionalism of real estate licensees.

This page intentionally left blank.

**Please Note -**

We intend to improve the *Primer* with each edition. Your comments and suggestions are appreciated. Please write to the *Primer's* editor:

> **David D. Westcott**
> **1400 Sixth Avenue**
> **Suite 203**
> **San Diego, CA 92101**
> **(619) 239-6104**

*Typeset by Westerfield Typesetting & Graphics, San Diego, CA (619) 574-1132*
*Artwork by Art Gottlieb, 1742 Garnet Avenue, Suite 140, San Diego, CA 92109*
*Cover Design by Paula Schlosser Design (510) 524-5341*